CUT THE
CLUTTER

Cynthia Townley Ewer
of OrganizedHome.com

CUT THE CLUTTER

Speed your cleaning
and calm the chaos

LONDON, NEW YORK, MELBOURNE, MUNICH, and DELHI

For Steve, who knows why

Project Editor Diana Craig
Project Designer Ruth Hope
Senior Editor Jennifer Latham
Project Art Editor Sara Robin
Managing Editor Penny Warren
Managing Art Editor Marianne Markham
Operations Publishing Manager Gillian Roberts
Art Director Carole Ash
Publishing Director Mary-Clare Jerram
DTP Designer Sonia Charbonnier
Production Controller Sarah Sherlock

First published in Great Britian in 2006
by Dorling Kindersley Limited
80 Strand, London WC2R 0RL
Penguin Group (UK)

2 4 6 8 10 9 7 5 3 1

A CIP catalogue record of this book is available
from the British Library

ISBN-13: 978–1–40531–145–8
ISBN-10: 1–40531–145–2

Colour reproduction by Colourscan, Singapore
Printed and bound by Star Standard, Singapore

Discover more at
www.dk.com

contents

My journey to an
organized home

People who know me only through my work on the Web imagine a lot of things – that I'm blonde (sorry, brunette here), that I'm tall and willowy (I wish!), and, most of all, that I am naturally organized, tidy, and clean. That sound you hear is hearty laughter, and it comes from those who know me best – my husband, mother, daughter, and son. They know the truth: that I was playing truant the day that innate organization ability was handed out.

I am not naturally organized, but I have learned how to be – the hard way. I know the exact day when my journey to an organized home began: 25 December 1983. That's when I realized that I had a problem with clutter and chaos, and that I needed to find a solution to create an orderly and happy home for my family and myself.

It was the evening of Christmas Day. Recently divorced, I had sent my two young children to spend the day with their father, so I visited my parents' home for Christmas dinner. But when I returned to my little house late that night, broken glass littered the doorstep. Someone had tried to break into my house while I was away!

I called the police and waited, shivering on the step. A police officer responded, approached the house cautiously, and slipped inside my front door. A few minutes later, he emerged, scratching his head. "I don't understand it," he said. "Your mortise lock held and the door wasn't opened – but somebody got in and ransacked your upstairs."

Guilty secret

Embarrassed warmth flooded my face. "No, no," I protested, "that's just the way I left it!"

The policeman peered at me keenly. "Do you know what it looks like up there?"

To my immense shame, I did. The two rooms that served as my home office, bedroom, and sewing area were knee-deep in crumpled photocopies, legal pads, fabric scraps, piled-up clothing, wrapping paper, stacked files, spilled coffee, and dirty dishes. Dust festooned the corners and a narrow path wound through the mess to the islands of my desk and my bed.

New order

That night, I confronted the truth. I had a problem. I wanted to bring up my children in a clean and comfortable home, but the place looked like a crime scene. I needed to learn what to do, how to do it, and when to do it to create the organized home my children and I deserved.

Next day, I began to search libraries and book shops for guidance. I read books. I tried many different organizing methods. I learned about cleaning and began to plan and schedule housework in the same way as my business activities. Little by little, I learned how to conquer clutter, do housework, and run an organized home.

Did it work? Fast-forward five years to September 1988. I'd met a young trainee doctor at the medical school library the week before, and this was to be our first date. My house was clean and orderly. My school-aged children were eating dinner at the kitchen table, as clean and orderly as it was in their nature to be. All was well as I opened the door.

My date followed me to the kitchen as I made coffee and, to my amazement, he began to ask me about my calendar, my To-Do file, and my family information centre. I showed him my lists, my cleaning schedule, even the little note with the date and time of our date.

He seemed impressed, but I had a little sinking feeling when the evening was over. How could I have shown this man my housekeeping system? What could he be thinking about my schedules and file cards and notebooks? They seemed a long way from the hip image I wanted to project.

Homemaking skills

Later, I learned that he was, indeed, impressed. On the night he proposed marriage, my husband Steve told me that he knew I was right for him from that very first evening. A fourth-generation doctor, he understood that a doctor's wife has to be organized, self-reliant and independent in order to deal with the demands of her spouse's profession. Nothing could have shown that capability more clearly, he felt, than the visible evidence of my skills as a homemaker that he saw when he came to my house on our first date.

Sharing the journey

Since 1998, I've taught those skills to the thousands of people who have visited our Web community, OrganizedHome.Com – and along the way I've learned much more than I've shared. Male, female, older, younger, the members of our community travel together towards a single mission – to help one another get organized at home.

In this book, we'll take that same journey together. Our goal is a clean and organized home. The methods offered here work. They worked for me and they've worked for the numerous people who've become members of our Web community. As you put them into practice, you will begin to realize that they are working for you too.

There's hope. There's help. Come and join us!

Cynthia Townley Ewer

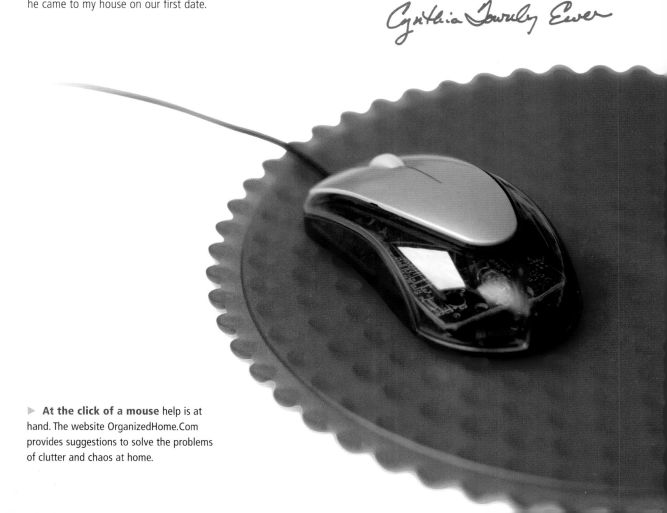

▶ **At the click of a mouse** help is at hand. The website OrganizedHome.Com provides suggestions to solve the problems of clutter and chaos at home.

around
the house

The problem:
clutter disorder and dirt

How do you really feel about the state of your house? Here's a quick test. Imagine that the front doorbell rings. Is there panic in the pit of your stomach at the thought of unexpected guests? You're not alone. For many busy families, clutter, disorganization, and dirt interfere with the workings of life on a daily basis.

Identifying domestic disorder

You know you have a problem with clutter and chaos in your home when:

- **You spent 10 minutes** searching the house for lost keys this morning. Again.
- **You have to rearrange** your bed to find room to sleep at night.
- **There's enough money** to pay the bills, but you can't find them.
- **You open cupboard doors** very slowly, prepared for an avalanche.
- **You run out of** must-have staples like milk and toilet paper. Regularly.
- **Your kitchen cupboards** are choked with empty margarine tubs and foil dishes.
- **Your cat can't find** the litter box, and your dog can't reach his doggie bed. With predictable, smelly results.
- **You buy replacement** items, only to find the one (or two or three) that was missing.
- **Dinner's been fast food** three times this week, and it's only Wednesday.
- **You're limping** because you tripped over items on the floor in the middle of the night.
- **There's a funny smell** in the house every time you return from holiday.

Sounds far-fetched? Not for the nearly 40 per cent of us who find it difficult to maintain a clean and organized home. In 1997, the Soap and Detergent Association in the US surveyed women's attitudes about cleaning. Of the respondents, 21 per cent, termed "Strugglers", spent the most time cleaning, yet felt the most discouraged about the state of their homes. Another group, the "Dirt Dodgers", who made up 18 per cent of the results, cleaned only when absolutely necessary – and found it difficult to keep their homes neat and organized.

Impossible standards

Add them together and you get us – the four out of ten people who are challenged by our lives at home. For all our numbers, we may as well be invisible. The modern media pummel us with misleading standards of perfection.

Even in real life, we seldom see the truth about our neighbours' clutter and chaos. At a friend's open-house party, we admire the beautiful home, but don't realize that it was achieved only by throwing dirty clothes, surface clutter, and stacks of newspapers into a padlocked bathroom.

Perfect pitch: the haves and have-nots

Take heart. You are not lazy, crazy, or stupid. You just need to learn the skills necessary to create a clean and organized home. Think of innate organizing ability as a kind of musical pitch. Some people have very little – they're the "tin ears" of the musical world. Others have perfect pitch – an inborn and accurate sense of which note is which, and the relationships between them. The rest of us struggle somewhere in between.

In the same way, some people naturally have an orderly relationship with their stuff. They keep things tidy without thinking, and they breeze through domestic life without turning a hair. They have the home management equivalent of perfect pitch hard-wired into their brains.

The rest of us have to work at learning organizational skills. But, just as we conquered musical scales and intervals, we can master planning and scheduling, cleaning and clutter control. And, like a well-rehearsed recital piece, our organizing abilities strengthen and become part of us as we use them.

"Most of us are not born with organizing skills. They are something we must learn."

▲ **Children's toys** are one of the prime spawning grounds for clutter and disorder. Learning the necessary skills can help even the organizationally challenged keep the problem under control.

Doing what doesn't come naturally

Problems arise when the two camps try to communicate. Tell someone who was born with a big dose of organizational ability about your new weekly menu plan, and you're likely to get a puzzled, "Well, doesn't everyone do that?" On the other hand, it's not always possible to benefit from the experience of a naturally organized person. For them, it comes easily, so they can take short cuts, assuming that the rest of us can follow.

Naturally organized people write far too many books about home organization. It's easy for them, so it should be easy for the reader, right?

Wrong. It takes one to know one – and to teach one.

The solution:
skill sets and cycles

How do you go from chaotic to calm and from cluttered to clean on the home front? Learn four simple skill sets, then apply them to the cycles of housekeeping. In this book, we'll start with the basic skills needed to declutter, organize, clean, and plan a happy home life. Then we'll apply these skills to the cycles of life in every home – food, clothing, surroundings, rooms, and paper.

Part One: Housekeeping Skill Sets

In home economics classes at school, I learned to make bound buttonholes, lay a pretty table, and bake a dozen biscuits that were all the same size – but I wasn't taught the real skills needed to create a clean and organized home. How to keep clutter under control. How to organize and do housework. How to plan my time and family activities.

Think of Part One of this book as a home economics class for the real world: an introduction to the four basic skill sets everyone needs – declutter, organize, clean, and plan.

Decluttering your home Fundamentally, the problem isn't about "stuff". It's about the habits, personality traits, and thought processes that encourage the build-up of clutter.

In the declutter skill set, we learn a 20-minute method to banish clutter anywhere. We gain a deeper understanding of personality traits that encourage cluttering, and we explore ways to fight the thought processes that tie us to our stuff. Finally, we share tips to deal with other people's clutter.

Organizing your home A well-organized home makes life flow smoothly, speeds cleaning and means you'll never have to look for misplaced items again … well, most of the time.

In the organize skill set, we focus on the three basic rules of home organization. We establish a place for everything, bring the family on board, and create activity centres to focus space and possessions. Finally, we look for storage solutions to contain clutter and make living spaces work.

declutter ▲ see pages 18–35

organize ▲ see pages 36–47

Cleaning your home It's not how long you clean. It's not how hard you clean. It's how efficiently you clean that makes the difference between grimy and gleaming.

In the clean skill set, we cover the basics of speed cleaning – materials, tools, and methods. We find out how to clean the way the pros do – fast and well. We stress teamwork, explore ways to involve the children, and share tips to speed things up so we can all get on with other things.

Planning your home It's an old saying: if you fail to plan, you plan to fail. Planning daily routines, housework schedules, and family activities is key to the smooth running of a home.

In the plan skill set, we explore the secrets of checklists, calendars, schedules, and to-do lists. We share timesaving tips and point out time-traps to avoid. Finally, we discover the organized family's power tool – the Household Notebook.

Part Two: Cycles of an Organized Home

Around the house, the calendar turns – and so do the basic cycles of home life. Food and cooking. Clothing care. Dealing with clutter, cleaning, and organizing. Paper handling and bill paying. In Part Two, we apply our new-found skill sets to each of these major cycles.

Food In this first section, we tackle all aspects of food: menu and meal planning, food shopping and storage. We declutter, organize, and clean the kitchen, setting up activity centres to make it easy and quick to get the family fed. We also tackle basic issues of energy efficiency, kitchen appliances, and setting up a store cupboard.

Clothing Section Two takes us into cupboards, dressing tables, and drawers as we organize all aspects of keeping ourselves clothed. We plan wardrobes, declutter and organize the clothes cupboard, clean out clothing clutter, manage seasonal storage, and learn the best ways to launder and care for our clothing investment.

Surfaces and systems In Section Three, our surroundings start to shine. Here, we learn to care for walls, windows, floors and furnishings, maintain bedding and mattresses, and get acquainted with household systems that keep us comfortable and safe. We focus on home safety and energy savings, too, as we make the home a clean and comfortable place to be.

Room to live Section Four offers room-by-room help for clutter, cleaning, and organization issues. Whether it's the family room, children's areas, bedroom, or bath, we cut the clutter, get organized, and clean up quickly and well.

Paper Section Five tackles the paper chase: sorting, organizing, and filing the paper in our lives. We learn which documents to keep and how to keep them, and we create centres for efficient bill paying, deskwork, and paper handling.

clean ▲ see pages 48–71

plan ▲ see pages 72–87

The solution:
do it your way

Learning basic skills – how to declutter, how to clean – is only the first step on the road to better home management. To reach the goal of a clean and organized home, we must craft our own personal home-management habits and routines. Any method we select must work with our unique personality, lifestyle, and strengths.

In home management, as with nylon tights, there is no such thing as "one size fits all". One person's list-based routine seems scattered and annoying to someone who prefers the tighter structure of a daily planner. Your neighbour swears by the scheduling advice she found online, but the tight blocks of time in her day don't work with your more casual approach. Your sister thinks it's essential to have all counters and surfaces bare of distractions; you can't work well unless you can see your tools and supplies.

Get personal

Knowledge is power – but self-knowledge is empowerment. Moving from disorder and chaos to effective, orderly living requires more than simple information or one person's example; it requires personally devised solutions that will work for you as an individual – not for your sister or your neighbour or anyone else.

"There is only one right way to get organized: yours."

Throughout this book, we'll help you tailor advice and recommendations to suit your own personality and family lifestyle. We'll identify your "clutter personality" – the habits and thinking that have caused you to become a clutterer (*see pages 30–31*) – and offer strategies to help you work in harmony with it.

Instead of establishing one level of "clean", we'll help you assess your own family's needs and constraints so you can reach the right state of "clean enough" for your home.

Where do I start?

It's easy to pick up a book about home management, read along, laugh at the jokes, and put the book down again. Translating that experience into a cleaner, more organized home is another matter.

Most visitors to our Web community have a single question: "Where do I start?" The answer is simple: you start where you are, then take a single step.

Getting organized isn't a race – it's a journey. On a journey, what matters is the trip, not where you start or how fast you make it, or where other people are along the way.

Too often, people frustrated by the condition of their homes see getting organized as a hundred-metre sprint: an activity with a beginning and an end and a lot of heated pounding in between. "I will clean things up," they vow, "and this time, it's going to stay that way!" A week later, they have little to show for all the effort because they haven't effected the real change that will solve the problems of disorder and chaos.

To make that change, take a single step towards better organization, right now. Tomorrow, take another step towards better home life. And another. And another. Just as chaos and disorder didn't spring full-blown into your home in a single day, so it won't be conquered in one day, either. The important thing is to take the first step, make the first change – and just keep travelling.

▶ **Start small.** Developing good habits, like clearing up clutter that has accumulated at the end of each day, provides easy-to-see results that will help to keep you motivated.

Find fellow travellers

Anyone who's gone on a walk with friends knows that sharing and friendship make even the roughest climb easier. It's no different in your journey to better home management. Look for like minds to walk with you and lighten the way.

There are a number of places where you could find potential fellow travellers. In your community, be alert for friends or neighbours who might form a support network for your efforts. Seek out a "declutter buddy" – a friend who brings a detached view to your decluttering. Without the ties that bind, she'll help you see your possessions in a new light

> ## "The important thing is to take the first step – and just keep travelling."

and help you release them. Next week, it's your turn to help her clear out her cupboard. Check with church groups, clubs or parents' associations to find other people with whom to share your progress; their support will make all the difference and will help to keep you motivated and enthusiastic.

Dedicated support groups can be a wonderful source of accountability and motivation. In North America, for example, Clutterers Anonymous (CLA) applies the Twelve Step program first modelled by Alcoholics Anonymous to issues of clutter and hoarding. Other clutter recovery support groups are offered by counselling centres or volunteer organizations. Community education services or church groups may offer classes and workshops on home management.

Our online community, OrganizedHome.Com, (http://organizedhome.com) offers an interactive support group to help members inspire one another as they get organized together. Have a success story? Come and share it with others who understand. Having trouble parting from your clutter?

We'll give you a pep talk. Wondering where to get started? We'll cheer you on as you take your first steps.

Online or in real life, change is easier to come by when it's shared. Look for others to travel the road with you, to encourage you when you are flagging, and to inspire you with their example, as you move towards your goal – better home and personal organization.

housekeeping
skill sets

"Getting organized" means different things to different people, but in most disorganized homes, you'll find clutter.

Clutter gets between you and the things you want to do. Living in a cluttered home, nearly every action is handicapped and impeded. Either you're wasting time looking for something you need, pushing clutter out of the way to create a workspace, or you're just distracted by the scatter of out-of-place items.

The problem is, attacking the clutter itself won't resolve the issue because the "stuff" is just a symptom. What causes clutter is a cluster of personality traits, thinking, and behaviour. To rein in clutter at home, you have to start with you: your thoughts, your habits, and your day-to-day behaviour patterns.

Reversing the tide of clutter is a slow and steady job, but the rewards are great. In this section, we'll focus on basic methods to STOP clutter and retrain the family to a new, uncluttered outlook.

Clear clutter:
the STOP clutter method

Household clutter is made, not born. Its hidden cause? Deferred decision-making. Each item of clutter in your home represents a frozen decision or an incomplete action. Worse, the stale energy of piled-up clutter attracts more clutter, accreting together into an avalanche of pent-up "must-do, should-do, want-to-do" decisions that are tiring even to contemplate.

For example, going through the post, you notice a catalogue you'd like to look through, so you set it aside on the counter. Next day, three more catalogues, a stack of bills, and a pile of takeaway pizza offers land in the pile, and by the end of the week, the lone catalogue has mushroomed into an unwieldy stack of magazines, letters, bills, flyers, and shopping receipts that will take an hour to sort, file, and finish – and you still haven't found time to peruse the new catalogue. The STOP clutter method fights clutter at the heart by thawing the decision-making

◀ **Keep it brief.** To prevent flagging spirits, declutter in short sessions of between 15 and 20 minutes.

process. It's short, sweet, and powerful, and is designed to help you blast through all those frozen decisions quickly – no more sitting on the fence in the face of chaos! By forcing you to make decisions rapidly, you cut through the mass of clutter and regain your organized home. Using the STOP technique, you'll attack clutter in four easy steps: Sort, Throw out, Organize, and Put away (*see opposite*).

STOP clutter tools

The tools you'll use for each STOP clutter session are simple. They're designed to set limits, encourage decision-making, and make it easy to wrap up each session of cutting clutter. You will need a kitchen timer, three large cardboard boxes, and a rubbish bag.

sort ▲

throw out ▲

A timer Stopping clutter, like acquiring it, is a long-term process of short steps. Too often, the initial excitement of attacking the clutter problem causes people to bite off more than they can chew – or decide, store, or put away in a single session. Result: messed-up drawers, stacks of "I-don't-know" items, and a sense that the job is never finished. Using a timer to keep STOP clutter sessions short and complete keeps the declutter momentum going and prevents burnout. You'll use your timer to start – and stop – each session so that you can finish the put-away step and leave the newly decluttered area clean and ready for use.

Three boxes The put away, storage, and sell/donate boxes lie at the heart of the STOP clutter method. Labelled "Put Away", "Storage", and "Sell/Donate", they're the decision-making engine that drives the declutter process.

Use sturdy, good-sized boxes, preferably with handles and lids. Look for cardboard storage boxes (sold in office suppliers), or scour supermarkets for fruit and vegetable boxes with lids. Handles make it easy to go round the house at the end of each STOP clutter session, emptying the Put Away box. Lids help you stack the Storage and Sell/donate boxes as you gather out-of-season items or set aside boxes for donation or a car-boot sale. Lids help to cut the temptation to peep inside and return decluttered items to their old haunting grounds. Out of sight is out of mind!

A rubbish bag An opaque bin bag or waste bin is star player in a STOP clutter session. Here's where you'll entrust all the true rubbish, and the quicker the better. Black bin bags prevent the declutterer (or family members) from having a change of heart. If it can't be seen, it won't be returned to the scene.

Taking it a step at a time

To harness the power of the STOP clutter method, assemble your boxes and bin bag and set the timer for 15 minutes. The timer's bell will tell you when it's time to stop deciding and start putting away. Working in 15-minute increments (plus another 5 minutes to return put-away items and store the tools), you stay fresh and motivated to do the job.

1 Sort Turning to the day's chosen clutter cache – the area around the telephone, for example – take the first step and sort the items being decluttered. Quickly move through the pile of clutter that surrounds the phone, making a quick decision about each item: should I keep this here, put it away, sell it, or throw it away?

If the item belongs in the area being decluttered, sort it into a pile of like items: pens with pens, paper clips with paper clips, and notepads with post-it notes. If the item is an intruder that must be put away in another location, such as a pair of socks, consign it

organize ▲

put away ▲

to the Put Away box. Surplus items that can be donated to charity or sold are thrown into the Sell/Donate box, the proper place for the plastic flower pen and the ghastly shopping list holder. Items that more appropriately belong in household storage areas – such as light bulbs left over from Christmas holiday decorations – are tucked into the Storage box.

2 Throw out As you sort, throw rubbish straight into the bin bag. Expired coupons, old receipts, scribbled bits of paper, non-working pens – all go straight in.

3 Organize When the entire area has been sorted and the rubbish thrown out, it's time to organize. Take a good look at the newly decluttered area, and find ways to organize the items that belong there. Corral pens next to the phone in a pretty coffee mug. Place the phone book neatly beneath the phone base. Consider ways to organize the area for best use; can you replace messy message slips with a hanging write-on/wipe-off white board?

4 Put away When the timer rings or the area is cleared, it's time to put away any misplaced items found during the STOP clutter session. Take the Put Away box and go round the house, returning items to their proper places. Throw the bin bag into the bin, and return the timer and boxes to a cupboard or shelf, where they'll await the next STOP clutter session. As the Storage boxes fill, add them to a storage area and begin a new box. Decide when you'll attack your home's next clutter magnet and note it on your calendar (*see Planning Your Home, pages 72–87*). Finally, admire your new, organized telephone area. Using the STOP clutter method, you've created a working centre for phone calls and messages.

STOP clutter step by step: the junk drawer

All homes have at least one of these – a drawer for small, often-needed items. The contents of this catch-all arena seem to expand like bread dough, multiplying at will whenever the drawer is closed. When the mess reaches the top of the drawer, it's time to STOP clutter.

1 **Sort.** Assemble your tools: timer, boxes, and bin bag. Set the timer for 15 minutes. Open the junk drawer, and begin the sort step. Sort items that belong in the drawer into like piles, and keep sorting until the timer's bell rings or the drawer is cleared.

2 **Throw out.** Throw any broken or valueless items into the bin bag. Place items that belong elsewhere in the Put Away box, and tuck any items for storage in the Storage box. Surplus items that are still useful go to Sell/Donate.

3 **Organize.** Once the drawer is empty, organize the survivors in the cleared space. Use drawer dividers to separate batteries from postage stamps, pens from shopping coupons. Bundle or bag small items to make them easy to find.

4 **Put away.** When the timer bell rings, stop the session and put away the items in the Put Away box. Store the timer and boxes for the next STOP clutter session. Throw the bin bag in the bin.

STOP clutter around the house: **declutter strategies**

Just as clutter builds up gradually, reversing the flow takes sustained effort. There are limits to what you can achieve in a single STOP clutter session. You may make quick work of the mess on a shelf, in a drawer, or on a work surface. But where do you start to tackle a whole house full of clutter? Answer — one step at a time. Use the following strategies to take your battle against disorder to a global level.

Where the shoe pinches

The process of cutting clutter can be psychologically uncomfortable, so bolster motivation by putting your first STOP clutter efforts where they'll bear the most fruit. Look for the places where the shoe pinches, and focus your clutter-busting efforts where they'll count the most. If it's a challenge to get out of the house to work each day, for example, tackle the jumbled cosmetics on the bathroom shelf, attack the wardrobe, and clear clutter away from the key rack.

Front Door Forward

The most straightforward path through whole-house clutter? Use the Front Door Forward method. Start at the front door and move to the right around the house, decluttering as you go. Start each session next to the last area you cleared.

The advantages of Front Door Forward are that you always know which location is next in line for a clear-out. Better still, the house's public areas are decluttered first — no more wincing at the sound of a neighbour's knock at the door!

A Clean Sweep

Overwhelmed by a house full of clutter? Try doing a Clean Sweep. Once a day, grab a binliner and go round the house looking for rubbish that can be thrown out without the need for decision-making. Old plastic bags, unmated socks, broken kitchen tools, foods past their "use-by" dates, and makeup more than a year old are among the suitable candidates. When the binliner is full, throw it out!

The Penicillin method

One day, you declutter the small table in the hallway. By the following week, a whole new species of clutter has infected the same area. One online declutterer, Ellen, likens it to a dish of mould, to which a lab technician daily adds a single drop of penicillin. Next day, only the area around the drop is mould-free but, as the steady drip-drip-drip of the penicillin continues, the clean areas begin to grow together until the entire dish is cleared of mould.

To apply the Penicillin strategy, use the STOP clutter method to clear clutter from a small area each day. The following day, check to see that the first area is still clear, then move on to liberate another cache of clutter.

A Drawer-a-Day

Practitioners of Feng Shui believe that clutter and accumulated rubbish are traps for stale "chi", the energy that flows throughout home and life. Liberate the trapped chi step-by-step with the A Drawer-a-Day method — fighting clutter by attacking it in small, daily nibbles.

Simply put, take 15 minutes to use the STOP clutter method (*see pages 20–3*) on a single drawer, shelf, work surface, or corner each day. Visualize restoring a free flow of life-giving energy as you declutter and clear each storage area or counter.

▶ **Decluttering** is physically and emotionally demanding. By tackling it in small steps, you'll maintain the energy and enthusiasm you need to work your way around the whole house.

Short and sweet, a quick evening sweep makes for happy mornings. Before bed each night, patrol the house for misplaced belongings. A stout cardboard box or basket with handles makes it easy to gather up discarded shoes, magazines, plates and glasses, toys, television remote controls, and schoolbooks. Go round the whole house and return items to their proper place.

Families with children should build family "put-away" time into the routines of daily life. Just as in any good nursery or kindergarten, returning playthings to their places at the end of the day trains children to habits of order — and stops parents stubbing their toes on scattered toys in the middle of the night!

Keep clutter from
coming back

Getting rid of existing clutter is only half the job; you'll need new habits and a new outlook to prevent clutter from gaining a toehold in your organized home. Try these strategies to keep the clutter monster at bay for good.

Sell It!

Cut the ties and free yourself from clutter by selling unused items for ready cash:

- **Target a jumble sale or car-boot sale.** Be sure to note big-ticket items. Use group pricing – one price for four items or per bag – to encourage sales. Take any unsold items at the end of the sale to a local charity shop and make sure you get rid of everything.
- **Sell online.** Online auction sites make it easy to find buyers for surplus books, craft supplies, collectibles, or electronics. For easiest online selling, consider using an auction reseller, who will advertise your goods, handle the sale, and see to postage and packing in return for a cut of the proceeds.
- **Pass it on.** Secondhand shops aren't just for clothing any more. Fitness equipment, baby items and children's clothing shops now offer an easy way to sell surplus items.
- **It pays to advertise.** Place low-cost classified ads when selling expensive items. Many newspapers and community centres offer free or low-cost classified ads for private sellers. Use this service for a quick way to find new homes – and a few extra pounds – for unneeded appliances, furniture, or fixtures.

Home, home on the range

A primary cause of clutter? It's the homeless ... post, toys, newspapers, and so on. Without a home, common household items wander, lose their way, meet bad companions, and make the transition to clutter.

Establish good homes for your stuff. Newspapers may be folded and stacked on a coffee table before being read, then given shelter in a box while they wait for recycling. Devote prime domestic space to use as a Launch Pad (*see pages 186–7*) for each family member: a location for handbags, school papers, rucksacks, and briefcases. Give paperwork proper files so it never has to huddle in lonely stacks on kitchen counters. With a home to go to, good stuff will never become bad clutter.

One-In, One-Out Promise

The simplest way to deny clutter houseroom? Make the One-In, One-Out Promise. For every new garment, game, DVD, or magazine that enters your home, resolve that one older garment, game, DVD, or magazine must leave. For example, when this month's issue of your favourite magazine arrives in the post, set aside an older issue to pass on to a friend. Pretty new towels may enter your home only if the older set is recycled for use as car-wash rags or put in the charity bag.

The No-Buy-It Diet

Go on a No-Buy-It Diet to build clutter-free habits and avoid buying more "stuff". The No-Buy-It Diet is simple: find ways to rent, borrow, or swap for items you need, rather than buy them. Try these No-Buy-It strategies to share the wealth and cut the clutter without buying new:

■ **Equipment for parties.** Having a party or reunion? Borrow special equipment like punch bowls or coffee urns from friends or community sources. Churches, community groups, and some fast-food restaurants offer clutter-free access to specialized equipment for your celebration; at the end of the event, the items are returned for others to use.

■ **Children's sports equipment.** This can be costly and is often outgrown from season to season. Get together with other parents to organize swaps of uniforms and equipment for children's sports activities. For example, ski swaps can outfit youngsters inexpensively before each season and can find new homes for outgrown ski boots at the end of the year.

"Without a home, common household items wander, lose their way, and meet bad companions."

■ **Maternity and baby clothing.** Expecting a baby? Other mothers are an excellent source of gently worn maternity and baby clothing, so swap and recycle instead of buying new. Circulate a "maternity box" of maternity clothing among a group of young-mother friends. After the child is born, remove worn-out items, and add any new clothing before handing the box on to the next expectant mother.

Observe oosouji

To hold the line against clutter and start the New Year fresh, borrow a Japanese custom. To prepare for a happy and prosperous New Year, the Japanese perform *oosouji*, cleaning and organizing their homes and offices in the run-up to New Year's Day. By this practice, they tie up the old year's loose ends and outstanding projects, and make room for the blessings and challenges of a new year.

Take a tip from the Japanese and ring in the New Year from a clean and decluttered home. At the end of the year, create space in each shelf, cupboard, and wardrobe for the new possessions that will come with a new year.

▲ **Make a one-in,** one-out promise. When you shop for new clothes, make sure that you donate, for example, one older shirt to charity for every new shirt you buy.

■ **DVDs, videos, and computer games.** Rent DVDs, videos, and computer games rather than buying them. Rental DVDs by post bring films to you without creating video clutter at home – and you'll have access to a far larger library of new films than that offered at your rental shop. Borrow DVDs and videos from your local library, or arrange a video swap with friends and neighbours for a free film experience.

What's your
clutter personality?

It's silent. It's sneaky. It creeps about in corners: clutter. While it's tempting to launch an all-out battle in the war against clutter, it's best to know your enemy first. There are as many reasons for household clutter as there are clutterers. Target your household's clutter problem by going to the root of the problem: your own thinking.

The hoarder:
"This might come in handy one day."

Know a hoarder by his or her collection ... of the most unlikely objects. Hoarders save everything, and I do mean everything – plastic shopping bags, newspaper flyers, and worn-out clothing. Hoarder creativity knows no bounds. Ask a hoarder why she's holding onto three years' worth of local newspapers, and she'll describe the papier-mâché angel figure she hopes to make from them. The problem is, hoarding knows no limits, so our friend can't see that she has enough materials to make angels for each home in the neighbourhood ... and then some!

Hoarding is rooted in insecurity, financial or otherwise. Deep down, hoarders are afraid that they'll never have the resources they need if they let go of any possession, no matter how worn, useless, or superfluous. If kitchen cupboards are crammed with cracked margarine containers, small kitchen appliances that haven't been used in decades, and old catalogues, it's likely there's some hoarding behaviour underlying the clutter.

Hoarders need to remind themselves that resources will always be available. Where can a hoarder look outside the home for a substitute hoard? No problem! Stuff will be with us always. Find magazines at the library, kitchenware marked down at car-boot sales, and every small appliance known to man can be found (cheap!) at the pound store. Think of these off-site treasure troves as attenuated household storage areas. Dare to bin it!

The deferrer:
"I'll think about that tomorrow."

Those of the deferral mindset are guilty of the great set-aside. Bills, flyers, old newspapers, items that need cleaning or repair, and household projects are all set aside to be dealt with another day. The deferrer will leave dirty dinner plates in the sink, wet laundry in the washing machine, and dropped fruit underneath the apple tree in the garden.

Deferrers need to be reminded that tomorrow has no more time or energy than today – and that deferring decisions drags down each new day with yesterday's unfinished business. Since this behaviour is grounded in procrastination, apply the best remedy: action. For deferrers, simply making a start creates the momentum needed to finish the job. Remember, it's easier to keep a rolling stone in motion than it is to pick it up and start it rolling the first time!

How to push the inner deferrer into action? Set yourself a cut-off date. For example, when you find an unfinished cross-stitch project, circle a date on the calendar and make a note. If you haven't finished the cross-stitch by that date, the item must go – but simply by making a start on the project, you're liable to keep going until you finish it. The jump-start of taking action is often enough to spark even the most confirmed deferrer's battery, so harness this effect to resume momentum on stalled clutter issues.

The rebel: "I don't want to and you can't make me!"

Somehow, it's all Mum's fault. Rebels were forced to pick up after themselves as children; as adults, they're still expressing the mute and stubborn determination of a four-year-old who refuses to pick up his toys. Rebel clutter can be anything, but often centres on household activities. No, the rebel won't put his or her clothes in the laundry basket, cereal bowl in the dishwasher, or car in the garage – even when the clothing gets wrinkled, the cereal bowl hardens into yellow gloop, and the car gets damaged by passing traffic.

Rebels need to remind themselves that the war is over. They don't live at home with Mum and Dad anymore – and their own family deserves an adult on the job, not a sulky child. Tell that inner rebel, "It's okay – I'm the parent now, and I want a house that's nice to live in." By switching places with the old authority figure, it is possible that the Rebel can find a way out of his or her "I don't want to!" mindset. By reminding yourself that you are in control of your decisions, you can defuse the inner rebel's imaginary power struggle.

The perfectionist: "Next week, I'll organize everything ... perfectly."

Perfectionists are wonderful people but they live in an all-or-nothing world. They do wonderful things – when they do them! Perfectionism forms an inner barrier to cutting clutter because the perfectionist simply cannot abide doing a less-than-perfect job. Without the time to give 110 per cent to the project, the perfectionist clutterer prefers to let matters – and the piles of stuff – slide.

For example, plastic food containers may be overflowing from their kitchen cupboard, but the perfectionist clutterer won't sort them out until he or she can purchase the perfect shelf paper, lid-holder organizer, and colour-coded folders and labels. As a result, the massed and crowded containers stay put, falling down onto the feet of anyone hapless enough to open the cupboard door.

Perfectionist clutterers need to remind themselves of the 20–80 rule: 20 per cent of every job takes care of 80 per cent of the problem, while fixing the remaining 20 per cent will sort out 80 per cent of the job. By giving themselves permission to do only 20 per cent, perfectionist clutterers get going. It is perfectly fine to tell the inner perfectionist, "Today, I'll do the important 20 per cent of that job – sorting, stacking, and organizing those food containers. Later, I'll do the other 80 per cent – buying organizers and lining the shelves with shelf paper." If later never comes? Well, you've outwitted your inner perfectionist clutterer...congratulations!

The sentimentalist: "Oh, the little darling!"

Sentimentalists never met a memento they didn't like – or want to keep. Children's clothing and school papers, faded greeting cards, souvenirs from long-ago trips, and jumbled keepsakes crowd the environment of the sentimental clutterer. The problem is, there's so much to remember that the truly endearing items get lost in a flood. Who can find the first-year school report in an attic full of boxes of paper?

The sentimental clutterer needs to reduce the mass of mementos to a more portable state, changing his or her mindset from an indiscriminate "Awwww!" to a more selective stance. Remember, what are important to the sentimental heart are the memories and emotions. So, for example, a sentimental clutterer can corral each child's school papers into a single box by selecting one best drawing, theme, or project each month – everything else must go in the rubbish bin.

Other ideas for reining in rampant sentimental clutter include scrapbooking the very best photos and papers, or photographing surplus sentimental clutter before letting it go. Sort it out, choose the best, keep the memories and bin the rest!

Fighting clutter
from the inside out

It isn't just our homes that are clogged with useless stuff. Clutter takes hold of our minds, too. Psychological issues like fear or sentiment can prevent us from getting rid of our excess. Solution: confront the inner forces that stand between your clutter and the rubbish bin. Try these counter-measures to release your grip on clutter.

Scarcity thinking: "I might need it one day."

People with scarcity thinking refuse to part with clutter out of fear that they will not have – or will not have enough of – the goods and items they need at some future time. Result: drawers filled with folded aluminium foil and stacked egg cartons, garages drowning in bent nails and broken tools.

Deal with scarcity thinking by dragging your fear into the open and staring it down – then move past it to release the hold on your thinking. For example, confronted with a cupboard full of empty yogurt containers (no lids), ask yourself, "When was the last time I ever used one?" An answer that ranges from "never" to "about 25 years ago" means that scarcity thinking is behind the clutter problem.

Face the fear! Remind yourself that the world is full of empty yogurt containers. Your belief that they might all disappear is just that – only a fear. Out they go, both the containers and the fear behind them.

Protecting an investment: "I paid good money for that."

Financial issues often bond us to clutter; a mental refrain of "But I paid £15 for that!" can keep us from releasing items we no longer need or want. The problem is, yesterday's purchase price no longer has much relationship to today's value. Take computer equipment. Three or four years after purchase, the actual value of a personal computer is only a fraction of the original price due to rapid advances in technology.

It's not what you paid for the item that matters; it's what it's worth today – and that is the value you must assess when considering whether to give the item houseroom or let it go as clutter. Online auction sites are wonderful allies here; they'll give you a quick, realistic value for any product. Knowing what something is worth today will shift your thinking and make it easier to part with the item and move on.

Thrill of the chase: "It's a collection."

Collecting can be fun but it can also lead to immense clutter problems. In the thrall of pursuit and acquisition, little else matters – until you have to find homes for the new additions on already-crowded shelves. By the time a cherished collection must be stored in dusty attics or on high shelves, it's crossed the line and become clutter.

To break the bonds of collection clutter, assess your collection with an eye to finding the heart: those three or five or seven items with a true tie to your affection. Only those items with meaning, use, and value deserve a place in your home.

All in the family: "It was my grandfather's."

Family: it's the tie that binds – and binds you to unwanted stuff in the form of "heirloom clutter". Heirloom clutter is any item you don't want, don't need, don't use, and don't value, but which you keep because it once belonged to a family member.

We're not talking about true heirlooms. I have one: a beautiful quilt hand-made by my great-grandmother Kirchener. Each time I find the tiny squares of "ABC" fabric, salvaged from a childhood dress of my mother's, I feel the love of four generations in my hands. My quilt tells a story, and I will pass it – and its story – on to my own grandchildren.

▲ Be selective. True family heirlooms deserve a place in an organized home, but not all inherited items qualify. Do keep your grandparents' love letters, but find a shredder for their utility bills.

Heirloom clutter is more like Grandpa's old sofa. It's tattered. It's ugly. You can't sit on it for fear that it will fall apart but you can't get rid of it either. Why not? "Because it's an heirloom!" Learn to distinguish between a true heirloom and heirloom clutter. To help, ask these questions:

■ What do I know about this item?
■ Do I have a memory related to this item?
■ Does the item have use or value in my everyday life?

Identity crisis: "Those beer kegs were in my room at uni."

Identity clutter is possessions we no longer use, but hold onto because they symbolize a younger, earlier identity. Identity clutter is easy to spot because it's usually branded closely with its time and place. The macramé wall hanging you made at evening class. An LP record collection from the 1980s.

To cut the bonds of identity clutter, remind yourself that you are not your stuff. The memories and the growth are the true gift of these earlier identities. The leftover stuff no longer has a use, except to tie us down and hamper our current, richer life. To retain the memories, save a symbol of that stage of your life, and then release the identity clutter. Write a journal entry about your evening class and ditch the dusty macramé. Frame two or three LP covers, hang them on the wall, and give the rest of the collection to charity.

Dealing with
other people's clutter

Clutter issues, like red hair or blue eyes, tend to run in families. While an occasional brown-eyed, naturally organized joker does sometimes enter the pack, chances are that household clutter is a family problem. When you're taking the first steps down the road to order in your own life, other people's clutter can create major roadblocks. What can you do to deal with the clutter created by others?

Establish clutter reserves

There's no such thing as clutter-free living. Even the tidiest among us still throws clothing on the floor from time to time.

Accept reality by establishing dedicated clutter reserves. Like wildlife reserves, these are limited areas where clutter may live freely, as long as it stays within boundaries.

- **In a bedroom,** one chair becomes the clutter reserve. Clothing may be thrown with abandon, so long as it's thrown on the chair.
- **A kitchen junk drawer** can house vitamin bottles, rubber bands, clipped recipes, expired coupons, and shopping receipts that are unwelcome outside their clutter reserve.
- **A large magazine bucket** in the living room is fair game for magazines, so long as they can fit inside the bucket.
- **Craft, sewing,** or hobby projects create instant chaos – but too-rigid pick-up rules invade scarce craft time. Dedicate a small folding table or fit out a spare cupboard for craftwork to keep inspiration flowing. To keep the clutter within bounds, close the cupboard doors or screen the table between sessions.

Where to start? Change begins with you!

You've worked for weeks to declutter the television room and kitchen, and once again, you wake up to wall-to-wall mess. Other people's mess. Tempting as it may be to call a family meeting and lay down the no-clutter law, resist the urge. Any forced regime of clutter-free living will last only as long as you stand over family members and nag them to pick up their socks, newspapers, and toys.

Instead, recognize that change must begin with you. Only when you have met and mastered your own clutter challenges can you turn your attention to helping other family members along the path to order. Moreover, their progress will be just like yours: made in small steps. Just as you must make slow and steady progress towards building new habits, setting up activity centres, and cutting off new clutter at the source, so with other family members.

Tips for the family clutter consultant

Fighting over disorder and disorganization gets nobody anywhere – and it doesn't clear the clutter. Instead, adopt the role of clutter consultant to help other family members get a grip on clutter. Acting as a helper takes the heat off the dispute, and creates a sense of teamwork. Try these tips to inspire others to order in your household:

Work with the clutterer's personality "My way or no way" clutter fixes are based on a faulty premise: that there's one right way to cut clutter and get organized. Wrong!

Personality styles dictate the shape of successful clutter solutions. A clear-desk strategy that works for a visually-oriented parent won't have meaning for a child who prefers his tools in view. Contain his coloured markers in a cheerful mug on the desktop, rather than in a closed drawer, to respect his personality style.

Attack the problem, not the clutter Clutter is only a symptom; the true problem lies within the clutterer's relationship to stuff, space, and order. As a clutter consultant, your job is to attack the problem, not the stuff. Picking up a child's scattered papers after she returns home from school is a one-time symptom fix; setting up a Launch Pad for the child (*see pages 186–7*) and teaching her to visit it before and after school offers the true solution.

Be flexible Spouses, roommates, or housemates often disagree on what constitutes clutter. One person's rubbish is another one's treasure, so why waste time defining your terms? A successful family clutter consultant is flexible, and reaches for solutions rather than confrontation. In my home, husband Steve's poker materials had become an unwieldy collection of books, printouts, and scraps of paper that drifted from sofa to table to floor, depending on where Steve had been studying last. To my eyes, it was clutter. To him, it was his poker library: an indispensable resource for a man who hopes to compete at a world-class level some day.

Solution: I designated a small shelf unit for his poker library. By making a home for the poker library, Steve has easy access to his reference materials – and I no longer have to see them piled across the breakfast table or heaped on the sofa.

▲ **Family mess?** Get-organized efforts are doomed to fail if they're based on one family member's idea of "tidy". Stress the benefits to all family members of a neat and organized space.

▲ **Organized success.** An organized entertainment area helps family members find and replace videos and DVDs, or find a good read. Seeing a benefit helps the entire family learn to be organized.

Getting organized isn't about how the house looks – it's about how it works. How quickly can you wrap a gift, pay the bills, or change an ill child's bedding in the middle of the night? In an organized home, stuff and surroundings are arranged to make it easy to carry on the work of daily life.

Organization is more than simply putting items neatly into boxes, cupboards, or drawers. It's about storing a household's supplies, tools and materials in a meaningful, logical pattern – and in a way that makes it easy to return them after you're finished with them. Good organization speeds and simplifies every daily task.

In this section, we'll learn the basic principles of home organization, how to create activity centres to focus everyday tasks, and how to use containers to create an organized home. We'll also look at ways to involve all the family in organizing the home. Our goal – to create liveable, workable space and storage that makes daily life flow smoothly.

How to
organize a home

Home. It's where the heart is, where you belong, come to recharge your batteries, and rest your head – and, for most of us, there's no place like it. Our homes are more than shelter from the elements – they are the stage on which we live our lives. Sentiment aside, however, just how well does your house work for you?

Think back to the last 24 hours. Did you leave the house without delay ... or did you lose the car keys again this morning? At mealtimes, was it easy for family members to help set the table or were the dishes stored too high, too low – or were they sitting, still unwashed, on the kitchen counter?

"Getting organized is not about how things look: it's about how things work."

When you went to bed, was it a relaxing transition from a busy day, or did you have to shove aside a pile of clothing and evict the dog from your pillow to rest your weary head? If daily life is getting you down, it's time to get organized.

Think function, not appearance

First, we need to get clear about what organizing is and what it isn't. Organization is not a decorating style – it's about how well your home functions, not how it looks. A home organized with mismatched homemade containers can be far better organized than one fully outfitted with pricey built-in organizing "systems" that don't work. The paradox is that tidy houses are not always organized houses. Neat stacks of paper can hide

◀ **Getting organized** means having everything you need readily to hand so that you can perform the everyday tasks that keep home and life running smoothly.

unpaid bills and missed appointments. A clean and streamlined bedroom won't show the ripped and crumpled clothing jammed into drawers or crammed into wardrobes. By contrast, a busy desk may be the best evidence of an organized household: bills paid, papers filed, letters answered.

One can be tidy without being organized. Tidying is the process of returning misplaced possessions to their homes. But what if those items don't have the right homes in the first place? Then you're back at Chaos Point One, still looking for the house keys, your wallet, or the dog's lead. "Put away" does not necessarily equal "organized". So don't fall for the organized look. Go for the organized function – it's what makes the difference between chaos and calm.

Think process, not product

Pick a car-boot sale, any car-boot sale. Chances are, some pretty pricey organizing products will be featured for sale: rotating plastic turntables, bathroom shelf units, specialized organizers like tin holders, tie racks, and shelf extenders. All on sale for a tiny fraction of their retail price – and all mute witnesses to a would-be organizer who has confused "getting organized" with "buying stuff".

There's a difference between organization and the products you'll use to achieve that goal. Organization is a process, not a product. It involves time and thought, effort and motivation – and you can't buy these factors in any shop. No tangible item, no matter how useful, can set you on the road to better organization all by itself. The moral is: nobody got organized by buying stuff. Instead, they ended up at a car-boot sale.

The rules of
home organization

The bottom-line test for organization is function. Does your house work for you? Can you find things, carry out tasks, and live daily life without stress? To organize a home, follow the three rules of home organization: a place for everything, bring the family on board, and create centres for household activities.

1 A place for everything

It's an old saying, but it's still true: "A place for everything, and everything in its place" is a mantra for home organization. Possessions, like people, need homes. Find them that home, defend their turf with labels, dividers, and organizers, and you've won most of the battle.

> ## "It's an old saying, but it's still true: 'A place for everything, and everything in its place.'"

Be creative when it comes to finding homes for household stuff – and rearrange your thinking. So what if shops sell towels in sets of three? Break up the trio and store them where they're needed: hand towels stacked in a lavatory near the living area; bath towels and face cloths in the bathroom where they're most used. Don't hide takeaway pizza vouchers and menus away in a kitchen drawer where they'll get forgotten: store them in a folder near the phone where they'll be most useful.

2 Bring the family on board

Getting organized is not simply a matter of domestic space allocation; it's an integrated process involving all members of the household. Any organizing scheme or system will fail unless all family members understand it and can follow it. Bring the family on board as you organize your stuff and your surroundings. For example, when organizing where to put items in the kitchen, store plates, bowls, and unbreakable glasses in low cupboards. Younger family members can lay the table only if they can reach the crockery; by storing tableware in an accessible place for them, you'll be helping all of the family to help you.

3 Create "centres" for household activities

Looking for a model of a well-organized home? Go back to pre-school! Pre-school teachers are model organizers because they have to be. Without a plan for classroom structure, 18 or 20 energetic little people could create plaything havoc in mere moments.

To keep their classroom running smoothly, pre-school teachers apply the concept of "centres" – dedicated areas for a single activity, like building blocks or dressing up, with storage for all the things required by that activity. In the Wendy house, kitchen toys, pots, and pans encourage role-playing; at the art table, paper, paints, and brushes are within easy reach. At home time, children know to return clothes to the dressing-up box and toy cars to the designated "car park" area.

On the domestic front, you can set up centres that work the same way, to focus and support the everyday activities that are carried on in the home. To create them, you'll designate:

- **A focus.** Allocate one focussed activity to each centre.
- **A specified area.** Set aside a single place to perform the activity.
- **Storage for tools and supplies.** Ensure that all items needed are present and available in the centre.

Creating centres

Consider establishing these activity centres for your home. Tailor them and their contents to your family's needs.

■ **Telephone** (phone directory, family address book, family calendar, message pad, pens, folder containing takeaway coupons and menus)

■ **Grooming** (skin-care products, shaving tools, cosmetics, and hair-care implements near a bathroom sink and mirror)

■ **Outdoor clothing** (coats, hats, gloves, scarves, umbrellas, and boots in a cupboard near the door)

■ **Cleaning and caretaking** (mops, broom, and vacuum cleaner, cleaning carryall with tools, replacement light bulbs, cleaning cloths and sponges, specialized cleaning products)

■ **Paper handling** (desk, telephone, computer, file box or file drawer, pens, paper, and chequebook)

■ **Correspondence basket** (stationery, selection of greetings cards, pens, envelopes, and stamps)

■ **Children's play areas** (floor mat or cushion, toys in plastic bins)

■ **Reading** (comfortable chair, reading light, small table for beverage, reading glasses, pillow, highlighter pens, and page markers)

■ **Homework** (table, good lighting, pens and markers, paper, reference books)

■ **Entertainment** (television, remote controls, TV schedule, seating, snack trays, place mats)

■ **DIY area** (workbench, lighting, toolboxes, organizers for hardware such as nails)

■ **Laundry** (washing machine, tumble dryer, folding space, stain pre-treatment, bleach, detergent, fabric softener, laundry sorter)

■ **Arts and crafts** (workspace, lighting, storage for paints, paper, glue, and embellishments)

■ **Mending** (sewing machine, iron and ironing board, sewing tools, fabrics and supplies)

■ **Planning and scheduling** (desk area, computer, planner or electronic organizer, office supplies)

■ **Wrap and post centre** (cardboard boxes, padded envelopes, bubble wrap, brown paper, postal scales, gift wrap, ribbon and gift cards, scissors, tape, pens, and marker pen)

bathroom centre ▲ see pages 190–1   **play centre** ▲ see pages 210–11   **paper centre** ▲ see pages 226–7

The concept of "activity centres" isn't set in stone – and it's not necessary to set up each centre in a distinct and specific space.

Often, particularly in a kitchen, activity centres will have to overlap. In small spaces, don't try to mark off each centre with fixed lines and rigid dividers; instead, see the concept as a fluid one that depends on the chores being performed.

Keep centres flexible

A cutting centre, focused on the sink area, may overlap almost completely with the dishwashing centre in a small kitchen. Each centre's tools should be stored in the most logical space for the centre's purpose, and they may share drawer or counter space with other equipment. The goal is to make each activity as convenient as possible, even when the grater and juicer must reside in the same cupboard as the plate drainer!

First principles:
organizing basics

As we get organized room-by-room around the house, keep these basic principles in mind. Whether it's crammed cupboards or cluttered work surfaces, these central organization strategies will help keep order on the home front.

Hot, warm, or cold?

It's a simple but powerful premise: items that are used the most should be easiest to reach. Think of organized spaces as having storage locations that are hot, warm, and cold, and store tools and supplies according to how often they're used.

■ **Hot zones**, like the fronts of drawers, shelves at eye level, and storage space on a work surface, are home to the most used items. These are areas your hand can reach with little or no effort, such as the kitchen tool holder next to the stove. This is where to store your favourite spoons, whisks, and ladles for easy access to these cooking best friends.

■ **Warm zones** are a bit harder to reach – such as the space at the back of the drawer or the shelf near the top of the cupboard. You'll need to stretch or bend, or open doors wider to reach a warm zone. Send items you need infrequently, such as once a week or once a month, to the warm climes. Potato peelers, large pots, and baking tins can all live here happily. You'll know where they are when you need them, but they won't impede your work the rest of the time.

■ **Cold zones** (otherwise known as Outer Siberia) are those storage places that must have been designed by a chiropractor to encourage business. They're dark. They're obscure. They're hard to reach without a small pair of steps or assuming a posture on your hands and knees. The back recesses of the bottom shelf or the cupboard above the refrigerator that can only be reached with a ladder, are cold-zone territories. Here's where you put those items that you use least, such as jelly moulds, seasonal cookware, and serving platters for big parties. Think of it this way: the cold will keep them fresh!

Label, label, label

In the middle of a sort-and-throw-it-out session, an organizer's design seems obvious, but over time, that data can be lost. Faced with a linen cupboard, our mental outline of "I'll stack the children's sheets here, the beach towels over here and the winter blankets down here ..." lasts only until the first late-night rummage for clean sheets jumbles the tidy piles.

Solution? Labels, labels, and still more labels. Picture labels for children. Computer-printed labels. Labels by the sheet, or labels created one-by-one by electronic label-makers. Repeat after me: "There is no such thing as too many labels".

Labels make any organizing scheme crystal-clear. They show everyone, not just the organizer, where things belong. Baby-sitters or house guests will always know where to find the towels – and where to replace them – when the linen cupboard shelves are labelled.

When moving, labels on boxes help to get the contents to the right place in the new house. For seasonal storage, labels prevent the need to open-and-dig for the Christmas-tree lights. In the fuse cupboard, labels can show exactly which fuse to remove to shut down the leaking hot water heater.

Harder to get out than to put away

Professional child-carers, such as day-nursery staff or child minders, know a simple secret: to keep things neat, make it harder to get something out than to put it away. It's just human nature. When we want something, we want it, and we'll work hard to get it, too. But when it comes to putting it back…. Take advantage of human nature and make things harder to get out than to put away.

For instance, store children's books upright in a flip-file – a plastic rectangular washing-up bowl in which they can be stood on end. To retrieve a book, the child will need to flip through the titles to find what she is searching for – but to put it away, she need only slide it back into the bowl.

"Repeat after me: 'There is no such thing as too many labels'."

Go vertical

For books, files, or papers, vertical storage beats horizontal storage every time. What is horizontal storage? It's a pile. A stack. One thin, rectangular object stored on top of another one. A stack of books on a coffee table. Files in a tray on a desk. Magazines stacked next to a table, on the floor. To reach one book, one file, one magazine, you must move them all – and chances are, you won't bother to move them all back.

Vertical storage, such as that offered by hanging files or bookcases or table-top file boxes, makes it easy to find the file or letter you need. Simply flip through the hanging files, peeping at the papers within. In a vertical magazine file, it's easy to find the issue you want – and you won't disturb the rest of the magazines when you pull it from the storage box.

Our child's book flip-file illustrates the principle perfectly. Finding the right book is a matter of flipping through the covers; replacing it doesn't require moving the other books. Similarly, sewing enthusiasts know that hanging fabric lengths from clothes hangers makes it much simpler to find the fabric they're looking for – and with no need to disturb other lengths folded in a pile.

In geometry, there's no preference, but when organizing, choose the vertical over the horizontal any day!

▶ **Top to bottom** DVDs, stored vertically in a box with labels facing up, make it easy to find cinema favourites. Photo labels provide a peep inside closed storage containers and help you find just the right shoes for an evening out. Hanging file folders allow quick search-and-replace options for stored paperwork.

Choosing
organizing products

Boxes, baskets, containers, and gadgets of all kinds offer great solutions to many household storage problems – but they're not solutions in themselves. Buying them may make you believe you're tackling a problem, but buying the wrong organizer at the wrong time is worse: it just creates more clutter.

Organize, measure, buy

Take a common problem: magazine storage. Faced with a bookcase filled with favourites, it's tempting to say, "Oh, I must do something about those stacks of magazines", grab the car keys and head to the shops. Once there, buying a set of 12 plastic magazine holders (in the same colour as the living room curtains) appears to be the right solution.

Home you go – only to find that the holders are too big for the bookcase, and that the whole collection will require eight more containers to hold the entire stack. Wallet drained and energy depleted, you drop the whole project, leaving the new holders to swell the population of household clutter.

Smart organizers understand how the process works: they organize first, measure next, and buy – if they buy – last. First, they assess and sort the magazines, keeping only 20 per cent: those periodicals to which they refer often.

After recycling the rejected 80 per cent, our organizer plans and measures available storage areas. Only then does she shop for organizational products – and she does so with a list that enables her to buy exactly what she needs.

Put organizers to work for you by following these tips for making the most of the storage products available.

Corral and contain
Cartons, boxes, baskets, and containers are the organizer's foot soldiers in the war against chaos. Use them to sort and store magazine collections, children's toys, and arts-and-crafts materials. Open containers are ideal for often-used items, making them available but keeping them from spreading over living areas.

Climb the walls
Hooks, pegs, and hangers provide bonus storage in tight places. Pegs near an entrance allow children to hang coats and hats when they enter the house. The dog's lead and the car keys will never go missing if they have designated hooks near the back door. Narrow picture shelves intended for displaying picture frames are ideal to hold nappies and skin-care products near baby's changing table.

On the shelf
Wall-mounted shelf units are hard-working members of the get-organized team. Over-the-door shelving provides an instant larder when stocked with tinned food. A shelf above the washing machine stores laundry products so they are accessible to adults but safe from children and pets.

For maximum storage power, combine plastic containers or wicker baskets with shelves. Colour-coded containers help children keep their play spaces tidy. Low, flat wicker baskets make it easy to see and access toiletries in the bathroom.

Divide and conquer
Drawers are wonderful friends. There's only one tiny problem: open and close a drawer ten times, and you're apt to find a scrambled mess thereafter. Fix the problem with drawer organizers. Use short, straight lengths of cardboard or plastic to create divided areas or go for ready-made drawer organizers: some offer different-sized trays that interlock to create custom dividers.

▶ **Sort the sock drawer** with dividers, and you'll never again have to dig through a tangle of tights or stockings to reach the cotton socks you need for the gym.

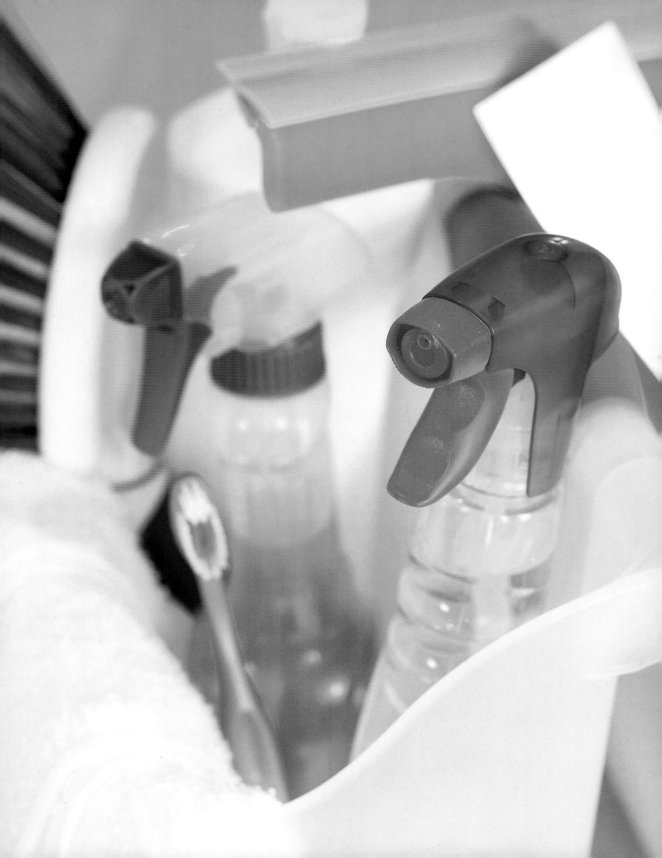

Cleaning the house. It's a dirty job, but somebody has to do it. Chances are, dirt and disorder have taken over your home. Do you have the cleaning skills you need to keep a sparkling house?

Setting the right standard for "clean enough" brings a realistic goal to the task of keeping a clean house. Learning to clean efficiently speeds house-cleaning chores. Tapping talent in the form of family teamwork provides extra manpower (and woman- and child-power) to get the job done fast, and trains younger family members in cleaning skills. Choosing the right cleaning products, selecting the right cleaning tools, and using them effectively helps keep cleaning drudgery at bay. Scheduling cleaning chores helps you attack dirt early, before it becomes entrenched and stubborn.

In this section, we'll learn the basic cleaning skills that keep a household healthy and happy. Got your apron and your cleaning tools? Ready, set ... clean!

Setting standards for
the "clean-enough" home

How clean is your house? It's a matter of choice: yours. While it may sound like heresy to the "cleanies" among us, the happiest families establish a standard for household cleanliness that suits their family composition, cleaning style, and personal preferences.

Set the right standard – for you

Some families – such as those with crawling babies or immuno-compromised older family members – will need to reach for a very high standard of cleaning. Others, such as a clan of healthy young adults, can live quite happily in a home with a more-relaxed cleaning style. While nobody advocates ignoring cleaning to the point of health and safety problems, a realistic view of your family's cleaning standard prevents frustration – and helps get the work done faster.

Reach for family agreement on the issue of a cleaning standard. If most household members err on the "relaxed" side of the equation, there'll be cleaning trouble if one member pushes for higher standards.

Negotiate a commonsense compromise. Food preparation areas require a high level of sanitation but a teen's bedroom poses fewer health and safety concerns. Better to pick cleaning battles carefully, with an eye to general well-being, than to fight it out over every speck of dust.

▲ **Clean smart** by setting a realistic cleaning standard. Schedule chores to keep the house clean every day.

▲ **Be realistic** about where to insist on a higher standard. Children's rooms and kitchen areas demand a higher level of cleanliness.

▲ **More relaxed** cleaning standards are appropriate in less-used areas. Go easier on the chores in guest bedrooms or utility areas.

Where does your family fall on the cleaning spectrum? Try this quiz: it will help you assess the sweet spot of "clean-enough" for your home. There are no right or wrong answers.

1 When dinner is over, what's the state of the kitchen?

A Pristine, of course. I load the dishwasher as I cook, and the washing-up is done promptly. I can't relax if the kitchen doesn't sparkle when I turn out the lights. Who wants to come back to a dirty kitchen in the morning?

B I let the dinner plates soak until next day. Who wants to ruin a good meal by spending time with their hands in hot water afterwards?

C What's the difference? The kitchen counters are still covered with dirty dishes; I just washed the ones we needed before the meal.

2 How's your relationship with the vacuum cleaner?

A Who needs a man when I have my high-speed vacuum cleaner? Even the cat has learned to stand still for the daily vacuuming.

B Love–hate. I show it the carpet every week or so, or when friends are coming over – but I do wish it would learn to lower its voice.

C What vacuum cleaner? I'm still hoping a cleaning reality show will call by and dig us out. Public exposure would be a small price to pay!

3 Getting to the seat of the problem, how often do you scrub the toilet?

A As often as I use it, of course. Who wants to park themselves on anything less than sparkling?

B Hit or miss – a couple of times a week, more often if the men in the house forget to aim.

C Only when something snarls at me when I lift the lid … say, every few weeks?

4 For sweetest dreams, how often do you change the sheets?

A Once a week – or twice a week in warm weather. I love the feel of crisp, fresh bedlinen.

B When I remember or when the smell gets to me. Say, every couple of weeks or so.

C Only when I have a new boyfriend, if you know what I mean. Why waste good laundry powder and water if I'm going to be too sleepy to notice?

5 Are you a duster or a dabbler? How often do you remove dust from the home?

A Daily, of course; it's a ritual. Some of my finest ideas come to me while I stroke the furniture with my duster.

B Once a week or so – or whenever the household joker writes "Dust Me" on the dining-room table with his finger.

C I'm a fan of the blow-it method. If I pick something up and it's covered with dust, I blow it off. Great household hint, no?

If you answered mostly A, congratulations! You are a Clean Extreme and happy to be so. Your house shines and any dust mote so unwise as to assert its presence is shown the door, pronto. Just be careful that militant cleaning doesn't come between you and other family members, who don't necessarily share your enjoyment of the process.

Mostly B answers show you're a Moderate Mopper, with a house that is clean enough to be healthy yet dirty enough to be a home. Most of the time, you're happy with the balance between time spent cleaning and the domestic results, but occasionally you slip a bit too far towards slapdash. Try a more scheduled approach to clean less and enjoy it more.

More than three C answers? You're a Dirt Dodger. Too often, you're discouraged about life on the home front. Remember this truth: if you don't want to, you aren't going to. To pull the household back from the dusty brink, focus on small changes: clearing kitchen counters once a day, setting aside an afternoon each weekend for cleaning chores.

Choosing and using
commercial cleaners

Have you looked down the cleaning aisle at the supermarket lately? An explosion of new cleaning products has created a dizzying array of cleaning choices. Cut through the confusion by sticking to the Big Four of household cleaning products.

Along with a few specialized products, spray window cleaner, spray degreaser, tile and bathroom cleaner, and cream cleaner will handle everyday cleaning needs cheaply and well.

Window cleaner Don't be misled by the name "window cleaner"; this spray-on product cleans windows and a whole lot more, evaporating quickly and leaving no residue behind. Applied to glass or mirrors, it loosens surface dirt so you can remove it with a squeegee or cleaning cloth. Use on glass, mirrors, kitchen counters, sink fixtures, appliance fronts, refrigerator shelves, cupboard doors, and any other liquid-safe surfaces with light, non-greasy soiling.

Degreaser These spray cleaners dissolve grease so it can be lifted away and removed. Also known as "all-purpose cleaners", they will remove food residues from kitchen counters, greasy fingermarks from walls, doors, and light switches, oily dust from skirting boards and mouldings, and hard-to-remove dirt on outdoor furniture. Polish surfaces with a dry cloth to remove the slight film they leave behind.

Tile and bathroom cleaner The bathroom poses multiple cleaning challenges – sticky film from body oils, soap and shampoo; mould and mildew from moisture and condensation; yellow, chalky, hard-water residues on fixtures

▲ **Spray cleaners** make it easy to apply cleaning products evenly to soiled surfaces. An extra spritz on heavier soil helps loosen and remove dried-on dirt.

▲ **Elbow grease** provides even more cleaning power, but hold back. Allow cleaning products time to work before you scrub. Save your energy for other chores!

and fittings. Cut tough bathroom dirt with a tile and bathroom cleaner: a potent, three-in-one product designed to fight soap film, mineral deposits, and mould and mildew.

A thick liquid, this cleaner requires to be left on for a while to sanitize surfaces, dissolve minerals, and cut greasy dirt. Apply a thick coat using a squirt bottle. Leave it on for the time recommended on the product label and then scrub with a brush. Rinse thoroughly.

Abrasive cleaner Chemical-based cleaners – such as window cleaner or degreasers – rely on chemical reactions to dissolve, lift, or loosen dirt. Sometimes, though, you need to add additional scrubbing power to deal with tough or dried-on dirt. Enter scouring powders and cream cleaners. These also contain small abrasive particles designed to enhance the scrubbing action. Like sandpaper, they use friction to remove hardened dirt.

Abrasive cleaners are made in different strengths. Kitchen cleaner is designed for most sinks; "delicate surface" cleaners feature smaller abrasive particles and are recommended for special finishes. Abrasive cleaners may be formulated with other cleaners, such as bleach, to fight stains; be sure to read labels and choose the appropriate type for the job.

Because these products can be difficult to rinse clean, use them inside sinks, baths, and toilets where rinsing is easier.

Special cleaners for special jobs

These special-use products are formulated for specific cleaning issues or specific surfaces. Be sure to read the labels and use as directed by the manufacturer.

■ **Oil and grease stain removers.** Petroleum-distillate products designed to remove the greasy residues left by chewing gum, oil, or adhesives.
■ **Lime and scale remover.** A highly corrosive solution for hard-water scale deposits.
■ **Rust removers.** Designed to remove the rust stains in sinks, baths, and toilets that can occur in areas where the water supply has a high iron content.
■ **Stainless steel cleaner or polish.** Special products designed to clean, protect, and shine stainless-steel sinks, surfaces, pots, and pans.

Safety tips for cleaning products

Cleaning products are designed to fight dirt – and like all weapons, they can be dangerous if misused. Follow these tips to stay safe while using commercial cleaners.

■ **Check the label.** Go ahead – read the fine print. Cleaning product labels spell out what you need to know to use the product safely and effectively.
■ **Use as directed.** No, more is not better; using too much cleaning product is as counterproductive as using too little. Follow manufacturers' recommendations.
■ **Don't mix and match.** Cleaning products are designed to work – but not necessarily together. Mixing them can create dangerous fumes that are harmful to health.
■ **Store safely.** Follow recommendations on the product label for safe storage. Store cleaning products in their original packaging in a cool, dry area away from foodstuffs, and be sure they are inaccessible to small children. If you decant cleaners for use in spray or squirt bottles (*see page 57*), label appropriately.
■ **Dispose of properly.** Cleaning products are hazardous by nature. Even empty containers can create a health hazard if not disposed of properly. Don't leave empty containers in open wastepaper baskets where they could be found by children or pets. The rise of throwaway cleaning wipes has created disposal headaches for landfill operators and sewage treatment plants. Do not flush disposable wipes; they do not dissolve in water and can clog pipes and drains. Treat disposable cleaning products and their containers with all the respect you give their traditional cleaning cousins.

Green alternatives:
cleaners from the larder

Commercial cleaners are effective, but they contain harsh chemicals and can produce irritating fumes. Green cleaners use ingredients from the larder to make cleaning products that are kinder to hands and surfaces – and the environment.

Diluted white vinegar

Mildly acidic white vinegar dissolves dirt, soap scum, and hard-water deposits, yet is gentle enough to use in solution to clean hardwood flooring. White vinegar is a natural deodorizer, absorbing odours instead of covering them up. (And no, your bathroom won't smell like a salad. Any acid aroma disappears when dry.) With no colouring agents, white vinegar won't stain grout on tiled surfaces. Because it cuts through detergent residue, white vinegar also makes a great fabric-softener substitute for families with sensitive skin. In the kitchen, use vinegar-and-water spray (*see recipes, page 55*) to clean countertops, lightly soiled oven surfaces, and splashbacks. In the bathroom, spray countertops, floors, and exterior surfaces of the toilet. For really tough bathroom surfaces such as shower walls, pump up the cleaning power by heating the solution in the microwave until barely hot. Spray shower walls generously with the warmed solution, leave to stand for 10–15 minutes, then scrub and rinse.

▲ **A mild acid,** lemon juice can be used instead of vinegar for general cleaning. Use the outer rind to polish porcelain surfaces and release fragrant lemon oil. If you have a waste disposal unit, grind the rind in it while running cool water down the drain. The oils in the rind clean the disposal unit and sharpen the blades.

▲ **Keep bathroom drains** running freely and smelling sweet by pouring 20–40g (¾–1½oz) baking soda into the drain and dribbling in just enough hot water to wash the solution down. Leave to stand for 2 hours or overnight and then flush thoroughly with hot water. (Do not use on blocked drains.)

Undiluted white vinegar

Used straight from the bottle, undiluted white vinegar makes quick work of tougher cleaning problems involving hard-water deposits or soap scum. Use it to clean the inside of the toilet bowl. Before you begin, pour a bucket of water into the toilet to force water out of the bowl and allow access to the sides. Pour undiluted white vinegar around the bowl and scrub with a toilet brush to remove stains and odour. Use a pumice stone to remove any remaining hard-water rings.

Clean showerheads that have been clogged with mineral deposits with undiluted white vinegar. Place 60–120ml (4–8 tbsp) vinegar in a plastic food storage bag and secure the bag over the showerhead with an elastic band. Leave to stand for 2 hours or overnight, then rinse and buff.

White vinegar softens clothes and cuts detergent residue. For family members with sensitive skin, add 240ml (½ pint) to the rinse cycle instead of commercial fabric softener.

For general cleaning purposes, you can substitute lemon juice for white vinegar (*see caption on page 54*).

Baking soda

Baking soda's mild abrasive action and natural deodorizing properties make it a powerful replacement for harsh commercial scouring powders. Sprinkle baking soda onto a damp sponge to tackle grimy rings in the bath, scour vanity units, or remove food deposits from the kitchen sink.

For tougher grime, make a paste of baking soda and water, apply to the bath or sink, and leave to stand for 10–20 minutes until the deposits have softened and can be removed.

Rubbing alcohol

Rubbing (isopropyl) alcohol provides the base for an evaporating cleaner to rival commercial window and glass cleaning solutions. Use it on windows, mirrors, chrome fixtures, and for a shiny finish on hard-surface ceramic tiles (*see box, right*).

Ammonia

An alkaline solution, clear ammonia creates stronger window and all-purpose cleaning recipes than acidic vinegar (*see box, right*). Choose a non-foaming type: foam may look as if it's working, but it's difficult to rinse and remove.

Homemade green cleaners

Homemade cleaning products offer many advantages to cost-conscious households. Using household ingredients can be far less expensive than buying commercial cleaners, won't generate discarded product packaging, and the family avoids exposure to harsh chemicals or toxic ingredients. Try these cleaning recipes as a starting point, increasing or decreasing their strength as your household's cleaning needs require.

■ **Homemade spray cleaner recipe**
Try this recipe to harness the cleaning power of white vinegar. Mix in a spray bottle:
240ml (½ pint) white vinegar
240ml (½ pint) water

■ **Homemade glass cleaner recipe**
Try this recipe to harness the cleaning power of rubbing alcohol. Mix in a spray bottle:
240ml (½ pint) rubbing (isopropyl) alcohol
240ml (½ pint) water
1 tablespoon white vinegar

Try the following formulations for spring cleaning or tough chores.

■ **Strong glass cleaner recipe**
Mix in a spray bottle:
240ml (½ pint) rubbing (isopropyl) alcohol
240ml (½ pint) water
1 tablespoon clear, non-foaming ammonia

■ **Strong all-purpose cleaner recipe**
Mix in a spray bottle:
1 tablespoon clear, non-foaming ammonia
1 tablespoon clear washing-up liquid
480ml (1 pint) water

What's in your
cleaning holdall?

Nothing lengthens a cleaning session like having to run back and forth to the broom cupboard. Stay on the job – and make short work of it – by carrying commonly needed tools and supplies with you in a holdall as you clean. Begin each cleaning session with a fresh stack of white cotton cleaning cloths.

A cleaning holdall is a housecleaner's best friend. A plastic bucket or tidy tray, it holds the tools and supplies needed to clean it right and clean it fast. What's inside? Check your cleaning holdall for these top tools:

■ **Cleaning apron.** An apron protects clothing, keeps tools to hand, and has pockets to hold extra binliners and collect rubbish or small misplaced items. Choose a sturdy, comfortable, machine-washable apron.

"A cleaning holdall is a housecleaner's best friend."

■ **Rubber gloves or washing-up gloves.** Protect hands from harsh cleaning products with rubber gloves. New colours make rubber gloves a bright addition to the cleaning holdall – but steer clear of frou-frou decoration. Fur cuffs or rhinestone embellishments are fun to look at but are not meant for serious cleaning.
■ **Cleaning cloths.** White cotton cleaning cloths are the cleaner's mainstay. Fold them for easy access, and then use them to wipe fixtures dry, make mirrors gleam, and remove fingermarks fast.

◀ **Take your cleaning holdall** with you as you move from room to room. You'll have everything you need to hand and can speed through the job in double-quick time.

■ **Household sponge.** This dual-purpose sponge has an absorbent side and an abrasive side. Flip from soft to tough to remove stubborn, dried-on deposits from the sink.
■ **Squeegee.** Clean windows, mirrors, and glass the way the pros do. A rubber-bladed squeegee removes cleaning solution and dirt with one quick swipe. Wipe the blade dry with a cleaning cloth between strokes.
■ **Scraper.** Dried-up gunk comes off fast when tackled with a smooth metal or plastic scraper. Keep the scraper handy in an apron pocket; it'll make quick work of blobs of jam or dried-on porridge.
■ **Tile brush.** Any handled brush with thick bristles cleans tiles, bath surrounds, and sanitaryware in a flash. Bristles reach into corners; the handle keeps your hands free and clear of the cleaning fray.
■ **Toothbrush.** Tiny spaces attract big-time dirt. Tackle them with a firm-bristle toothbrush. Use it to clean out gunk from around sink fixtures, sink rims, or tight corners.

In addition to the above, if you are planning to buy cleaning products in bulk, you will also need the following:
■ **Squirt bottle.** Tile and bathroom cleaner works best when applied evenly and thickly. Use a funnel to decant the cleaner into a clean squirt-top bottle to get the right amount of product in the right spot – even underneath toilet rims.
■ **Spray bottle.** Whether you spritz it for light coverage or spray it for harder jobs, adjustable spray bottles make it easy to apply window cleaner or degreaser to surfaces. Use a colour code or label bottles to tell them apart.

Choosing
cleaning tools

Supermarket specials may seem like bargains and the latest "as seen on TV product" may hold out the promise of easier cleaning – but don't be lured by their siren call. It pays to buy durable, good-quality cleaning tools. Avoid gadgets or single-use items in favour of these tried and tested workhorses of the cleaning world.

Floor cleaners

Mops Whether used for wet or dry cleaning, mops are the foot soldiers in the battle for clean floors. Every organized home needs at least two: a wet mop, to pick up wet spills and wash hard-surface floors; and a dust-control mop, to collect dry dust, dirt, and pet hair.

When choosing a mop for wet cleaning, bear in mind its purpose – not only should it dissolve dirt, but it must also lift the dirt from the floor and remove it. For this reason, avoid string mops. They are heavy to lift, awkward to use, and nearly impossible to rinse clean. Mops with non-woven strands provide the modern alternative. They are lightweight, highly absorbent, and easy to wring out, particularly if you use the manufacturer's matching bucket.

Other alternatives are a large-headed mop with a swivel base and removable terry cover (*see Resources, page 248*), or a mop with a replaceable microfibre cover. These tools are dual-purpose; a dry cover makes quick work of spilled liquids, while a cover wrung out in cleaning solution dissolves and lifts dirt easily. As the cover becomes soiled, simply replace it with a freshly wrung-out one.

To finish off the floor, a dry cover polishes away the last of the water – and since both types of cover can be washed and dried, and then reused, you'll avoid the expense and environmental problems of disposable mop covers.

◄ **Wet mops** with flat large heads (*top*) swoop easily under furniture; reusable terry-cloth covers add versatility. Choose sponge mops with a hands-free wringing action (*bottom*) to stay dry.

▶ **The corn broom** (*back right*) has flexible bristles that reach easily into corners. A sweeping broom (*front left*) clears large spaces quickly. A hand brush makes short work of crumbs.

Sponge mops, too, offer efficient cleaning for spills and floors. Larger cleaning heads make the job go faster. Because these mops get a workout, make sure hinge mechanisms are made of metal; plastic won't stand up to the job.

Dust-control mops are available in many forms. Some have wax-impregnated dusting fibres, rather like the fibres of a string mop. Others consist of a frame to which you attach an impregnated dry-mop pad. Yet others use disposable non-woven sheets. Use any of these on dry dirt and to sweep up crumbs in the kitchen.

When buying a dry mop, examine the handle and hinge assembly to make sure it is sturdy.

Brooms and brushes These come in three basic types: sweeping, hand, and corn. Sweeping brooms are made from synthetic bristles set in a wide flat base. They're used to sweep large areas like the centre of indoor rooms, garages, and patios. Brooms with rougher bristles tackle irregular surfaces.

Choose a sweeping broom with tacked-in bristles, avoiding brooms that are merely glued together. Look for a metal coupling between the handle and the head; the stresses of sweeping will wear out plastic fittings quickly.

Hand brushes are lightweight and work well to clean near skirting boards, behind furniture and in corners. Use them indoors, as their lighter weight makes them impractical for heavier outdoor jobs. Store hand brushes head-up to avoid bending the bristles.

Corn brooms are made from natural bristles, and they're the all-purpose solution for sweeping chores. Pair them with a dustpan for quick kitchen clean-ups; the rough bristles do a superior job on flooring material with a coarse or pitted surface that holds dirt, such as brick or concrete.

When buying a corn broom, look for a smooth, strong handle and multiple rows of stitching to hold the bristles in place. Store the corn broom head-up to prevent the bristles from bending. As the broom ages, trim the bristles about 2.5cm (1in) to restore it to youthful vigour.

Vacuum cleaner Equipped with proper filtration, a vacuum cleaner swoops up dust finally and forever, and removes it from the home. Vacuum cleaners come in two basic styles: cylinder and upright. Generally, upright vacuums do a better job on carpeting, are less expensive, and are easier to store, while the cylinder cleaner does a superior job on hard flooring, stairs, and hard-to-reach places, such as car seats. For dusting, use the vacuum's extension hose and attachments, such as an upholstery brush, dust brush, or crevice tool.

A hand-held vacuum cleaner comes in handy for stairs, tight corners, and small spills. Choose a hand-held model with disposable bags for best air quality. Rechargeable hand-held cleaners are cordless – and convenient.

Dust-busters

Where there's life, there's dust! Household dust is an airborne mix of soil particles, lint, insect parts, animal dander, pollen, moulds, and fungi. Dust comes in through the open window or door, or hitches a ride inside on shoes and clothing. It is stirred into the air by walking or careless dusting. Airborne dust irritates breathing passages, and triggers allergic reactions in sensitive people. As it falls, it settles on fixtures, surfaces, and floors, and clogs central-heating boiler filters and refrigerator coils, causing these appliances to work harder and consume more energy. Because dust is abrasive, walking on dusty floors can damage carpet, vinyl, or hardwood floors.

Regular dust removal is essential for a clean and well-kept home. Try the following tools and techniques to control dust.

Dusting cloths What's the pedigree of a great dusting cloth? It's white, and it's made of 100 per cent cotton. Cotton is absorbent, trapping dust instead of scattering it, and it won't scratch fine furniture. White dusting cloths show the dirt as you work and are washable, reusable, and may be bleached. Old-fashioned unfolded muslin nappies work just as well. So do white cotton flannels, scraps of recycled terry towelling, or soft damask napkins.

Lambswool duster A lambswool duster with a long handle extends your reach and is useful for dusting delicate, detailed items. Long wool fibres attract and hold fine dust until you release it outside by twirling the wand firmly between your palms.

How to clean a "dry" room

Cleaning a "dry" room – one with no sinks or water sources – comes down to a single word: dust. Because dust and dirt tend to fly around when disturbed, a dry room is cleaned from top to bottom. As the dust falls, the cleaner has a multiple chance to trap it and show it the door ... or the vacuum! Use your cleaning carryall as you work, a section at a time. Working around the room only once saves steps and makes cleaning chores whizz by. Try this step-by-step method to clean a dry room.

1 Empty the bin. Place the wastepaper basket outside the door to be emptied. When team cleaning, a team member empties all the rubbish. If working alone, empty and replace the wastepaper basket at the end of the cleaning session. For team cleaning, divide chores between the duster, who goes round the room dusting, and the vacuumer, who empties the rubbish and vacuums.

2 Move around the room in sections, starting at the top. Using a long-handled lambswool duster, wipe down cornices, the top of door frames, and the tops of hanging photos and pictures. Brighten photo glass and clean windows with a cleaning cloth lightly sprayed with glass cleaner; use degreaser to remove smudges and fingermarks.

Electrostatic dry cleaning cloths These are composed of long, triangular-shaped fibres that attract and trap dust particles. While pricey, they will give superb results when dusting electronic equipment or coping with fine dust.

Tools to avoid Paper towels contain wood-pulp products that can scratch delicate surfaces. Feather dusters move dust into the air instead of collecting it, they can't be washed, and a broken quill can scratch delicate surfaces.

Dusting rules

■ **Collect, don't scatter.** The number one goal for dusting: to collect and remove dust, not scatter it. Forget images of flapping dusting cloths. Instead, dust with the calm and controlled motions of a Tai Chi practitioner. Coax dust motes into your tools – don't disperse them into the air so that they resettle on the surfaces you are trying to clean.

■ **Dust top to bottom.** When dusting, it's inevitable that some dust will fly, no matter how careful the cleaner. Give yourself a second chance to collect escaped dust particles by starting at the top and working down: light fixtures, wall-hung pictures, window and door frames, furniture, and skirting.

■ **Dust damp.** Use just-damp dust cloths as you work. The moisture will attract and hold dust. But beware of too much moisture. It can harm wood furniture and delicate surfaces. As an alternative, spritz your cloth with an aerosol dusting spray. Never spray surfaces directly; spray the cloth instead to avoid build-up and overuse of these products.

> "Forget images of flapping dusting cloths. Dust with the calm and controlled motions of a Tai Chi practitioner."

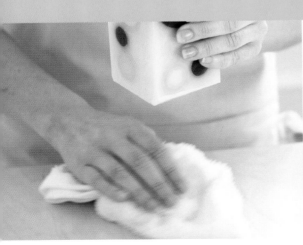

3 Horizontal surfaces next. Gently dust knick-knacks or decorative items on mantelpieces, shelves, or tabletops with a white dusting cloth, then dust the surface beneath them. If needed, apply a light spray of cleaner to loosen dirt on windowsills or surfaces. Lean down to dust furniture legs and wipe dust from skirting boards.

4 The final stage – centre, vacuum, and out. After going round the room and working top-to-bottom, dust or clean any freestanding furniture in the centre. Vacuum the floor from the room's furthest corner to the door ... then take the vacuum cleaner out of the room. Empty and replace the wastepaper basket. As a finishing touch, spray room freshener as you exit to leave the room smelling sweet.

Tools for wet cleaning

When it comes to cleaning, some household areas are all wet: rooms such as the bathroom or kitchen, which contain a water source and are home to food preparation, bathing, or grooming activities. Water splashes, soap film, air-borne grease and smoke from cooking, and excess spray from using personal-care products combine with household dust to up the cleaning ante in a wet room.

To clean a wet room, you'll use a greater number of cleaning products and cleaning tools than when cleaning a dry room. In the cleaning holdall, rely on degreasers/all-purpose cleaners to cut through oily dirt and dissolve dried-on stains. Pair a degreasing spray with a good supply of fresh cleaning cloths; using a fresh cloth makes sure you remove

the loosened dirt, not just spread it about in a more even layer. Hang cleaning cloths over your shoulder for quick access while cleaning a wet room; when thoroughly saturated, retire them into the holdall in favour of a dry cloth.

Keep specialized tools like scrapers and abrasive sponges at the ready; they'll help you deal with sticky smears and blobs on counters and fixtures. Always spray the area generously with degreaser spray before scraping; the cleaner helps loosen dirt and protects the surface from scratching. An old toothbrush reaches into cracks and crevices; use it in corners, the grout between tiles, and around the rim of sinks and fixtures. The toothbrush's long handle will keep your knuckles out of the fray; stiff bristles work best to scrape out hardened food or entrenched mould.

How to clean a "wet" room

"Wet" rooms – kitchens, bathrooms, and utility rooms – present more complex cleaning challenges than dry ones. Hard-water film, soap scum, and greasy deposits require amplified cleaning power; food preparation and personal care areas need to be sanitized. Instead of moving around the room in stages, stagger chores to give cleaning products time to work. This step-by-step method shows how to apply maximum power to cleaning a bathroom.

1 Place the waste bin outside the room, to be emptied and replaced last. Add sanitizing pine cleaner or toilet-bowl cleaner to the toilet bowl, and leave to stand. Apply a generous amount of bathroom spray or pine cleaner to the shower or the inside of the bath. Leave the cleaners to stand so they can get to work dissolving grease while you turn your attention to the sink.

2 Dust any light fixture or mirror frame over the sink. Spray and squeegee the mirror, using glass cleaner. Spray and wipe towel racks or toothbrush holders, then spray the taps and bathroom surfaces with bathroom cleaner. Let the cleaner stand while you scrub and rinse inside the sink, using cream cleaner. Wipe the surfaces and polish taps dry.

The presence of water often requires special cleaners. Depending on the content of the water supply, you may need to use limescale remover to treat hard-water deposits, or rust remover for reddish stains in areas with iron in the water supply. Handle these power cleaners with great respect, following the directions on the label.

Dressed to clean

A casual approach to cleaning can be risky – to your clothing! Tackling cleaning chores dressed in a nightdress or in office clothes isn't just haphazard – it's dangerous.

Take cleaning seriously and dress for the job. Avoid loose clothing that will catch on handles or interfere with tools. Comfortable clothing that provides a free range of motion keeps the cleaner on the job longer, and more happily. Washable clothing is a must; a white cotton T-shirt or top will be easiest to keep stain-free.

Wear sturdy, supportive shoes; these protect feet from injury. Avoid wearing footwear that is easy to slide out of, such as flip-flops, especially if using a step stool. Springy sneakers or lace-up walking shoes keep you on your feet, and protect toes from splashed cleaning solutions or a dropped tool. Add a cleaning apron with pockets for further protection, and to keep tools and cleaners close at hand. If your apron has side loops, hang spray bottles of cleaning solution from them ready for use. Line apron pockets with plastic bags to gather up bits of rubbish. Stockpile a stack of cleaning cloths in one pocket, a cleaning sponge in another. You're dressed to clean.

"Wet rooms – kitchens, bathrooms, and utility rooms – present more complex cleaning challenges than dry rooms."

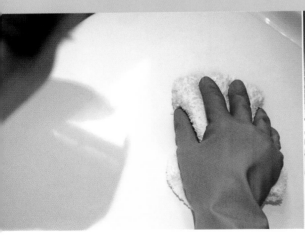

3 Spray toilet surfaces with sanitizing bathroom cleaner: the cistern, toilet lid top, toilet lid underneath, toilet seat top, and finally seat underside. Leave the seat up while you scrub and rinse inside the bowl. A good toilet brush makes it easy to scrub under the rim, where mildew hides. Wipe toilet surfaces dry in reverse order with cleaning cloths.

4 Using a tile brush or abrasive sponge, scrub to loosen deposits on shower walls or inside the bath. Rinse clean. Use cream cleaner or pine cleaner to scrub the bottom of the bath or shower tray, then rinse. Polish fixtures dry with a cleaning cloth. Using cleaning cloths or a small mop, clean and dry floors. Wipe dust from skirting boards. Empty and replace the waste bin – and admire your gleaming bathroom!

Top cleaning tips
from the pros

Professional cleaners are masters of the art of speed cleaning. They're in and out, with only sparkling clean surfaces to show for it. Career cleaners work efficiently to get each job done as quickly and easily as possible. To clean your home in record time, try these tips from professional cleaners.

1 Schedule cleaning

Nobody hires a cleaning service that promises to arrive "some Saturday or other when nothing else is happening". Take a tip from the pros, and set up a regular cleaning schedule. The pros don't stop until the job is done, and neither should you. Schedule the job and stick at it to get the work done in record time.

2 Get motivated

You won't find paid cleaners pausing to watch television programmes or check their email. Use motivators to prevent distraction and avoid boredom. Play upbeat music for an energy boost. Bookworms look forward to cleaning when a recorded book plays on a personal stereo. Clean as a team with friends or family members to stay on track.

3 Dress for success

Professional cleaners dress for the job in comfortable, washable clothing designed for work. Supportive shoes and kneepads spare their bodies. Goggles and gloves protect against chemicals.

End the era of bleach-stained sweatshirts and set aside a "cleaning uniform" instead – including shoes, gloves, and eye protection – and wear it!

◀ **Professional cleaners.** They have the tools, the talent, and the know-how to make short work of cleaning a house. Learn their secrets to speed cleaning chores in your organized home.

4 Invest in proper tools

Professional cleaners don't use gadgets. You'll never find them using specialized, one-use tools, or the latest gizmo they have seen advertised on the shopping channel. Buy good tools, once, and use them – and you'll be finished in record time.

5 Carry your tools with you

How does your cleaning session go? Is it fast and focused or more like this? Ooops! Forgot the cream cleaner. Must go downstairs. The toilet brush? It's in the kids' bathroom down the hall. Run to the utility room for more cleaning cloths, to the kitchen for a box of tissues. Where's the vacuum cleaner? Did someone take the squeegee to wash the car?

Professional cleaners carry their tools with them – all their tools, cleaners, brushes, and rags needed to finish the job are right there in the holdall. Vacuum, mop, and hand-held vacuum cleaner wait in the doorway. A plastic bin bag is tucked into a pocket, next to the lambswool duster. That's why the pro has finished the entire bathroom before our amateur gets back upstairs with the cream cleaner.

6 Simplify supplies

There's a reason the pros can carry all the products they need in one container: they've simplified their cleaning products. Professional cleaners go to work carrying the Big Four:

- Light-duty evaporating cleaner (glass cleaner or multi-surface cleaner)
- Heavy-duty degreasing cleaner
- Tile and bathroom cleaner
- Cream cleaner or scouring powder

That's it! No soap scum remover, no special worktop spray, no single-use products designed to clean only blinds or fans or walls. The professionals know that with these four simple products they'll be able to handle any ordinary cleaning chore.

7 Make every movement count

Professional cleaners don't go round a room more than once. Taking their place before the bathroom sink, they'll spray and wipe the mirror, scrub the sink, wipe down counters, and polish taps before they move to the right or left.

Don't get physical with your cleaning sessions – make every movement count. Stand fast and clean everything in your path before you move on.

8 Two hands are better than one

Professional cleaners don't work as if one arm is in a sling, and neither should you. Get in the habit of using both hands to attack cleaning tasks.

Spray a mirror with one hand; wipe it down with the other. Scrub counters with two sponges or cleaning cloths. Dusting goes twice as fast when a lambswool duster in one hand cleans nooks and crannies while the cleaning cloth in the other skims flat surfaces.

9 Pick it up

Professional cleaners come to clean – not to tidy – worktops, furniture, appliances, and floors. They can't do the job if each horizontal surface in the home is covered with papers, toys, dirty dishes, and just plain clutter.

Pretend that you've hired an expensive cleaning crew. You wouldn't make them relocate the clutter just to be able to do their job. Give yourself the same head start you would give professional cleaners: pick up before you clean.

10 Think teamwork

Two people make a bed four times faster than a single cleaner working alone. Watch the pros at work. Working in teams of two or three, they make short work of an average home.

Where family circumstances permit, make cleaning a family affair. Family members are more reluctant to mess up a clean house when they have been part of the cleaning effort!

Live as a family, clean as a family? When it comes to housework, there can be a big divergence between husband and wife, parent and child. Who gets stuck with the dirty end of the broom in your home?

Make a family cleaning plan

Creating a family game plan for house cleaning can help negotiate the chorus of "I don't want to!" resistance. Set a realistic cleaning standard, schedule cleaning chores, focus on teamwork, and you will pull the emotional sting from discussions over the household cleaning routines.

Agreement on a cleaning standard avoids arguments over "how clean is clean?" Chores done according to a schedule – not according to the dictates of a harassed parent or a spouse – remove fuel for a power struggle. Tackling cleaning chores as a team takes the drudgery out of the job. Sharing and cooperation make cleaning fun!

Scheduling: the solution for
a clean and happy home

Clean houses have one thing in common: cleaning chores are tackled according to a schedule. Haphazard cleaning isn't only ineffective – it takes longer. The quickest and simplest route to a clean house is to schedule cleaning tasks on a daily, weekly, monthly, and seasonal basis.

I know, I know – you have a million reasons why you don't want to clean on a schedule. You're a free spirit. You're pregnant. Your spouse works odd shifts. You're an artistic type and sticking to a schedule would dampen your creativity.

Trust me; in over 10 years of teaching these skills, I have heard every rationale ever offered for resisting this truth. But truth it remains. There's only one reason to schedule housework: because doing so gets the job done fastest and most easily.

Little and often

Housework delayed is housework multiplied. Dust the breakfast area weekly, and it's a quick-swipe, two-minute job. Wait a month, and enough air-borne grease has settled over the dust to require (a) soft soap, (b) elbow grease, and (c) an energetic half-hour to return the furniture to a state of clean. Better to schedule two easy minutes a week than to catch up with a sweaty half-hour once a month.

Whatever your mental roadblock to the idea, consider establishing a cleaning schedule. By scheduling chores so they're performed regularly – before the problems mushroom exponentially – the house stays cleaner, and the house cleaners do less work to keep it that way. Use these sample checklists as a starting point to develop one that's right for your household:

Daily cleaning checklist
- Make beds
- Place dirty clothing in laundry basket
- Wash, dry, and put away one load of laundry
- Clear kitchen counters and wipe down the cooker top
- Clean kitchen sink
- Take out kitchen rubbish
- Sweep kitchen floor
- Clear television and play areas (put away toys, stack newspapers, remove clutter)

Weekly cleaning checklist
- Change bedlinen and bathroom towels
- Clean bathrooms
- Clean kitchen counters and wipe inside of microwave oven
- Wash or dust hard-surface floors
- Dust furniture
- Vacuum carpets and rugs
- Check entrance or doorstep; sweep if needed

The case against spring-cleaning

In Grandmother's day, spring-cleaning was mandatory. It marked the end of the winter, when the entire house was scrubbed clean of the smoky film given off by fireplaces and stoves. With today's heating technology, this rationale no longer applies. Modern lives, too, cannot sustain an old-fashioned cleaning marathon.

So how do we replace spring-cleaning? With a workable household cleaning schedule. Homes cleaned according to schedule stay reasonably clean all the time. A cleaning schedule integrates seasonal cleaning chores into daily or weekly cleaning sessions, and no task goes too long without being done. Result: a clean home all year round.

Even the best-run households experience rocky patches from time to time. Illness, special work assignments, absence of a family member, or outside commitments can all throw a spanner into the workings of a home.

There's a solution for busy times – a minimum maintenance shortlist to keep your home running smoothly. Think of it as a Magic Minimum: those essential tasks that must be done come hell or high water, or football play-offs. Every family has different needs, but most Magic Minimums provide for:

■ **Basic accounting chores** (making bank deposits and paying bills)
■ **Meals and menus** (cleaning the dishes, food shopping)
■ **Laundry** (necessary clean clothing)
■ **Home management** (once-a-day pick-up, weekly cleaning of bathrooms and kitchen)

To make your own Magic Minimum plan, list the absolutely essential maintenance jobs that need to be tackled to keep the household clean, fed, and running on time.

A sample list might look like this:

Every day:
■ Load and run dishwasher
■ Tidy kitchen
■ Wash one load of laundry, fold, and put away
■ Family pick-up time

Every week:
■ Review chequebook and pay bills
■ Shop for groceries
■ Clean bathroom(s)

Next step: delegate! Assign one or more minimum chores to each family member. Every family member has a stake in keeping the household functioning, so everyone should be expected to help.

Finally, post your Magic Minimum list in a public place. Families using a Household Notebook (*see pages 84–7*) will include their list under the "home management" divider. Another choice is the refrigerator door, but use whatever area is central to your family. The written list aids accountability, because everyone knows what must be done to keep the household functioning during times of stress.

laundry ▲ see pages 142–55

meals and menu planning ▲ see pages 92–7

Teaching
children to clean

"Clean your room!" It's the cry of parents everywhere. Toddlers to teens, it's a battle to get kids to help. The scenario is familiar: a dirty house, un-cooperative children, and frazzled, frustrated parents. What can parents do to create peace on the home front? Try these strategies to chill the chore wars.

The buck(et) stops here

An ambivalent mindset can stop us from successfully gaining children's cooperation around the house. Perhaps we grew up in a home that was heavy with sex-role stereotypes. Maybe we feel guilt because we work outside the home.

When ambivalence strikes remind yourself that, just as we prepare our children for adult life by sending them to school, so we need to prepare them to manage a home.

■ **Start small.** The easiest way to secure your children's assistance is to train them to it from the time they are small. A one-year-old will giggle if handed a clean nappy to dust the the furniture. Nothing can be such fun as washing a car with a five-year-old. Problem is, these little ones' efforts aren't yet much help. In truth, you'll probably have to follow behind that one-year-old with his nappy duster, removing the specks of dirt he's rearranged. Even when you match the chore to the child, the early years require some extra work from you. Listen up, parents of tiny children: just do it! An investment in your child's learning now will reap rewards in just a few years.

■ **Invoke change slowly.** Your children are at an age to be of help around the house – but their idea of "helping" is lifting their feet from the floor so you can vacuum beneath them. Resist the big bust-up and get children involved in chores slowly. For example, this month, decide that one of the children will assist with pre-dinner preparation, the other will help with cleaning up. Next month, begin a Saturday morning family "cleanathon." Gradual change gives you time to teach a child your household's standard for each task.

■ **Tap the power of choice.** Children who are given a choice of chores do them better and more happily. A child who dislikes the feeling of wet hands and gritty cleanser may be the World's Best Duster-and-Rubbish-Emptier. Another, with sensitive ears, may prefer bathroom duty to using the vacuum cleaner. A chore list of scheduled chores makes it easy to allow children to select the jobs they'd prefer.

■ **Make housework a partnership.** The best motivator for a child is to work together with an adult. From a child's point of view, it's downright lonely to be sentenced to clean a bathroom each afternoon after school. Better to institute a family

"Invest in your child's learning now and you will be implanting skills for life."

Pick-Up Time each day, a family Clean-Up Time each week. Even if that same child is alone in that same bathroom, he knows that all the other family members are hard at work, too.

■ **Focus on the big picture.** Cleaning methods are a frequent bone of contention between parents and children. A parent's insistence on "the right way" can add another element of conflict to the housework issue. The answer? Avoid this by focusing on the "good-enough" job. A 10-year-old's skill with the vacuum cleaner will increase with practice ... if he's not derailed by arguments over too-high standards or demoralized when a parent redoes the work.

Who says children can't do chores? Check this listing of age-appropriate chores to help children learn responsibility and habits of order:

Two- to three-year-olds can:
- Pick up toys
- Help make beds
- Help feed pets
- Dust lower shelves and furniture legs
- Place spoons, napkins, and unbreakable dishes on the table
- Carry dirty clothing to the laundry area
- Sweep floors using a lightweight dust-control mop

For four- to five-year-olds, add these chores to the list above:
- Make beds (if using duvets)
- Set the table
- Dust table tops
- Unload and put away groceries

Between six and eight years of age, children can master these additional tasks:
- Keep their play areas or bedrooms tidy
- Water house plants
- Make beds (using bedspreads)
- Sort laundry
- Put clean clothing away
- Assist with simple food preparation (tear lettuce, make sandwiches)
- Fold socks, shirts, and trousers
- Help wash the car

Nine- to ten-year-olds are ready to:
- Change sheets
- Clean bath and sinks
- Help cook meals

- Prepare simple snacks
- Wash dishes
- Load the dishwasher
- Polish silver
- Vacuum
- Sweep floors with broom and dustpan
- Help with gardening (rake leaves, weed)

From eleven and up, train teens to do "adult" chores. They'll squawk on the outside, but feel pride on the inside as they master real-life skills. With teaching, teens can:
- Plan and cook family meals
- Do their own laundry using the washing machine and dryer
- Wash windows
- Replace light bulbs
- Polish furniture
- Wash hard-surface floors
- Clean garages and outbuildings
- Wash, wax, and vacuum cars

family teamwork ▲ see also pages 66–7

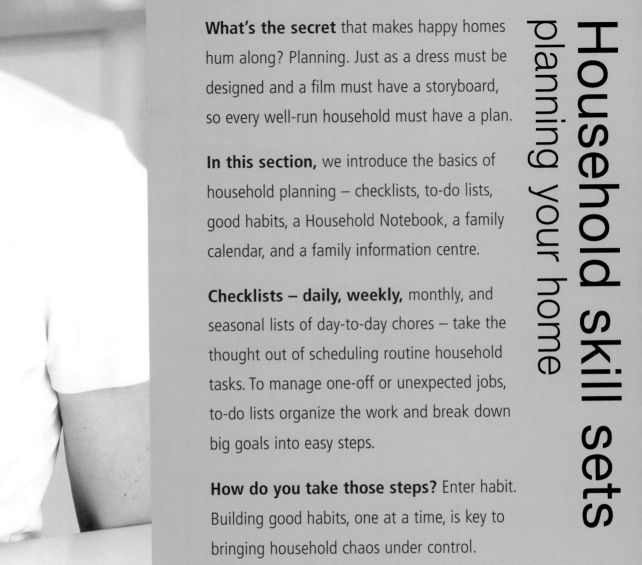

What's the secret that makes happy homes hum along? Planning. Just as a dress must be designed and a film must have a storyboard, so every well-run household must have a plan.

In this section, we introduce the basics of household planning – checklists, to-do lists, good habits, a Household Notebook, a family calendar, and a family information centre.

Checklists – daily, weekly, monthly, and seasonal lists of day-to-day chores – take the thought out of scheduling routine household tasks. To manage one-off or unexpected jobs, to-do lists organize the work and break down big goals into easy steps.

How do you take those steps? Enter habit. Building good habits, one at a time, is key to bringing household chaos under control.

To keep track of planning, we create a family organizer – the Household Notebook. Add a family calendar and place them at the heart of a family information centre to guide the doings of life in an organized home.

Plan to succeed
for an organized home

Planning. It's the strategy that separates the hapless house from the happy home. Without a tool to plan your time and schedule your life, everyday life slides into disorder and chaos. Homework goes missing, each and every week. You regularly have overdue library book or DVD rental fines to pay.

Chores don't get done, laundry doesn't get washed, and dinner doesn't get cooked on time. You wake each morning to a sink full of dirty dishes, and you go to bed each night, mind buzzing with "Did I remember?" and "Did I forget?" worries, a true symptom of failure to plan.

The four tools for planning

A basic plan for an organized home meshes four powerful planning tools: checklists, to-do lists, good habits, and a family organizer. Together, they put the whole family on the path to orderly living.

1 Checklists These are simple-to-follow reminders of the routine tasks of each day – or each week, month, or season. Checklists cover recurring jobs: cleaning chores, personal care, exercise routines. They cut through mental clutter and distraction, and make clear what needs to be accomplished each day.

Checklists promote delegation and family teamwork. Are the children bursting to spend Saturday at the park? The morning checklist sets out the chores that need to be done before the fun part of the day can begin. Once the list is completed, bring out the picnic basket!

2 Master to-do lists What checklists do for recurring tasks, to-do lists accomplish for one-off chores or larger projects. Can't sleep at night because your head is ringing with thoughts of what you need to do, want to do, must remember? Large or small, entrust clamouring "mind clutter" to a to-do list for a good night's sleep.

Working from a Master To-Do list, you'll record a mix of nagging jobs, little reminders, home improvement projects, and personal goals. Moving Master To-Do list items to a running to-do list breaks down big projects into achievable tasks, and integrates those tasks into the coming days, weeks, and months. Tackling projects via the organized approach of a to-do list takes your aspirations out of the mental clouds and makes them happen.

3 Habit Checklists and to-do lists organize efficient living, but they don't get the work done themselves. How do you follow through on your good planning? Enter habit: the secret engine of an organized life at home. Once formed, habits are like the little engine that could, pulling family members along in their (orderly) wake.

Encouraging good habits and banishing bad ones is key to streamlining life and getting rid of chaos and disorder.

> "Planning – the strategy that separates the hapless house from the happy home."

Best of all, habits are self-sustaining. Once you form them, they will work for you without further effort. Bring a brace of good habits to work for your organized home. As you plan, incorporate checklist items or to-do entries into existing routines to maximize the power of habit.

4 The Household Notebook What's a blockbuster tool for a well-organized home life? A family organizer: a personal planner for the household. I call it the Household Notebook, and no home should be without one.

The Household Notebook is a simple three-ring binder that contains all the information needed for daily life in an organized home, in an easy-to-find, easy-to-use format. It's a family calendar, an address book, and an information resource all in one. The Notebook is designed to gather together all the handouts and schedules, post-it notes, and slips of paper, and give back answers: when is the football team end-of-season party? What is the telephone number for the judo club? How much will it cost to order pizza for Friday night supper – and what's the number to call?

Flip it open to a listing of emergency numbers for the babysitter. Use it to keep product manuals organized, to stay on top of sports team practices, and track each day's checklists.

▲ **Household planning** is as critical as planning in any other area of life. Winging it leads to disorder, chaos, and stress. Planning is a powerful tool for an organized home.

It will be home to the to-do lists, the family calendar and the checklists that bring order to the household. The family calendar will keep all household members on the same page for appointments and commitments.

Finally, give your planning tools a home by creating a family information centre, a central location for household planning and information. The family information centre works for everyone in the household, and is a valuable resource for babysitters, helpers, or extended family members. With a central location for paperwork, it's a simple matter for anyone to locate a takeaway menu, call this week's school-run parent, check dates for forthcoming events, or work out what's for dinner from the weekly menu plan.

Checklists: from daily do-its
to routine chores

Checklists exist to free the brain from "mind flies" – those little buzzing "I need to, I have to" thoughts. Whether it's daily lists of routine chores or more long-term tasks, checklists pin down buzzing thoughts and put them on paper, where they're easy to convert into action.

Daily Do-Its checklists

Build your own checklists for planning success; these lists should get you started:

Sample Morning Do-It checklist
- Check the day's calendar and checklist
- Exercise
- Shower and complexion care
- Make bed
- Read email
- Wake children and make breakfast
- Do one load of washing
- Fold one load of drying
- Place breakfast dishes in dishwasher
- Clear kitchen counters

Sample Evening Do-It checklist
- Empty dishwasher and set table for breakfast
- Set up programmable coffee or tea makers for morning beverages
- Make lunches for next day
- Empty kitchen rubbish and clear counters
- Select the next day's clothing
- Exercise
- Pray or meditate
- Complexion care
- Review next day's calendar and checklists

Daily Do-Its

Do you plan your day? Or does each morning dawn in a whole new world – and go downhill from there? We all have days that slip through our fingers without a plan. Perhaps the alarm clock fails to wake us. Frustration and aggravation mount as we slide from one crisis to the next. Forgotten appointments. Nothing for dinner. Without a road map for the day, the smallest distractions will lead you off the path of order and into the quicksand of delay and disorganization.

The cure? Daily Do-Its, simple morning and evening checklists designed get the family up and out, and cover the routine needs of daily life. Meals. Clean clothing. The morning exodus to work and school. Do-Its won't deep-clean your house, redecorate the living room, or clean out the garage for you, but they will cover the basics and keep your household running smoothly.

To create Daily Do-It checklists, divide a sheet of paper into two columns, one for Morning, one for Evening. Next, list the simple chores needed to get out of the house in the morning, cover meals, and provide clean clothing. Slip the Do-It list into your Household Notebook (*see pages 84–7*), inside a plastic page protector for easy reference.

Morning Do-It checklist In the morning, focus on the day ahead. List reminders to check your calendar so you won't be surprised by unexpected meetings or missed appointments. Include personal care tasks such as exercise, complexion care, and grooming. Caring for yourself first just makes sense – and for most of us, self-care won't stand a chance unless it's at the top of the list! Add early-morning chores related to meals and laundry, and resolve to clear the kitchen counters before you leave the house. You'll thank yourself at the end of the day.

Evening Do-It checklist Do-Its in the evening wrap up the day and prepare for the next. In the kitchen, clean up from the evening meal and set the stage for the next morning. Think ahead! Prepare what you need for the morning's coffee or tea, make lunches, and set the table for breakfast. Avoid last-minute clothing crises by planning the next day's outfits. At the end of the day, list personal chores that will tuck you into a peaceful night's sleep: complexion care, prayer or meditation, or reading. Last on the list, remind yourself to take a quick look at the next day's schedule.

Daily Do-It checklists are your personal road map out of the aimless disorder of an unplanned day. Morning and evening, they'll remind you to do those basic, necessary minimums that keep life humming along.

"Daily Do-It checklists are your personal road map out of the aimless disorder of an unplanned day."

Weekly, monthly, and seasonal planning checklists

If Daily Do-Its keep each day running smoothly, weekly, monthly, and seasonal checklists get the big jobs done. What's on the checklist? Everything! From scheduled cleaning chores to menu planning to voluntary work. If you have to do it routinely, it belongs on your checklist.

Like the Daily Do-It, file your weekly, monthly, and seasonal checklists in plastic page protectors in your Household Notebook. Each week, month, and season, check the appropriate checklist to stay on-task and organized.

Use the sample checklists in the box (*see right*), as a guide to create your own checklists for routine chores to be done each week, month, and season.

Long-term checklists for weekly and seasonal chores are home to recurring to-do list items. Check your Master To-Do list to compile your household's checklists.

Weekly checklist
■ Review calendar for the forthcoming week
■ Check Master To-Do list and add items to the running to-do list (*see pages 80–1*)
■ Plan weekly menus
■ Collect cut-price coupons from the paper
■ Pay bills
■ Shop for groceries
■ Run errands: visit the drycleaner, the bank, the photo developers

Monthly checklist
■ Review calendar for the forthcoming month
■ Check Master To-Do list and add items to the running to-do list
■ Balance chequebook
■ Check larder and freezer inventories; rotate foods

Seasonal checklist
■ Review calendar for the forthcoming season
■ Check Master To-Do list and add items to the running to-do list
■ Make medical appointments
■ Rotate seasonal clothing and review family clothing needs
■ Note holiday or travel plans and make travel arrangements, if needed
■ Arrange for central-heating system maintenance
■ Check smoke/carbon monoxide detectors

Checklists for the long term

Checklists and schedules organize the work, but they won't get the job done on their own. Even the best checklists won't help if you don't check them regularly. Stay on track with your planning system:

■ **Check in each morning and evening.** Consulting your calendar, schedule, and checklists each morning gets the day off to a productive start. At the end of the day, reschedule any unfinished tasks and review the plans for the next day. You'll go to bed prepared for a good morning.

■ **Be flexible.** Life happens, and when it does, the best-laid plans can fall by the wayside. That's the time to lighten the domestic load. Drop back to minimum maintenance (*see pages 68–9*) when illness, a heavy workload, or holidays intervene. Written checklists and schedules make it easy to return to the plan when life calms down again.

Beyond the routine:
to-do lists

If checklists are a road map for the predictable activities of daily life, to-do lists organize the unexpected: one-off chores, extraneous jobs that must be done around the house, or ongoing projects. Working together with checklists, they'll make sure you tackle those jobs that don't show up on lists of routine chores.

For example, routine kitchen chores – clean the fridge or scrub the sink – are daily or weekly checklist items (*see pages 76–7*). "Install wallpaper border in kitchen" is a to-do item, a single job broken down from the larger goal: "redecorate kitchen". You'll use to-do lists to identify these one-offs and schedule them into an organized life, and to break down and schedule bigger projects.

There are two kinds of to-do lists: a running to-do list for daily reference, and a Master To-Do list. The running list sets out a list of high-priority to-do items that must be done in the short term. The master list is the source: it's the place where you dump, sort, organize, and carry out the to-dos.

The Master To-Do list
To start a Master To-Do list, get a sheet of lined paper and make three columns: assigned date, item, and completed date. Move to the middle column and list it all – and I do mean all – every must-do, should-do, want-to-do thought that crosses your mind.

A good Master To-Do list is a mix of goals and aspirations, errands and minutiae. It's a place to put those "oh yes!" reminders that circle your brain into concrete form. Don't worry if your list stretches for pages and pages. Better to put down buzzing thoughts on paper, than to carry them around with you. Better still, the Master To-Do list shows progress at a glance. You'll see what jobs you've completed, what tasks you're working on, and which items remain to be done.

You'll use the Master To-Do list to make frequent, short running to-do lists. As you add an item to the running to-do

Date assigned:	Item:	Date completed:
June 15	Return overdue library books	June 17
June 29	Repair floor in children's bathroom	
July 1	Make vet appointment for the cat	
July 10	Call about dance team costumes	July 14
July 14	Buy glitter trim for costumes	
August 1	Finish status report for event committee	

▲ **Power planner.** The Master To-Do list holds it all, big or small. By putting "must-do" jobs down on paper, it's easy to assign dates and translate them into action.

list, write the date in the "date assigned" column; when a job is completed, note the completion date. As time passes, you'll have a record of the good work you've accomplished.

Run with it: making the running to-do list

From the Master To-Do list comes the running to-do list: a short-term list of things to do that is consulted – and changed – often. Consult it daily along with your checklists to keep on top of goals and must-do jobs.

"A good Master To-Do list is a mix of goals and aspirations, errands and minutiae."

Making the running to-do list is simple. Check the Master To-Do list, and transfer two to ten "to-do" items to the running list. Some items will be time-sensitive: the "have-to-do" stuff that looms on the horizon. Sweeten the list by adding a few "want-to-do" jobs, those to-do items that forward a goal. As you add items to the running to-do list, note the date assigned on the Master List – and when you complete a job, cross it off the list! Add the list to your Household Notebook, calendar, or personal planner. Together with checklists for routine chores, to-do lists guide efficient day-to-day planning for an organized home.

Daily To-Do Basics: Go, Call, Buy, and What's for Dinner?

Each day's to-do list has an internal rhythm that can help you get the work done fast. Most to-do lists set out where you need to go, whom you need to call, what you need to do, a list of things to buy, and what's for dinner.

Make your to-do list easy to follow. Group items on your list under these headings: Go, Call, Buy, and Do. Review dinner plans in a section labelled "What's for dinner?" (*See Daily To-Do form on page 242.*)

By grouping chores and reminding you about the evening's dinner plans, your to-do list gives an instant update on the important work of the day.

Time-saving tips for every day

Time is a democratic asset; everyone is given the same 24 hours each day. Save your precious time with these tips:

■ **Don't go empty-handed.** Whether going upstairs, leaving the room, or going outside, take something with you to put away as you go. Take newspapers to the recycling bin when you go to the garage, carry a pair of shoes to the wardrobe when you go upstairs, take out a bag of rubbish when you leave the house.

■ **Use small bits of time to do small jobs.** Fold socks during a commercial break. Give the sink a quick wipe-down as you leave the bathroom. Little efforts mount up.

■ **Do chores while you chat.** During telephone conversations, look for "busy hands" jobs that can be done while talking. Prepare a salad, sort a drawer, or return misplaced items to their homes while you talk with family or friends. A cordless telephone or headset makes it easier to make good use of telephone time.

■ **Double up on errands – or stay out of the shop.** Never make a special trip to do a single errand; instead, group them together. Visit the dry-cleaner nearest the bank, or go to the supermarket on the way home from work.

■ **Make good use of travel time.** Audio books are good companions for a driving commute; use trips to and from school to discuss the day's plans with the children. Don't talk on the mobile while driving, however, unless you have a hands-free set; it's illegal and the saving of time isn't worth the safety risk to yourself and others.

Habit, the household
wonder worker

Imagine the television pitch: "Special offer! The amazing Household Wonder Worker will take your house from chaos to castle in only 21 days. It'll speed your cleaning, calm your chaos, and cut your clutter. Backed by scientific research, our product is guaranteed to bring order and serenity to your disorganized home."

Habits: where to start?

You're sold on the power of habit, but where to begin? While every family's climb out of chaos will be different, focus on building these first habits for an orderly home:

- **Check your lists.** Review each day's checklists and to-do lists each morning and evening. They'll keep you on track and organized each day.
- **Make the bed.** Invest 45 seconds in straightening duvets and tucking sheets in to start the day on an organized note.
- **Take time for self-care.** Morning or evening, no matter how busy, take 20 minutes for grooming and self-care. Care for yourself first; it'll give you confidence throughout the day.
- **Welcome each morning.** The night before, check clothing for the next day. Lay the table for breakfast, and put out items needed to prepare morning beverages.
- **Keep meals in their place.** Clean kitchen worktops and wash dirty dishes after each meal. Don't let clearing-up jobs from one meal invade cooking energy needed for the next one.

You say you have the phone in one hand and a credit card in the other? Sounds that good, does it? Sorry, television viewers. The Amazing Household Wonder Worker is the most powerful secret weapon in the war against disorganization and clutter, but you can't buy it, not in the shops, or anywhere. You have to build your own, but it's free for the making. Put it to work for you, and it'll lead you, step-by-step, out of the darkness of disorganization and into the light. What is it? Habit.

Let the force of habit be with you

Habit is a small word for such a powerful force. It may start small, but habit works like a snowball, perched at the top of a snow-covered mountain. It takes a tiny little effort to push the snowball over the edge, but look out! By the time it reaches the bottom, that little snowball has gained the power of an avalanche.

So, too, with the habits we build into our daily life. Small steps forwards, barely noticed, have a powerful effect on our homes and our lives. What's the secret? Momentum. It takes energy and thought to form a good habit, just as it takes energy and intention to push that little snowball over the edge. Once in place, however, a habit gains in strength and effect with each repetition, building strength and power behind it — and you don't even have to think about it.

Anatomy of a habit

Habits are powerful, but they're not mysterious. We all have a brace of them, for good or bad. Does each day begin with two cups of coffee and the newspaper? Habit! Do you sweeten weekly supermarket trips with an almond croissant from the supermarket bakery? Habit! Do you always place your handbag or briefcase on the floor of the car, behind the driver's seat? There's that habit again!

If habits are familiar creatures, why are they so very difficult to start – or to change? Go back to the snowball. Yes, it's a bit of a nuisance to make it, isn't it? You have to get your hands wet, cold, and numb, and pack the snow tightly. You must perch the snowball on its ledge just so, and then give the silly thing a push. Once you do, though, look out!

"Once in place, a habit gains in strength and effect with each repetition, building strength and power behind it."

The analogy explains why good habits can be so difficult to start, and bad habits so difficult to end. Setting up good habits means creating conscious, intentional change. Ending bad ones means countering the tremendous, built-up force of a thousand repetitions.

21 days to success

How do you form a good habit? The concept is simple: decide what you want to do, and do it each day for 21 days. By the time you've repeated the habit daily for three weeks, you own it – or rather, it owns you. Put it in place and your habit will carry on without further thought.

Dr Maxwell Maltz, author of the book *Psycho-Cybernetics*, first noted the significance of this 21-day time period. A plastic surgeon, Dr Maltz knew that it took 21 days for amputees to stop feeling phantom sensations in the amputated limb. When he began working to help patients change their attitudes, not their appearance, he found that this time period applied to changes of thinking, too. It's a hard-wired interval needed to grow any change to fruition.

If the idea is simple (do it for 21 days!) the devil is in the details. Establishing a new habit is hard work. Each new habit

must turn aside the formidable energy of an entrenched old habit in order to survive and thrive.

Old habits are not so easily dislodged. In practical terms, fresh new habits must be tended carefully and guarded from intruders. During their infancy and youth, good habits can be extinguished by a single episode of "Mañana, mañana – I don't want to do it!" You have to cherish the new, good habit and fight the old bad one at the same time.

On the trail of good habits

Ready to bring the power of habit to your side in the war against domestic chaos? Try these three tips to help you form new habits:

■ **One habit at a time.** Tempting as it is to decide that today, you'll change your entire life from top to bottom, resist the urge. It's better to build a single helpful habit than try for a total overhaul of life – and fail.

Changing a habit takes undivided energy and commitment. To succeed, focus on a single habit. Only after you've established a new habit should you move on to another. Take heart, though. With 52 weeks in each year, you can build 17 new habits and still take two weeks holiday in a single year.

■ **Hitch your habit to a star.** A new habit stands a better chance of survival if it has a friend. Think of a habit you have now as a locomotive engine, and add the new one to the train. By building new habits in concert with established ones, you make the change easier to adopt.

Do you put your toddler down for a nap at 2 p.m. each afternoon? That's a perfect "prompt" to build your new habit – 30 minutes of daily inspirational reading – into your schedule at 2:05 p.m.

■ **Seek out support.** When it comes to building new habits, a support network is worth a thousand words. Agree to swap "nags" with a good friend: you hold him or her accountable, he or she holds you accountable as you work to build new habits together.

Look for habit buddies to conquer tough habits side-by-side. Have you decided to walk for 45 minutes each day? Walking with a friend, a neighbour, or your spouse will double the motivation (and the fun!).

The Household Notebook:
planning an organized home

Organized people use a personal planner: a small book that contains information, calendars, and schedules to help them stay organized. Organized households need a planner, too: a Household Notebook. Containing calendars, schedules, checklists, and information of all kinds, a Household Notebook serves as a command centre for the entire family. It's the place to go, when you need to know.

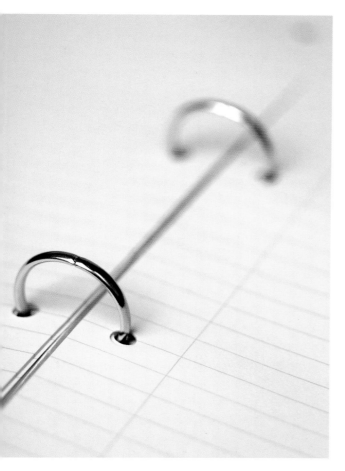

While each family's organizer will be unique, most are simple three-ring notebooks with several divider sections. Because they're infinitely expandable, household notebooks become as distinctive as the family that uses them. A family with school-aged children involved in dance, music, and sports will include organizer sections for rehearsal and practice schedules, summer

"A Household Notebook serves as a command centre for the entire family."

activity ideas, and videos to-rent lists. A two-career couple with preschool children may add baby-sitter and day-care dividers and an emergency telephone list to their household notebook. Empty nesters will rely on packing checklists for holidays, home repair records, and gift idea lists for far-flung children and grandchildren.

By compiling and storing family information in a central location, life at home benefits. No more searching for scraps of paper or mislaid parental permission slips. Information is always right where it belongs: in the Household Notebook.

Create Your Own Household Notebook
To create your family's Household Notebook, start with a three-ring binder, some clear plastic page protectors, paper, and tabbed dividers.

▲ **Simple, basic,** and low-tech, the Household Notebook is a high-powered information manager. Do away with scrawled post-it notes, in favour of a central source for household information.

Add dividers Using tabbed dividers from an office supply shop, set up dividers according to your family's needs. Each family grows their own family organizer; expect divider categories to change together with your family. Some suggested dividers are listed on the following pages, but your family is unique, so what you choose will reflect that. Be sure to place a few clear page protectors in each divider section.

Add paper Start with a calendar, and add pages or forms to record information. At OrganizedHome.Com, you'll find free printable calendars, forms, and checklists to jump-start your Household Notebook (*the most popular forms can be found on pages 238–47*). Computer users may use desktop publishing programmes to create information forms; others can use simple lined paper to create pages for their notebook.

Finally, add clear plastic page protectors to each section. These make it easy to track checklists, display schedules, and view product manuals.

Ready to begin Once the dividers and page protectors are in place and you've added calendars and basic forms, you're ready to begin. Gather all scattered slips and scraps of paper: pizza menus and business cards, school notices and church bulletins, class schedules and holiday activity brochures. Enter information in the Notebook, writing phone numbers on the correct phone directory pages, punching and filing club calendars, slipping magazine articles into page protectors.

Be creative! Add dividers that express your household's priorities and needs. Planning home-improvement projects? Add a "Home Improvements" divider, and store magazine cuttings and swatches in page protectors. Use Master To-Do and Daily To-Do lists (*see pages 76–7, 80–1*) in any divider to keep track of ongoing projects and goals, while blank lined pages hold information not covered by a specific form.

Keep your Household Notebook near the family's main telephone and calendar to guide family activities and decisions. A request for a cake from your Women's Institute? Note it on the calendar, and add "eggs and flour" to the shopping list. Planning Friday night out with your spouse? Go to the baby-sitter's information page and review emergency information with the baby-sitter before you leave.

Dividers for your Notebook

Every Notebook will reflect the unique family that builds it, but these suggested dividers will cover most information needs:

- **Emergency information.** Keep emergency information in the first section of the Household Notebook. Include a list of emergency phone numbers (including your home address, to assist rescue personnel, see page 240); baby-sitter's checklists with contact information; phone listings for health-care providers and information about emergency procedures.
- **Calendar and planning.** Calendar and planning notes are the heart of a Household Notebook, so set up a Calendar and Planning divider. What belongs here? A monthly calendar, a page protector with your checklists, and a section for to-do lists lives in Calendar and Planning. Use a three-hole punch to add work schedules, school calendars, and events lists for church and civic activities. Goal: to have a one-stop location for all planning information for each day, week, and month.
- **Telephone divider and address book.** Calling all telephone numbers! The Telephone Directory is the most useful, most-consulted section of any Household Notebook. The Telephone Directory is a single place to put the numbers of the school-run parents, takeaway telephone numbers, club directories, and lists of emergency telephone numbers. Include an address book in your Notebook, to keep track of family and friends. Don't stop with mere names, addresses, and telephone numbers. Add personal information like babies' names, birthdays, and email addresses to stay in touch with family and friends.

Make it yours

With basic address book functions tucked away, custom-tailor the Notebook for your household's needs. Your Notebook may include dividers for these activities:

Family and school Family is where the heart is – and deserves its own divider. This section tracks the information needs of family members and family life:

- Personal information page for each family member
- Clothing sizes tracker
- Master occasions list (birthdays, anniversaries)
- Gift suggestion list
- Birthday party ideas
- Family-friendly websites
- List of DVD/videos to hire
- List of books to read
- Library information

Families with school-aged children will want to add a school divider to hold:

- School timetables and holiday list
- Lunch menus
- School-run rota
- School information page
- School reading lists
- Summer activities information

Home management Bring it all back home! The Home Management divider holds information central to house and home. Cleaning, entertaining, decorating, and household storage information find a home here:

- Household cleaning schedule
- Seasonal chore checklists
- Children's chore checklists
- Home inventory
- Home decorating ideas
- Party planners
- Car maintenance schedule
- Stain-removal guide
- Recycling locations
- Home storage inventory

Meals and menus In the kitchen, the Household Notebook helps plan meals, create menus, and track how the larder and freezer are stocked. Use this section to hold:

- Weekly menu planners
- Grocery shopping lists
- Price book form
- Freezer inventory forms
- Larder inventory forms
- Recipes
- List of recipes to try

Money and finance A section for tracking pounds and pence makes sense. Keep track of household finances here:

- Budget/spending record
- Bills to pay
- Chequebook balance register
- Credit card list
- Online service/online account information
- Home inventory
- Insurance information
- Safe deposit inventory
- Utilities/services directory
- Magazine subscriptions
- Warranty information
- Vehicle records

Health and fitness Organize family health care with a Health and Fitness divider. Have a medical emergency? Grab the Household Notebook on the way to Casualty. Visit to a paediatrician? Use this section to record the children's illnesses, medication, and medical history. Types of information to file in the Health and Fitness section include:

- Diet trackers
- Blood-pressure record
- First aid kit checklist
- Medical information sheet for each family member
- Emergency directory
- Child health records
- Prescription drug record
- Insurance information
- Pet health records

Travel, hobbies, and activities Time for fun! The Travel, Hobbies, and Activities divider covers the extra-curricular activities that make life worthwhile. Hobby, place of worship, club, sports, voluntary, holiday, and travel ideas are included here. Your Household Notebook may have several dividers for this purpose. Do you sing in a choir? Give it a divider. Do the children play in a football team? Divide it up!

What belongs in these sections? Any and every piece of paper pertaining to that activity. Place of worship services timetable. Sports information sheets. Lists for travel and camping. These sections will vary from family to family, but here are some ideas:

- Picnic planner
- Travel packing checklist
- Before-we-leave checklist
- Camping checklist
- Holiday idea list
- House-sitter information sheet
- PTA newsletters
- Place of worship services timetable
- Scout or Girl Guide materials
- Craft materials inventory
- Sewing pattern list
- Books to read
- Videos to watch

Holidays and seasons Make the holiday season bright with the planning power of a Household Notebook. Our sister site, OrganizedChristmas.Com, offers free printable forms for holiday planning, or make your own pages to keep tabs on holiday events. Throughout the year, keep track of important days, gift-giving, and holiday decorations with pages to record:

- Family birthday calendar
- Birthday party planner
- Holiday gift list
- Seasonal greetings cards list
- Holiday menu planner
- Holiday decorations inventory
- Decorations to make list
- "Gifts to make" list
- Gift cupboard inventory for stored gifts

Life in view: the family calendar

What's the best way to keep track of hectic family schedules? A family calendar. Choose a large write-on calendar on which you'll track appointments, outings, children's activities, family dinners, and school-run rotas. Use coloured pens in a different colour for each family member to colour-code your entries.

If you can see the family's commitments at a glance, it will guide household planning. The week of football playoffs – with every night's dinner spent away from home at the football pitch – isn't the right time to tackle a new home-improvement project. A bonus: seeing family calendar dates in living colour helps you say "No!" to new obligations, when they clash with existing plans.

Create a family information centre
The best place to post your family calendar is in a family information centre: a designated space in your home to review checklists, take phone messages, add items to a to-do list, and check calendars.

A family information centre focuses on information handling and retrieval, so it should be located near a telephone, in a place that permits seating.

Hang the family calendar from the wall and place the Household Notebook near the telephone. Arrange pens and pencils in a pretty mug or holder, and add a pad of paper for phone messages.

Alternatively, use a bought "information centre" whiteboard to take phone messages. Coloured markers allow colour-coding, while the whiteboard eraser makes it easy to change an entry.

cycles of an
organized home

What comes closer to the rhythm of life itself than the cycle of food? As the kitchen is the heart of the home, so food and food preparation stands at the centre of our memories: holiday meals and special occasions; casual summer picnics and everyday family dinners. Make those memories happy ones with the ideas in this section, aimed to speed, streamline, and save money on the kitchen front.

Investigate menu and meal planning to save time and promote a healthy diet — while using smart supermarket strategies to keep the wallet plump. Learn proper food storage techniques to preserve your family's investment in foods for the larder.

Declutter cupboards, refrigerator, and freezer, then apply organizing principles to create kitchen "centres" that will speed food preparation and meal clean-up.

Harness the store cupboard principle for maximum savings — and to protect the family against natural disasters or hard times.

Planning
family menus

What are we having for dinner? It's the question of the hour. Too often, we find ourselves looking for answers in the supermarket at 5p.m. Harried and harassed by hungry children, we scan the aisles in desperation and rack our brains for a quick answer to the recurring dinnertime question.

Keeping the family fed can be daunting. Three meals a day. Seven dinners a week. From supermarket to larder, refrigerator to table, sink to cupboard, the kitchen routine can get old, old, old. No wonder we hide our heads like ostriches from the plain and simple fact: into each day, one dinner must fall. What's the answer? A menu plan.

A menu plan saves money, because it cuts out last-ditch trips to the supermarket. A menu plan saves you time. No dash to the neighbours next-door for a missing ingredient, no frantic searches through the freezer for something – anything – to thaw for dinner.

Most important, a weekly (or monthly) menu plan conserves a home manager's most valuable resource: energy. Follow these strategies to put the power of menu and meal planning to work for you.

Dare to do it

Often, making a menu plan is something we intend to do . . . when we get around to it. Instead of seeing menu planning as an activity that adds to our quality of life, we dread sitting down to decide next Thursday's dinner. "I'll do that next week, when I'm more organized."

Wrong! Menu planning is the first line of defence in the fight against kitchen chaos. It's better to do menu planning in a single, 10-minute weekly session than to do it nightly – and in despair – standing in the queue at the supermarket or peering into an open refrigerator.

Take the vow. "I [state your name], hereby promise not to visit the supermarket again until I've made a menu plan!"

Day	Main course	Pudding
Monday	Beef stew, baked potatoes, broccoli	Fresh fruit
Tuesday	Chicken breasts, steamed rice, stir-fried veggies	Apple pie and ice cream
Wednesday	French dip sandwiches (leftovers from roast), potato salad	Leftover apple pie
Thursday	Pasta with chicken and vegetables	Biscuits and ice cream
Friday	Freezer lasagne, green salad	Frozen fruit bars
Saturday	Chinese takeaway	Ice cream
Sunday	Baked salmon, wild rice, green beans	Layer cake

▲ **Plan it on paper.** A written menu plan doesn't take time – it saves it. Putting the week's meals on paper ends the "what's for dinner?" debate, saving time each day.

Start small and simple

Grandiose ideas of weekly new recipes and complex monthly schedules can scuttle the act of menu planning before it begins. Yes, it's fun to think about indexing your recipe collection, entering the data in a relational database and crunching menus until the next decade, but resist the urge.

"Take the vow: I promise not to visit the supermarket again without a menu plan."

Instead, think, "next week". Seven little dinners, one trip to the supermarket. Slow and steady builds menu-planning skills and shows you the benefits of the exercise. Elaborate and over-detailed menu plans become just another failed exercise on the way to an organized kitchen.

The power of advertising

Where to begin to make menu plans? The food flyers from your local newspaper. Try to make your menu plan and shopping list the day the food ads appear. Use the ads to get a feel for the week's sales and bargains. Use that feeling to guide your menu planning.

This week in my home town, for instance, two local chain supermarkets are offering whole chickens for a low, low price. To feed my family well and frugally, this is the week for Ginger Chicken and Fajitas, not a time to dream about Beef Stew and Grilled Pork Tenderloins. I'll serve those when roasts are the loss leader at the supermarket.

Menu-planning tips

Here are some points to ponder as you bring menu planning under control – and take the "desperate" out of dinnertime.

Build a family shopping list Look in any gift shop or browse mail-order catalogues and you'll find cute little shopping lists for all persuasions and occasions. Bear-shaped shopping lists. Long skinny shopping lists. Shopping lists with winsome graphics. Shopping lists with coloured borders.

OK, it's food ad day. Ready? Time to rough out a simple menu plan. The goal is two-fold: shop efficiently to obtain food required for seven dinner meals, while minimizing expenditure, cooking, shopping, and cleaning time. These are the bare bones of menu planning: make a draft plan, shop from a list, retain flexibility, firm up your plan, and hold yourself accountable.

- **Scan the food ads** for specials and sales. Rough out a draft menu plan: seven main dinner meals that can be made from weekly specials, side dishes, and salads. Use a blank sheet of paper, or a menu planner form (*see pages 246–7*).
- **Wander to the pantry** and the refrigerator to check for any of last week's purchases that are languishing beneath wilting lettuce or hardening tortillas. The best bargain is food you've already purchased – so plan to use it! Review your shopping list and note any condiments or spices that you will need for the week's meals.
- **Ready, set, shop** – but shop with an open mind. That whole chicken on special offer won't look like such a bargain next to a marked-down mega-pack of boneless chicken thighs. Be ready to substitute if you find a great offer.
- **Return from shopping** and stock your shelves. As you put away groceries, flesh out the menu plan. Match it up with the family's calendar, saving the oven roast for a lazy Sunday, the quick-fix pizza for football night.
- **Post the menu plan** on the refrigerator door. Refer to it during the coming week as you prepare meals.

Menu planning **basics**

Colourful freebies with pictures of kittens and teddy bears. Most homes have two or three pads of lists – or a dozen.

Only one problem: why aren't you using them?

Because they don't work, that's why. Teenaged sons play stuff-the-rubbish bin with the empty cereal box, but have you ever known one to write "Cheerios" neatly on a shopping list? Pre-printed lists, moreover, fit about as well as one-size-fits-all socks from the corner shop.

The solution? Build a family shopping list, noting all the foods and sundries your family consumes (*see Shopping list form on page 244*). Check your receipts. Computerized shop receipts can help jog memories for items to include on the list. Include a few blank lines for new foods or unexpected ingredients.

Organize your personal shopping list according to the aisles you visit frequently in the supermarket. Once you've made your family list, use a printer or copier to print 52 copies: a year's worth of shopping lists for the household.

Each week, post a fresh list on the refrigerator door or in the Family Information Centre (*see page 87*). When today's breakfast empties the carton of orange juice, circle that item on the list. Boys who don't circle "Sugar Gaggers" on the list when they empty the box will soon learn the principle of cause-and-effect – not making a note means that they'll be eating instant porridge for the rest of the week.

On shopping day, grab the list and take it to the supermarket. You'll know at a glance that you need to buy more juice, cereal, and bread.

Making a personal shopping list can be an interesting – and revealing – exercise. During the years when we still had teen children at home, cereal, milk, and biscuits headed the list, along with the entry "nuclear waste" – our family's slang for a cheap, luridly coloured punch beverage sold in the dairy cabinet. Sigh. The good old days. Now that our household is back-to-two (and we two are both a touch too round) "broccoli" and "salmon" head the list.

Court the calm of a routine Yes, there are some well-organized souls among us who don't make formal meal plans. But look closer and you'll discover that there's an underlying strategy behind this seemingly relaxed approach – the household meal service dances to a routine.

Sunday's a big dinner, and Tuesday gets the leftovers. Monday is burger night, and Wednesday sees spaghetti, year in and year out. Thursday's the day for a casserole, and Dad grills on Friday. Saturday night, it's a takeaway or pizza.

Create a routine around your menu planning. You can try new recipes – just don't let your enthusiasm for the glossy pages of the cookery book seduce you into doing so more than twice a month. Cooking tried-and-true dishes speeds dinner preparation and streamlines menu planning.

To do it, look for cues in the family schedule. At-home days with more free time can handle a fancy meal – or can signal soup, sandwiches, and Cook's Night Off. If it's your evening to do the usual kids' taxi service after swimming club, this is a great time to plan for takeaway burgers. Make the routine yours, and it will serve you well.

Stay flexible Menu plans aren't written in stone. So you're fighting fatigue on the "big" cooking day? Swap it with Pizza Night and go to bed early with a cup of herbal tea. Family members will forgive you, as long as they get their postponed favourite a day or two later. Building flexibility into your plan can also serve the aims of thrift with Cook's Choice Night. Traditionally held the night before the main weekly supermarket shop, you can slide a neglected dinner into Cook's Choice, or chop up the contents of the refrigerator for a clean-it-out stir-fry. Either way, you'll feel smug at your frugality and good planning.

Make it a habit Simple or not, a menu plan won't help you if you don't make one. Weekly menu planning is a good candidate for the weekly checklist. Get into the habit of planning before you shop, and you'll get hooked – one addiction that's worth cultivating!

Recycle not reinvent After you've made menu plans for a few weeks, the beauty of the activity shines through: you can recycle them! Your family won't mind, and you'll save even more time and energy. Instead of an ambitious plan for 30-day menus, tuck completed menu plans in a file folder or envelope. The next time chicken is on special offer at the supermarket, pull out the plan you made this week. Done!

Your family loves home-cooked meals, but with a busy life, who has time to cook a full dinner every night? Enter freezer cooking: an organized method to cook once and eat many times by stockpiling pre-prepared main meals and side dishes in the freezer.

Also known as once-a-month cooking or investment cooking, the concept of freezer cooking is simple. When you do cook, cook multiple portions and freeze extra servings.

The problem is, this method is a bit haphazard. Who hasn't known the virtuous feeling of cooking up a big saucepan of tomato sauce and tucking a container or two deep in the bowels of Moby Dick, the great white freezer? Where, sad to say, it remains. Months later, a freezer clean-out yields an icy mountain of anonymous dribs and drabs of pre-cooked food. Without labels, planning, or portion control, the cook-ahead effort goes to waste.

Use the following tips to fine-tune your freezer cooking skills and avoid mystery meals.

■ **Plan multiple meals.** Are minced beef or chicken pieces on special offer this week? Buy extra for freezer meals – but make it a plan. One kilogram (2lb) of beef will make four meals for your family? Great! That's what you buy, not a smidgen more. Too often, a weak "I'll freeze the extra" leads to overbuying and waste.

■ **Package the freezer meals first.** Back to our hungry family, faced with a huge saucepan of bolognese sauce. Before you know it, a meat-loving teen has gutted the pot and put a serious dent in your meal forward-planning. To avoid this hazard, fill freezer containers before you serve the evening's meal. You'll have a tighter handle on portion control – and there will be no more scant containers of sauce marooned inside the freezer.

■ **Freeze casseroles before cooking.** A twice-cooked casserole is nobody's friend. After dinner, who wants to scoop the leftovers into freezer bags? Efficient freezer cooks build their lasagna in three single-meal containers and freeze two while the current evening's dinner is in the oven.

■ **Package properly.** Ill-assorted margarine tubs and gaping plastic containers are for amateurs – and they won't protect your frozen assets from spoilage and freezer burn. Invest in three or four same-sized oven-safe casserole dishes. Is it beef stew tonight? Spritz the dishes with pan spray, and line with a sheet of foil long enough to wrap completely around the food. Spray the foil, too, then ladle in the stew. Gently tuck the foil up over the food. Freeze overnight, and then release the foil from the dish. Wrap, label, and freeze in freezer bags. To use, pop a foil-wrapped package into the casserole dish, thaw, and re-heat. Simple!

■ **Label, label, label!** An efficient freezer cook has assembled labelling supplies before he or she begins. Tuck a slip of paper with the name of the dish, cooking directions, today's date, and a use-by date to tell you how long to freeze the item, between the foil-wrapped package and freezer bag. Better, use a permanent marker pen to label freezer bags. Computer-savvy cooks can print computer address labels for easy labelling of frozen foods.

■ **Track inventory.** "Out of sight, out of mind" defeats many would-be freezer cooks. Introduce inventory control with a whiteboard. Adding three dinners' worth of macaroni cheese to your freezer hoard? Write them in. Visiting family has you drawing heavily on your inventory? Erase each meal as you use it. A small magnet-mounted whiteboard can be placed on the freezer door to track frozen assets. Or copy the freezer inventory form on page 245 and post it on the door.

Top tips for
grocery shopping

For most families, the food budget is the most elastic entry in the household budget. The rent is the rent, electricity costs may not change much from bill to bill, but smart shopping can reduce the cost of food – and cut the time and energy it takes to shop. Try these tips for frugal, efficient food shopping.

1 Never shop hungry
Hunger pangs make it easier for snack food and impulse purchases to jump into the trolley.

2 Shop less, save more
A quick stop for some milk usually turns into an hour's trip and a dozen grocery bags. Avoid small shopping trips.

3 Shop at home first
When making menu plans, assess the contents of the refrigerator, freezer, and larder or store cupboard before buying new foods.

4 Make a list, and live by it
Supermarket marketers depend on the impulse buy. Protect your budget by shopping from a list.

5 Time trips for best savings
Plan shopping trips for the day meat and produce managers mark down soon-to-expire items. You can save up to 50 per cent on those purchases if you time it right.

◀ **Take charge** of your shopping and trips to the shops become an exciting challenge – but travel alone. With kids in tow, you'll be distracted and may be persuaded to buy more than you intended.

6 Be fickle and shop around
Those who have a "favourite shop" usually pay a price for their loyalty. Peruse supermarket ads and shop in two or three shops in order to make the greatest savings.

7 Love those brand names? Get over it!
Own brand labels offer equivalent quality at a lower price than "nationally advertised" products.

8 Do the maths on unit pricing
Big boxes don't always mean big savings. Rely on the "unit price" – the item's cost per gram/ounce. It'll show you the product with the best price, regardless of size.

9 Shop with the season
Citrus in winter and strawberries in summer are much less expensive than the out-of-season reverse. Eat in season for freshness – and savings.

10 Buy in bulk …
but only if large sizes boast a lower unit price, and if your family can consume the product without waste.

11 Love those "loss leaders"
They're the sales items in the weekly food ads, offered below cost to lure consumers to the shop. Take the bait, but pass on higher-priced items.

12 Choose unprocessed
Fresh ingredients cost less than packaged foods, and contain fewer preservatives, less sodium and fillers.

13 Equip the boot
For easy shopping, put an ice chest in your car's boot for dairy products and frozen foods, and boxes to support plastic sacks.

Cutting costs with a price book

Even at the supermarket, knowledge is power – but how do you track prices and stay informed? With a price book.

A price book is a product-by-product record that tracks prices, sales, and buying opportunities for foods. Over time, you'll discover the "target price" for any item: the rock-bottom low price goal for purchases.

Second, the price book illustrates each product's sales cycle: the number of weeks between sales offering that target price. If tinned tuna is on special offer at the supermarket every six weeks, smart shoppers will buy six weeks' worth of tuna – and they'll avoid this product during the high-price weeks.

To make your price book, use a small notebook or printable price book form from OrganizedHome.Com. Assign one page to each staple product on your shopping list. On each page, list the date, shop location, brand, item price, and unit price. As you shop, note each new "low price" for each product.

Product: TOMATO SAUCE			
Date	Shop brand	Size/price	Unit price

Hint: Supermarket receipts make it easy to add entries to the price book. In the shop, shelf labels often list unit prices for goods.

FRESH FOOD STORAGE GUIDELINES

Food	Time	Temperature	Packaging and tips
DAIRY			
Eggs		Refrigerator (4°C/38°F)	Keep fresh eggs in the original carton; throw away any cracked or leaking eggs.
Raw in shell	3–5 weeks		
Hard-cooked	1 week		
Milk	7 days	Refrigerator (4°C/38°F)	Always buy milk and dairy products at the end of your shopping trip to keep them cold and fresh.
Butter	1–3 months (38°F/4°C)	Refrigerator	Butter is very susceptible to picking up flavours from other foods. Store in original carton or covered container to prevent flavour loss.
Yogurt	7–14 days	Refrigerator (4°C/38°F)	Store yogurt in the original container.
Sour cream	7–21 days	Refrigerator (4°C/38°F)	Once opened, use sour cream within 7–10 days.
Cheese			
Hard (Cheddar, Swiss)	6 months unopened	Refrigerator (4°C/38°F)	Wrap cheese tightly in original wrapping or plastic food storage wrap to protect against mold, flavour loss.
Soft (Brie)	3-4 weeks opened		
Shredded cheese	1 week		
Cottage cheese, ricotta cheese	7–14 days	Refrigerator (4°C/38°F)	Keep cottage or ricotta cheese tightly covered in the original container. Store the container upside-down to seal out air and preserve freshness.
MEAT, POULTRY, AND FISH			
Beef		Refrigerator (4°C/38°F)	Store meats in coldest part of the refrigerator. Store raw meat in original airtight packaging or plastic food storage bags.
Minced	1–2 days		
Joints	3–5 days		
Steaks	3–5 days		
Cooked beef (leftovers)	3–4 days		
Gravy and meat stock	1–2 days		
Poultry		Refrigerator (4°C/38°F)	Juices can contaminate other foods. Store chicken and turkey in sealed packaging in lowest part of refrigerator.
Whole chicken or turkey	1–2 days		
Chicken pieces	1–2 days		
Giblets	1–2 days		
Fish		Refrigerator (4°C/38°F)	To prevent odour, store fresh fish in sealed packaging away from other foods.
Lean fish (cod, sole)	1–2 days		
Fatty fish (salmon, halibut)	1–2 days		
Cooked fish	3–4 days		
Shellfish		Refrigerator (4°C/38°F)	Wash hands thoroughly with soap and water after handling raw shellfish.
Prawns, scallops, shucked clams or mussels	1–2 days		
Live clams or lobsters	2–3 days		
Cooked shellfish	3–4 days		

Food	Time	Temperature	Packaging and tips
FRUITS AND VEGETABLES			
Fruits (cold storage):		Refrigerator (4°C/38°F)	Keep fruit juices tightly covered. Wrap melons and cantaloupes to prevent flavour transfer to other foods.
Apples	1–3 weeks		
Berries and cherries	1–2 days		
Citrus fruit (oranges, lemons, limes, etc)	3 weeks		
Grapes	5 days		
Fruit juices	6 days		
Melons (cantaloupe)	1 week		
Fruits (room temperature)		Room temperature	Ripen apricots, peaches, and pears at room temperature; store in refrigerator when ripe.
Avocados	3–5 days		
Bananas	3–5 days		
Peaches, pears, and apricots	3–5 days		
Vegetables (cold storage):		Refrigerator (4°C/38°F)	Store asparagus upright in plastic container containing 2.5–5cm (1–2in) water. Rinse leaf or shredded lettuce with water and store in sealed plastic storage containers. Add a paper towel to absorb excess moisture and promote crisping.
Asparagus	1–2 days		
Beans (green or wax)	1–2 days		
Carrots and beets	1–2 weeks		
Celery	1–2 weeks		
Lettuce (head)	3–5 days		
Lettuce (leaf or shredded)	1–2 days		
Mushrooms	1–2 days		
Spinach	5–7 days		
Sweetcorn (in husk)	1–2 days		
Vegetables (cool storage)		Cool storage (7–10°C/45–50°F)	Onions need a dry storage space, so don't store them with potatoes, which release moisture. Don't store potatoes or onions in plastic bags. Better air circulation promotes a longer shelf life.
Onions	Up to 4 weeks		
Potatoes	2–3 months		
Sweet potatoes or yams	2–3 weeks		
Vegetables (room temperature)			Ripen tomatoes at room temperature away from sunlight.
Tomatoes	1–3 days		
BREAD AND CEREALS			
Breads		Room temperature	Store sliced breads in original packaging or plastic food storage bag. Bread may be stored in the refrigerator for longer shelf life, but will become stale and dry more quickly.
Sliced bread	5–7 days		
French bread or baguettes	1 day		
Rye or artisan breads	2–3 days		
Cereals		Room temperature	"Decant" opened boxes of cereal from original packaging into airtight storage containers for longest shelf life. Keep porridge oats in an airtight container to guard against moisture and insects.
Cold cereal, opened	Up to 2 months		
Cold cereal, unopened	Up to 18 months		
Porridge oats	Up to 3 months		

A well-laid table is a feast for the eyes – and the happy mood it creates can even overcome a mediocre offering. Bring a sparkle to day-to-day meals with pretty place mats and bright china. Cloth napkins add a colourful, environmentally friendly touch.

■ **Keep it simple.** For most meals, a setting of knife, fork and spoon, dinner plate, and beverage glass is sufficient. Keep table settings simple and functional.

■ **Lay it early.** Lay the table for the next meal immediately after you clear it from the present one, using freshly washed dishes straight out of the dishwasher. You'll save yourself the "put-away" step – and short-cut preparation for the meal to come.

■ **Delegate the job.** Laying the table with napkins and spoons can be a toddler's first household task, so bring the family on board. Allow children to add a simple centrepiece to create a happy family table.

Decluttering
the kitchen

It's not raindrops that keep falling on your head – it's the plastic tumblers when you open the cupboard. Time to declutter the kitchen!

Before you begin, clear worktops, empty the dishwasher, and bring your kitchen to an ordinary state of clean. Fill a washing-up bowl or sink with hot soapy water for quick clean-up and replacement of dusty items. Now begin, taking one step (drawer, cupboard, or shelf) at a time.

Decisions, decisions!

With each item you encounter you'll have to decide: keep, sell or donate, store, put away, or throw out? Stop the decision-making dam by holding each one in your hand and asking yourself a single question: "When did I use it last?"

- **"Never!"** Out it goes, into the bin, or for donation or to a car-boot sale – allow some other family the consumer thrill of possessing that genuine as-advertised-on-TV potato peeler machine.
- **"Within the last year."** Out it goes, with one exception. Seasonal cooking tools used only once a year, such as speciality cookie cutters, may be given houseroom if – and only if – they are removed from active kitchen storage and placed with the holiday decorations in a box marked Holiday Cooking Tools.
- **"Within the last month."** Candidate for a keeper. Deciding where the item should live will come during the organizing phase of the kitchen clear-up.
- **"Yesterday!"** Watch for these items; they're the backbone of an organized kitchen. Keep. Clean them if necessary and put them away where you found them. They will be the star performers of your new, improved kitchen.

STOP clutter in the kitchen

Label three STOP clutter boxes as follows: Put Away, Sell/Donate, and Storage. Also add a fourth box, labelled Put Away (kitchen). You'll use this for items that belong in another location in the kitchen, the first Put Away box for strays from other areas of the house. Add bin bags and set the timer to 20 minutes. Ready?

1 **Sort**
The sorting step is a powerhouse, designed to force a decision. Is this item rubbish? Into the bin bag it goes. Does it belong elsewhere in the kitchen, or in another room? Consign it to the correct Put Away box. Can it be donated or sold? Into the Sell/Donate box. Is it a speciality or seasonal item that should be stored? Place it in the Storage box. Sort until you empty the space or the timer rings – whichever comes first.

2 **Throw out**
Finished sorting? Throw out the rubbish. No pity, no mercy, no second chances! If you don't use it, it has no place in a lean, mean kitchen.

3 **Organize**
Assess the newly cleared space, wiping it free from dust or crumbs. Replace shelf liner if needed, or unroll non-skid padding to cushion kitchen dishes or glasses. Next, check the hardy survivors. Dusty or dirty items get a quick wash before being returned to their bright new home.

4 **Put away**
Check both Put Away boxes and return the items inside to their proper places. Take the Storage and Sell/Donate boxes to storage areas. Store your declutter tools until the next session. Done!

before decluttering ▲

after decluttering ▲

The rules of
kitchen storage

The basic principle that underlies organized kitchens? Use it most, store it closest. Less used items are reached with a bit of bending or stretching, while specialty or seasonal tools are sent to the kitchen equivalent of the Black Hole of Calcutta. Assess kitchen contents and storage options according to these three rules.

Sorting out the
kitchen sentimentalist

Visit a sentimentalist's kitchen, and you might be excused for confusing it with a shrine – or a museum. The refrigerator door bears multiple layers of curling photographs and water-specked children's artwork, the counter is lined with an unsteady parade of Granny's teapots, and cupboards are crammed with handed-down pots, dishes, and speciality plates.

Yes, the kitchen is the heart of any home, but a working kitchen is no place for sentimental overload. Too much memorabilia prevents the kitchen from being used efficiently – and the hot and humid environment is a hazardous place to store precious photographs or fragile mementos. Sort the sentiment from the kitchen stuff to get organized.

■ Group Granny's teapots on a mantlepiece where they can provide a decorative focus.
■ Store photographs in albums, where they can be enjoyed, away from the water dispenser's overspray.
■ Salvage the best of the children's artwork and hang it on the wall, and toss the rest.
■ Do a declutter and sort those handed-down pots, dishes, and plates using the A, B, C rules.

1 "A" is for every day

Every kitchen has a few best friends: dishes, tools, and equipment used each and every day. "A" kitchen items include plates and glasses, bowls and mugs, tableware and serving spoons, saucepans and frying pans, kitchen knives and cutting boards, a tin opener, kettle or coffee pot.

They've earned a home in the prime storage spots in the kitchen. "A" storage areas are those easiest to reach: kitchen worktops, the front areas of cupboard shelves, top drawers, and the fronts of lower drawers. Make the match, locating every-day kitchen tools in prime storage areas.

"It's easy: choose the most accessible areas in your kitchen to store the items you use the most."

2 "B" is for often

You love your slow cooker – but use it only once a week or so. It's a member of the "B" contingent: kitchen items that are used often but not daily. In their ranks are items such as graters, strainers, roasting tins, and mixing bowls.

Assign the "B" brigade to "B" level accommodations: lowest or highest shelves in the cupboards, or areas in the backs of drawers. To reach the land of "B," you'll stand on tiptoe or stoop a bit, but storage is reasonably accessible.

3 "C" is for seldom

In the kitchen, "C" items are those arcane tools, seasonal items, or single-use gadgets that just barely earn houseroom by being used once or twice a year. These also include small kitchen appliances which, left to multiply, can overtake even the largest kitchen, dangling cords and all. Give all "C" items a thorough clutter scrutiny before assigning them storage space in the kitchen – if you have never used that pasta maker, donate it to a fettuccine-loving friend. Most should be decluttered, but if everything on your shortlist of "C" tools manages to come into use once a year, well and good. This group includes seasonal cookie-cutters, holiday dishes, single-use gadgets such as potato ricers, oversized serving dishes, jars for homemade jam, or the waffle iron.

Consign "C" items to the dark reaches at the back of bottom shelves in the cupboards, or if they're decorative, perch them on top of soffits during the off-season. Small cupboards located over the refrigerator or oven, reachable only with a stool, are a natural home for "C" items. Alternatively, you can outsource them to other household storage areas. Store holiday dishes in the loft or basement, along with holiday decorations. Stack boxes of jars in the garage until time to make jam, or tumble "C" cooking gadgets into a lidded plastic container in the loft, labelled "kitchen gadgets".

▼ **Everyday items,** such as bowls used for soups or desserts, belong in "A" storage areas where you can reach them without undue effort, and where they can be easily replaced after washing up.

Kitchen
activity centres

In the kitchen, there's a primary rule: tools that work together should live together. Can you mix a cake, peel vegetables, or fry a burger without taking an extra step? Carry out this rule by creating activity centres in the kitchen: centralized places that group and organize tools needed for routine kitchen activities.

Each centre will be organized according to an activity focus, be assigned a designated space, and encompass storage for tools needed for that particular activity.

In most kitchens, activity centres will overlap. A sink/cutting centre – the zone for peeling, chopping, and washing food – may sit cheek-by-jowl with the cooking centre focused on the nearby cooker. Drawer and cupboard space may be shared between centres, and so may the tools and items they contain. Don't worry! The focus is on function, not boundaries. So long as you can get the job done without taking a step, overlap between activity centres is the norm.

Sink/cutting centre

You're making potato salad for a picnic. In the next 15 minutes, you'll drain freshly cooked potatoes, peel and grate hardboiled eggs, chop onion and celery, and mix a tasty dressing for your salad – and you'll do it all using the natural components of the kitchen's sink/cutting centre.

This centre's focus: washing, chopping, draining, and preparing food. Its designated area: the sink and a worktop next to the sink. Storage for this centre can include the worktop, sink storage areas, a drawer, and cupboard space.

Most-used cutting tools earn a home on valuable worktop space. Paring knives, serrated knives, and butcher knives are close at hand – and attractive – stored in a knife block. Hang a kitchen roll dispenser on the wall or beneath a cupboard to save space. To encourage hand washing and hygiene, decant liquid handwashing soap into a pretty pump dispenser, and assign it a home next to the sink.

Cleaning-up centre

The potato salad is sitting pretty, garnished, and ready to chill. It's time to clean up – and to do so, we'll call on the activity focus, designated space, and storage in the cleaning-up centre.

In this area is everything needed for cleaning up and rubbish collection. The designated location is under the sink, and includes the centre's storage; in households with young children, be sure to secure the cupboard with childproof locks or choose an inaccessible, high-up storage location close by.

Moisture is a persistent issue in a cupboard beneath the sink, so a cupboard liner is a must. Scraps of vinyl flooring, cut to fit the base of the cupboard, make it easy to wipe up spills and keep the area sanitized.

Large under-sink turntables make it easy to store items in the inaccessible back of the under-sink cupboard. Increase under-sink storage by mounting special organizers to the cupboard doors. A towel rack keeps hand towels at the ready; small shelves house washing-up liquid, sponge, and rubber gloves for easy access at washing-up time.

If you have an under-sink bin, plastic binliners are clean and convenient. Make it easy to change liners by storing a good handful at the bottom of the bin, underneath the current liner. When you remove the full bag, a fresh bag is always available.

Cooking centre

Focused on the hob and oven (and maybe a microwave oven), the cooking centre is the place to fry chicken, simmer chilli, or bake a batch of biscuits or muffins. It's home to the pots and

pans, whisks and spatulas used to heat, cook, and bake food. Because the cooking centre's tools are many and large, look hard for storage options near the cooker that can be included in this activity centre. Above the cooker, store baking sheets and biscuit sheets. Some cookers feature under-store drawers that are natural homes for the roasting tin and large bakeware. Put saucepans in their place with hanging racks that store cookware in plain sight – and within easy reach.

Spoons and spatulas are durable friends; store them in the easiest-to-reach drawer, or stand them upright in a container near the cooker. Affix a hook in the wall or underneath the cupboard for hanging oven gloves at the ready – but not too close to heat sources!

Store cooling racks, muffin tins, biscuit sheets, and roasting tins vertically on their sides in the cupboard. You'll be able to reach just the item you need, without having to lift, sort – and scratch – the rest of the group.

▲ **The sink/cutting centre** is where much food preparation begins. Here you'll house all the tools you'll need for slicing, chopping, cutting, grating, sieving, and squeezing.

Herbs and spices need to be conveniently located for easy seasoning, but make sure they are in a cool place: they'll lose their flavour stored under hot conditions.

Mixing centre
In the words of an old song, "Can she bake cherry pie, Billy Boy, Billy Boy?" She can – if her organized kitchen includes a well-planned mixing centre.

The focus: mixing, preparing, and assembling food. The mixing centre is the place where dough and piecrusts, marinades and muffins make their appearance. Star player in the drama will be the electric mixer, with supporting roles filled by kitchen scales, measuring jugs, baking supplies, and sifters.

The mixing centre is the most movable of all kitchen activity centres. Since it's not tied to a fixture, such as the sink or cooker, it can be located in any designated area with worktop space available. Storage includes cupboard, drawer, and wall areas around the designated worktop space.

Dishwashing/tableware centre

The meal is over and it's time to clean up — and turn to the dishwashing/tableware centre to get the job done. Chances are, this activity centre will lie right next to the cutting centre, since both share the kitchen sink as a designated space and use the same washing-up tools. The automatic dishwasher is the second compass point for this activity centre.

The centre's focus is the washing and storage of dishes and tableware — in a manner that will help family members to get the job done fast. Find storage for these items in drawers and cupboards convenient to the dishwasher. Shelf lining paper helps prevent scratching when putting dishes away; plastic skid-resistant shelf-liner cushions delicate china and glasses, preventing breakage. Assign dishes a home according to their function and use. Just because you purchase dishes as a set doesn't mean you should store them that way. A "breakfast shelf" holds cereal bowls, side plates, and mugs — and lets children lay the breakfast table each morning.

Seldom-used serving dishes live in the inaccessible way-back of the cupboard shelf, while plates and soup bowls enjoy the air and light of the shelf front.

Keep plastic food storage containers nested and handy. They'll help build the next day's lunches from the evening's leftovers. Keep lids separately in a plastic basket or drawer to prevent fallout — the descent of multiple containers onto your feet when the cupboard door is opened.

▼ **Keep children's bowls, mugs,** and other breakfast requirements together on a low shelf where they can be reached easily and quickly laid out in the morning.

Organizing the kitchen according to activity centres helps to speed cooking chores by storing tools in the area where they're most likely to be used. There's a natural logic to activity centres that makes it easy for others to find what they need – and to put them away. While some tools will span more than one centre, the categories below give a rough guide to who's who in the kitchen.

Sink/cutting centre

- Knives
- Cutting boards
- Grater
- Strainers
- Colander
- Juice squeezer
- Mixing spoons
- Rubber spatula
- Garlic press
- Vegetable peeler
- Vegetable brush
- Melon scoop/melon baller
- Kitchen paper
- Liquid handwashing soap

Cleaning-up centre

- Kitchen bin
- Binliners
- Washing-up liquid
- Dishwasher detergent
- Rubber gloves
- Washing-up bowl
- Dish drainer
- Cleaning cloths
- Cleaning supplies or cleaning holdall
- Cream cleaner (scouring powder)
- Sponge
- Silver polish
- Houseplant watering can
- Houseplant fertilizer

Cooking centre

- Pots, saucepans, and lids
- Baking trays
- Microwave cookware
- Loaf tins
- Flan tins
- Muffin tins
- Pie dishes
- Roasting racks
- Spice rack with spices
- Wooden spoons
- Spatulas and lifters
- Wire whisks
- Ladles
- Instant-read thermometer
- Meat thermometer
- Cooling racks
- Biscuit sheets
- Roasting tin
- Self-basting roaster

Mixing centre

- Electric stand mixer or hand mixer
- Food processor
- Automatic bread machine
- Mixing bowls
- Batter bowls
- Kitchen scales and measuring jugs
- Mixing spoons
- Rubber spatula
- Rolling pin

- Cookie cutters
- Biscuit cutters
- Canisters for bulk baking supplies (flour, sugar, brown sugar, yeast, cornflour)
- Baking staples: baking soda, baking powder, salt, vanilla, pan spray
- Herbs and spices
- Shortening
- Sweeteners (honey, molasses)
- Muffin papers
- Cake decorating tools

Dishwashing/tableware centre

- Plates
- Bowls
- Glasses
- Mugs and teacups
- Serving dishes
- Knives, forks, and spoons
- Serving utensils
- Plastic food storage containers
- Napkins (cloth or paper)
- Washing-up bowl/dish drainer
- Rubber gloves
- Washing-up liquid
- Automatic dishwasher detergent
- Hand towels
- Tea towels

Kitchen centres tools and equipment

Special kitchen
cleaning challenges

The kitchen. It's the heart of the home – and home to the household's toughest cleaning challenges. Preparing meals from day to day feeds the family – and the grime gremlins, too. Remove the dirt and bring a sparkle to the kitchen with these cleaning tips for ovens, hobs, and sink and worktop areas.

Oven

Heat plus grease plus food spills equal a tough cleaning job: the oven. Baked-on food and spattered grease require additional firepower in the form of special cleaners. Commercial oven cleaners do the job well – but are formulated with corrosive products such as sodium hydroxide (lye), and should be handled with extreme care.

■ **Safety first.** Whatever the cleaning method, protect eyes, skin, and clothing while cleaning the oven. Wear long sleeves and rubber gloves to protect arms and hands; safety goggles or glasses prevent injury to the eyes. A painter's mask guards against corrosive fumes, particularly when using spray oven cleaner products. Where possible, use a liquid formulation.

■ **Follow directions.** If using commercial oven cleaners, read the directions first, then follow them. Oven cleaners may be formulated to work on warm ovens or cold ones, so get the method straight before you begin. Newer versions offer fume-free cleaning for a healthier home.

■ **Rinse clean.** After cleaning, use a spray bottle filled with water to rinse the oven walls, then wipe them dry with a

> "Kitchen dirt heads straight for the sheltered hideouts offered by hobs, rings, and burner pans."

cleaning cloth. This process removes the last traces of oven cleaner, and prevents your next meal from tasting like cleaning chemicals! Similarly, be careful to remove all traces of oven cleaner from around the oven door gasket and seal.

■ **Try green alternatives.** If you don't like the idea of corrosive commercial oven cleaners, there is a greener option: baking soda. Sprinkle an even 5-mm (¼-in) layer of baking soda in the bottom of a cold oven, then lightly dampen the soda with water; it should be moist, but not wet. Spread the paste over the walls and ceiling.

Let the soda paste stand for 12–24 hours, re-wetting if it dries out. The paste dissolves grease and softens burned-on food, and makes it easier to remove the next day. You will need to apply some elbow grease to the job, but you'll avoid working with corrosive cleaners.

To clean oven racks and the drip tray the green way, soften them up with an ammonia bath. Place the racks and tray in a large, leak-proof black bin bag, and add 60ml (2fl oz) non-foaming ammonia. Seal the bin bag, and place it outdoors or in a garage overnight. The ammonia will soften baked-on food and make for easy cleaning the next morning. Rinse thoroughly and remove any remaining food, then dry the racks and drip tray before replacing them in the oven.

Cooker

The top of the cooker is a homing ground for kitchen dirt. Pans boil over and frying pans pop grease; stirring spoons deposit little lakes of dried sauce after the meal – and all of it

Cleaning the kitchen

Nothing says "good morning!" like a clean and sparkling kitchen. Achieving cleanliness in the face of an endless parade of hungry family members is another matter. Tackle kitchen grime and gunk quickly with this step-by-step guide to a clean kitchen.

  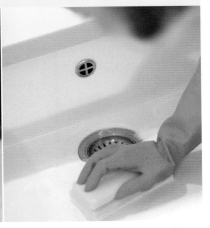

1 Empty the kitchen bin, and replace any binliners. Pre-spray all worktops and the hob before you begin to clean using a degreaser or multi-surface spray cleaner. Move around the room and spritz flat surfaces lightly.

2 Wipe down walls and splashbacks, cupboard faces, and the fronts of kitchen appliances with a cleaner-dampened cleaning cloth. Use an extra spritz of multi-surface cleaner to remove fingermarks, smears, and stains.

3 Scrub the interior of the sink with scouring powder or spray degreaser. Use a toothbrush to remove dirt from around sink rims and drains. Rinse, then use degreaser to clean fixtures and the sink edge. Wipe dry with a clean cloth.

4 Back to the worktops, this time to wipe them clean and dry. Use a scraper to remove dried-on foods, and a small stiff brush to loosen dirt where the splashback meets the worktops.

5 Return to the hob, and use the toothbrush to remove softened food from around burners, knobs, and dials. Tackle stubborn blobs with a scraper. Wipe dry with a fresh cleaning cloth.

6 Sweep or vacuum the floor, then damp-mop. Pay extra attention to the areas beneath the sink (water spots) and hob (grease). Shake and replace any mats or rugs. Put away tools, cleaners, and apron.

heads straight for the sheltered hideouts offered by the knobs, rings, and burner pans, where it dries and hardens.

- **Prevention, not cure.** As in the game of life, the best defence against hob dirt is offense. Wipe up food spills immediately, before heat has a chance to harden them. When not in use, place covers on the hob burners to protect them from kitchen-borne grease.
- **Take your time.** When you do have to clean, use tools and time to help the job along. Spritz cold hobs with a thick coat of degreaser spray, then give the product 10 minutes or so to soften the dirt. Use a toothbrush to get into nooks and crannies to remove the dirt.
- **Overnight treatment.** Spattered hob rings and drip trays may be cleaned in a similar way to oven racks. Remove them from the hob and place them in a large black plastic bin bag. Add 60ml (2fl oz) of non-foaming ammonia, seal the bag, and store it outside overnight. Next day, use a scrubbing sponge to remove the last traces of dirt.
- **Special needs.** Newer sealed hobs or ceramic hobs require special cleaning methods to preserve their beauty. Check with your cooker's manufacturer for the recommended cleaning products for these types of hobs.

Microwave oven

Because microwaves cook food from the inside out, there's less heat build-up to harden foods inside the oven. Take a gradual approach to microwave cleaning.

> "As in the game of life, the best defence against stove-top dirt is offense. Wipe up food spills immediately."

- **Steam-clean.** For light soiling, boil 236ml (8fl oz) water in a heatproof microwave container in the oven for 5 minutes. The steam will soften the dirt; wipe the oven dry with a cloth.
- **Degrease and deodorize.** For more cleaning power, use the steam-clean method above with a 50–50 solution of lemon

▲ **Shiny and safe.** A paste made up of a solution of 50–50 baking soda and water makes stainless steel fixtures sparkle and avoids the use of harsh abrasive cleaners.

juice and water, or vinegar and water. The acid will help cut stubborn grease, and the deodorizing properties of the lemon juice or the vinegar will help take away the lingering scent of last week's microwave popcorn.

- **Heavy-duty cleaning.** If there is dried-on food inside the oven which requires abrasive cleaning, use a baking soda paste (*see page 110*) to loosen and remove it. Take care to apply light pressure when wiping off the paste to avoid scratching the oven interior.

Sink and under-sink area

Sanitation is the name of the game when it comes to cleaning sinks and the areas beneath them. Moisture, food waste, and the hygiene challenges of meat and poultry preparation mean that the wet area of the kitchen can become a happy breeding ground for bacteria. Under the sink, drainpipes and waste

▲ **Cutting boards** require special care. To remove odours, rub with half a lemon; to clean and sanitize them, soak in a mild bleach solution (1 teaspoon chlorine bleach to 1 litre/1 quart of water).

▲ **Counter care.** Remove spilled food from kitchen worktops using disinfectant all-purpose spray cleaners. Allow the spray to sit for several minutes to loosen dried-on soil.

disposal units harbour germs and odours. The presence of moisture combined with holes necessary for plumbing fixtures creates an attractive home for insects, mould, and mildew.

■ **Spray and wipe.** Use a disinfecting all-purpose cleaner in a spray bottle to clean sink surfaces, fixtures, and rim. Remove dirt from the base of the tap, or around the rim, with a toothbrush, then wipe dry with a cleaning cloth.

■ **Get tough.** If stubborn deposits or stains require an abrasive cleaner, use a scouring powder on ceramic sinks — but only inside the sink. It's too hard to rinse scouring powder from sink rims or worktops!

■ **Keep the shine.** For stainless steel sinks, use a paste of baking soda and water applied with a cotton cleaning cloth, or use a commercial product specially formulated for cleaning these sinks. Avoid scouring powder — its abrasive qualities can scratch the surface of the steel.

■ **Out damned spot.** Use full-strength white vinegar to tackle water spots in the sink. Spray or pour it on generously, let it stand, then rub the spots with a scrubbing sponge.

■ **Clean and fresh.** Under the sink, clean the cupboard walls, doors, and the cupboard floor with a disinfecting all-purpose cleaner. Wipe them dry with cleaning cloths, then leave the cupboard doors open for at least two hours, to permit the area to dry completely.

Food preparation surfaces

Public health officials recommend sanitizing food preparation surfaces by washing with hot, soapy water. Rinse with clear water, then sanitize the cleaned surfaces with a solution of 1 tablespoon of chlorine bleach to 1 litre (1 quart) of water. Use this method on worktops, in sinks, and for cutting boards — wherever food may be placed during preparation.

Decluttering
the refrigerator

He's big, he's white, and he spouts water and icebergs: Moby Dick, the Great White Refrigerator. Staring into his chocked-up innards, you know what you must do. Plastic food storage containers pile in unsteady ziggurats in every corner. Leftovers huddle in back corners. Shrivelled fruit and wilted lettuce snuggle into the vegetable container. Time to declutter the refrigerator!

A refrigerator is not just an appliance: it's a central artifact of life. As you declutter it, you'll find evidence of your values (hospitality), aspirations (weight loss), resolutions (financial prudence), and self-indulgence (chocolate raspberry mousse cheesecake). A session of spearing the Great White does more than clear clutter: it can be a valuable peep into the state of the house in general – and of your mind.

To declutter the refrigerator, follow the STOP clutter in the fridge steps outlined on page 115. Before you begin, turn your refrigerator off – and unplug it, too, for good measure. The only shocks you want to receive are those from the expired use-by dates of some of the discarded food.

The moment of truth

You are standing in your kitchen, face-to-face with a clean and empty refrigerator, a rubbish bin brimming with discarded food, a dishwasher full of plastic food containers, and the few hardy survivors of your harpooning session. What can we learn from all this?

Lean back against the kitchen worktop and take a hard look at what the Whale has been hiding in its dark little innards. The implications will hit you in the face. Has your family changed – but your shopping habits haven't? The day I tossed out four jars of dried-out jam and a jar of peanut

butter manufactured in the last decade, it was clear that my children had turned a culinary corner, and the days of peanut butter and jam sandwiches were no more.

You'll wring a few unpleasant admissions from yourself, too. Look carefully at what foods have been wasted, especially from the fruit and vegetable container. Are you doing what I've been doing? I'm Miss Nutritional Virtue herself at the supermarket, but the baby carrots and low-fat margarine languish uneaten in Moby's dark corners.

▶ **Chill out** with a well-organized refrigerator. Spare and spacious, a clutter-free refrigerator helps speed food preparation, while free air circulation helps save on energy costs.

Use pen and paper to jot down your discoveries and track your new resolves. Is eating low-fat foods on your wish list? Then you'll want to toss the remnants of the butter and margarine and replace them with low-fat spreads and all-fruit jams.

Do you want to tighten the budget? Focus on the waste you've discovered. Do you buy grapefruit only to toss the shrivelled husks, months later? Are you overbuying milk, or

> "A session of spearing the Great White does more than clear clutter: it can be a peep into the state of your mind."

cheese, or meat? If you've tossed it out today, make a note to yourself to buy less – if any – on your next shopping trip. Have family members come to expect weekly cases of cola as a staple, not a treat? Cut back, and substitute fruit juices and cordials for those high-priced soft drinks. (I will maintain a respectful silence on the subject of chocolate raspberry mousse cheesecake. A rich life must have some indulgences.)

Staying organized

Now that you've sorted, tossed, cleaned, and replaced, you'll want your fridge to stay organized. These tips will help:

- **Create meal centres.** Make it easy to build a sandwich by tucking mayonnaise, mustard, cheese slices, and cooked sliced meat into a flat-bottomed plastic basket and storing them together. Ditto a "morning toast" grouping of butter, jam, honey, and Marmite; pull it out to top your toast.
- **Keep leftovers in the clear.** Don't bury leftovers in sealed containers; place them in clear food storage bags. If you can see them, they'll remind you of their existence and be more likely to be eaten.
- **Stay on top of the Whale.** A weekly refrigerator clean-out, done just before making menu plans, will keep Moby under control for good. Toss expired foods, wipe up smears and spills, and rearrange fridge contents before you shop.

STOP clutter in the fridge

Gather your tools: a lined rubbish bin, a sink-full of hot, soapy water, degreaser and window sprays, and cleaning cloths. Clear the kitchen worktops so you can spread out, and empty the dishwasher.

1 **Sort and toss**
Start at the top. Remove everything from the top shelf. Set aside what still has some life in it, but send all leftovers to the bin. Working your way to the bottom, you'll build up enough steam to tackle the vegetable crisper. Amazing, isn't it, how innocent little tomatoes and shy stalks of celery undergo such a malign transformation in that place? Unless you bought the vegetable desperado in question within the last week, throw it out. Then turn to the door shelves.

2 **Clean**
Rinse emptied plastic food containers and put them in the dishwasher. Shelves go directly to the sink's soapy water. While it soaks off the grime, use degreaser spray to clean the refrigerator's ceiling, walls, and door. Rinse, dry, and replace the shelves. Use spray window cleaner to remove greasy fingerprints from chrome and see-through plastic. Wipe down the door gasket and front, then clean the top of the Whale.

3 **Put away**
Time to replace the few food items that survived your scrutiny at the Sort and Toss stage. Done correctly, the Spearing of the Great White should all but empty the refrigerator. Don't be afraid of that stark look! A fridge is most energy-efficient when it has adequate airflow.

Declutter
the freezer

The freezer is a cold and lonely place, a natural refuge for forgotten food. Bulging containers with gaping lids join icy, unlabelled parcels in the Arctic wastes of this House of Mystery Food. The goal of a freezer declutter: to cull the contents to remove unusable food, and return the survivors to an organized space that makes the most of your household's frozen assets.

Freezer: to defrost or not to defrost?

Many modern freezers don't require defrosting, but you'll pay for the convenience of never having to haul out the pans of hot water. Automatic defrost freezers use up to 35 per cent more energy than comparable manual defrost models; the auto defrost cycle sucks moisture from frozen food and can adversely affect food quality. Defrost manual defrost freezers when ice build-up reaches 5mm–1cm (¼–½in), or when ice builds up on compressor coils.

Defrosting do's:

- **Cut the power.** Before defrosting, turn off the power to the freezer unit, and unplug the freezer from the wall.
- **Empty the contents.** Remove all the food from the freezer. Store it in ice chests while defrosting and cleaning the freezer.
- **Melt the ice.** Either leave the freezer door open until the ice melts naturally (be sure to cover the floor with newspaper to guard against melt water and falling ice) or add heat to speed the process. Use pans of warm water from the sink to melt ice, or wield a hair dryer to force warm air onto the ice (*see also Safety first on page 117*). As the ice melts, soak up drips with a sponge, tea towels, or cleaning cloths.
- **Clean up.** When the freezer is ice-free, scrub out the entire interior with a light paste of baking soda and water. Wipe clean and dry with a fresh cleaning cloth. The soda will absorb any lingering food odours and remove any food spills. If necessary, wash the shelves or the freezer baskets in warm, soapy water. Dry them thoroughly before returning them to the freezer.
- **Return to power.** Close the freezer door, plug it in, and turn the power back on. Let the freezer run for at least 15 minutes to allow it to cool before returning the frozen food stored in the ice chests.

◀ **Captive in ice.** Home freezers safeguard frozen foods, but there's such a thing as too safe. Defrost the freezer regularly when ice build-up interferes with organized access to frozen foods.

Defrosting don'ts:

- **Gently does it.** Don't use an icepick, knives, or sharp instruments to remove ice from the walls of the freezer. A slip can cause injuries, to you and to delicate freezer coils.
- **Safety first.** If using a hair dryer to melt ice, be cautious about electric shock. Do not stand in puddled water or allow watery drips to touch the hair dryer.
- **Skip the suds.** Don't wash freezer walls with soapy water. Soap is difficult to rinse clean; a soapy residue can affect the taste of stored food.

Organizing the freezer

Unlike refrigerators, which need a free flow of air to stay cool, freezers operate most efficiently when they are full. However, a full freezer is a dangerous landscape that allows food to go hidden until it is no longer edible. Keep an organized freezer with these tips:

- **Label, label, label!** Labelling frozen foods is key to keeping an organized freezer. Label each package – homemade or commercial – with the name of the dish or food, the number of servings, and the date it was added to the freezer. Use a permanent marker pen to write directly on zipper seal freezer bags; stick a computer address label on freezer containers. Hint for computer users: print label sheets of commonly frozen foods ("hamburgers", "spaghetti sauce", "chicken pieces", "beef stew") to make quick work of feeding the freezer.
- **Date everything.** To manage frozen foods efficiently, you need to know whether they are fresh. Remember to always write a date on every package added to the freezer. Make sure that you rotate foods so that new foods always go behind older packages.
- **Organize a large freezer by category.** Keep all casseroles in one area; frozen joints of beef and steaks in another part of the freezer. Frozen chicken and turkey should live in the bottom basket of the freezer where they are easy to grab.
- **Use freezer baskets.** Flat-bottomed baskets support floppy freezer bags and organize freezer contents. Place all frozen vegetables in one basket, upended loaves of sliced

STOP clutter in the freezer

Gather your tools: a double-lined bin for rejected foods, ice chests to hold declutter survivors, a sink of hot soapy water, baking soda, and cleaning cloths.

1 Sort
Turn off the freezer, and unplug it from the wall. Start at the top, and remove each parcel of food. One by one, decide if the container stays or goes. The freezer declutter rule is simple: if it's sealed, labelled, and fresh, it stays. If it's Mystery Meat of unknown age, freezer-burned, or an open container, out it goes.

2 Throw out
Declutter all foods with torn or open packaging, freezer-burned meat, or any item of food you can't identify and date. Run reusable containers holding the rejects under a hot stream of water to loosen the food-icicle from the carton. Pop the food into the double-lined bin, and soak the container in the sink's sudsy water. Tuck any keepers into the holding area of ice chests.

3 Clean and put away
When the freezer's empty, wipe it out with a paste of baking soda and water. Wipe dry with fresh cleaning cloths. If necessary, remove and wash shelves or organizer baskets in hot soapy water. Rinse thoroughly and dry before returning them to the freezer. Clean door storage units. Soak and rinse door racks, then dry before returning; wipe door compartments with baking soda paste, then dry. When the freezer is clean and dry, plug it in and turn it on for 15 minutes before replacing food.

bread in another. Special freezer organizers are designed to fit together, and won't crack in cold temperatures; they're a good option for chest freezers.

■ **Think square.** When freezing homemade soups or stews, use square or rectangular plastic freezer containers to store them in rather than round ones. Squared-off containers fit together neatly and take up considerably less space than cylindrical shapes.

■ **Rotate for freshness.** When adding new foods to the freezer, store them behind existing products, and use the oldest foods first.

freezer inventory

Item

Bread dough			✓	✗	✗
Bread rolls		✓	✓	✓	✗
Chicken casserole	✓	✓	✓	✗	✗
Beef, raw mince				✓	✗
Beef, sausage			✓	✗	✗
Ice cream, (chocolate)	✓	✓	✗	✗	✗
Soup, chicken			✓	✓	✗
Soup, lentil			✓	✓	✗

Use a slash mark to record each freezer meal or frozen item stored in the freezer. Cross out each item as used.

✓ **Item in**   ✗ **Item out**

▲ **Keep track** of freezer contents with a simple write-on, wipe-off whiteboard or with a freezer inventory form (see page 245). A free printable form is also available from OrganizedHome.Com.

Freezer inventory

When it comes to the freezer, out of sight is too frequently out of mind. Expensive frozen food goes to waste because no one remembers it's there to be eaten.

The solution: a freezer inventory (*see form below and on page 245*). Post the inventory on the outside of the freezer door or lid, and check it regularly when you make menu plans. Remember: the best bargain at the supermarket is the food you've already bought and paid for.

Selecting and buying a refrigerator/freezer

A refrigerator/freezer is more than a place to store food; it's a major financial investment and a big consumer of energy in any household. If you're in the market for a new refrigerator, keep these pointers in mind while shopping.

Capacity For the best value, match the refrigerator's capacity to your family size. Buying too large or too small costs money, both up front and in additional energy costs. A too-large refrigerator wastes energy cooling empty space; an over-filled, too-small refrigerator has to work too hard to keep food cool without proper air circulation.

Appliance manufacturers measure refrigerator capacity in litres (cubic feet). To gauge the correct capacity for your household, follow this rule of thumb: a household of two people requires 250–300 litres (8–10 cubic feet) of refrigerator space. For each extra person, add an additional 30–60 litres (1–2 cubic feet).

Size Your kitchen's built-in cabinetry and floor plan will determine the maximum size of a new refrigerator. Measure the space available, and shop with a tape measure. You'll avoid falling in love with a gleaming behemoth that's just a fraction too tall for the space available!

A refrigerator's depth is important, too; you'll need to make sure that there's enough room to open doors fully in your kitchen space. Note whether doors open to the right or left; some refrigerator models feature adjustable doors. When judging depth, be sure to allow for an adequate clearance from the kitchen wall. A refrigerator needs 10–15cm (4–6in) of air space for air circulation over the compressor coils.

FREEZER FOOD STORAGE GUIDELINES

Food item	Time at −18°C (0°F)	Packaging tips
BAKED GOODS		
Bread, baked	12 months	
Bread dough, (yeast, unbaked)	2 weeks	
Quick breads (nut bread, banana bread)	3 months	Wrap loaves tightly in plastic wrap, then insert in zipper freezer storage bags to avoid moisture loss.
Rolls, unbaked	2 weeks	
Rolls, baked	12–15 months	
Muffins	3 months	
Pancakes or waffles	6 months	
DAIRY PRODUCTS		
Butter, salted	3 months	The "salty" taste of salted butter may intensify with freezing; store unopened butter packages in moisture-proof freezer wrap or freezer storage bags.
Butter, unsalted	6–9 months	
Margarine	12 months	
Cheese (Cheddar, Swiss, Jack)	4 months	Thaw in refrigerator.
Cheese, cottage	3 months	Thaw in refrigerator.
Cheese (Roquefort, blue)	3 months	Freezing will affect texture, crumbling.
Cream (heavy, half-and-half, light)	2 months	Cream will not whip after freezing.
Eggs (raw and out of shell)	6–12 months	Do not freeze eggs in shell; freezing will affect texture. Freeze in covered container.
Ice cream, ice milk	2 months	
Milk	1 month	Allow room for expansion in freezer container; freezing will affect flavour and texture of milk.

Food item	Time at −18°C (0°F)	Packaging tips
MEAT, POULTRY, AND FISH		
Beef, raw mince	3–4 months	
Beef, roast	6–12 months	
Beef, steak	6–12 months	
Beef, sausage	1–2 months	
Beef, cooked dishes	2–3 months	
Pork, raw mince	3–4 months	
Pork, chops	4–6 months	
Pork, roast	4–6 months	
Pork, sausage (fresh)	1–2 months	
Pork, sausage (smoked)	1–2 months	
Ham, fully cooked (whole or half)	1–2 months	Do not freeze ham slices or canned ham; freezing will affect texture and flavour.
Casseroles with ham	1 month	
Bacon	1 month	
Chicken, whole	12 months	If freezing for more than 2 months, over-wrap original packaging with freezer wrap or freezer food storage bags.
Chicken, pieces (raw)	9 months	
Chicken, pieces (cooked)	4 months	
Turkey, whole	12 months	
Casseroles, poultry	2–3 months	
Fish, fresh (whole, fillets, or steaks)	6 months	Freeze fresh fish in sealed containers or wrap to prevent moisture loss.
Fish, cooked	3 months	
MISCELLANEOUS		
Pasta, cooked	3–4 months	
Rice, cooked	3–4 months	
Soups and stews (vegetable and/or meat)	2–3 months	

Setting up
a store cupboard

It's the secret weapon of the well-organized kitchen. A working store cupboard is a planned reserve of foods and household supplies that saves time, money, and stress in the kitchen. A reservoir of consumable goods, it can be set up anywhere – if there's so much as a spare roll of toilet paper tucked beneath a sink, your home boasts a store cupboard. Remember: a store cupboard is not a place, it's an attitude!

What's the goal of establishing and maintaining a store cupboard? It's two-fold: household convenience and protection against unexpected events. A well-planned store cupboard means that the household will never run out of commonly used products such as toilet paper. More important, a store cupboard is a reserve against hard times. Whether it's job loss, illness, or natural disaster, a store cupboard ensures that the family will continue to be fed, clean, and comfortable in the face of adversity.

Beginner, intermediate, or advanced?

A beginner's store cupboard focuses on convenience and contains back-up products for each storable item used in the home. The standard is simple: for each open bag, box, or carton, the store cupboard contains a second, back-up product. A good first goal: a three-day supply of food and hygiene supplies adequate to support your family plus one additional person.

More robust store cupboards serve additional aims. In the case of an emergency, a mid-range store cupboard can feed a family for a period of two weeks to a month. This store cupboard includes substitutes for fresh foods, such as powdered milk, dried fruits and vegetables, and protein products.

The most comprehensive store cupboards are designed to meet long-term food storage needs. This can be anything from six months to a year. This requires stocking versatile foods with a long shelf life, such as whole wheat berries, preserves, and dried foods.

Stocking the store cupboard

Whether it's bargain brand ravioli or expensive gourmet soups, build your store cupboard to suit your family, your finances, and the storage space you have available.

Single-income households with young children will build store cupboards replete with cold cereal, formula, disposable nappies, and child-friendly snack foods. Empty nesters with an active social life and his-and-hers diets will lean towards jars of artichoke hearts, low-sodium veggies, and tiny jars of cocktail nibbles for drinks snacks and hostess gifts. Non-cooks will rely heavily on microwave meals and freezer pizza. And just about every family can stockpile basics for kitchen and bath, such as toilet paper, toothpaste, detergent, and paper napkins.

Check the shopping list

Where's the best place to discover your family's store cupboard preferences? Your shopping list. If you buy it, use it, and it can be stored, it's a store cupboard candidate. Building a store cupboard from the shopping list is also a powerful antidote to Store Cupboard Mania: the indiscriminate purchase of case lots of tinned chicken curry or own brand soups that no one in the household will eat.

An expansive view of the store cupboard principle also allows for freezer storage and a limited amount of refrigerator space. Carrots, potatoes, oranges, and apples enter the store-cupboard zone when bought on sale and tucked into corners of the fruit and vegetable container, while freezer convenience meals qualify, too.

To work the store cupboard principle, you've got to get organized! Maximum store cupboard power requires that you know what you have, how long it will keep, and how to store it safely.

■ **Starting a store cupboard** does not require complex organization. Create it by buying twice as many of each item as needed for weekly use, then store the extras. When you've used up the mayo in today's tuna salad, retrieve the back-up jar from the cupboard, and add "mayo" to the shopping list.

■ **The beginner's store cupboard** can often be stored side-by-side with opened or in-use items. For example, stack the open box of detergent on top of a box of foods or line up tins of chicken noodle soup front to back on the tinned goods shelf.

■ **Rotate the contents** of the store cupboard by placing just-purchased items at the back of the stack or row; use the front items first.

■ **A dedicated store cupboard area** can be a big help. Set aside a cupboard or shelf to hold stored items. Organize them by category, stacking tins and boxes. Plastic bins support and contain bags of dried beans, rice, or pasta.

■ **Complete store cupboard meals** are one exception to the "store by category" rule. On a section of shelf, assemble all the makings for three to five store cupboard meals: pasta, a large jar of spaghetti sauce or pesto sauce, and ready-grated dried parmesan shelved together make it easy to spot the empty spaces after use, and restock.

■ **Larger store cupboards** require more storage space and may be sited in multiple locations around the house, depending on the storage needs of different foods. Root vegetables and apples need to be cool and dry; tinned foods can tolerate greater temperature fluctuations. A written inventory can remind forgetful cooks of the location of items.

larger storage guidelines ▲ see pages 122–3.

LARDER STORAGE GUIDELINES

Food item	Storage time	Packaging tips
Baking powder	18 months	Unopened
	6 months	Opened
Baking soda	2 years	Unopened
	6 months	Opened
Biscuit mix	12–18 months	
Breakfast cereals, ready-to-eat (corn flakes)	6–12 months	Unopened
	2–3 months	Opened
Breakfast cereals, hot (oatmeal, farina)	1 year	
Cake mix	1 year	
Chocolate chips, semi-sweet	12 months	
Chocolate, unsweetened	18 months	
Cocoa	Indefinitely	
Coconut, grated	1 year	Unopened in original packaging
Coffee, ground	2 years	
Coffee, instant	1 year	Unopened in original packaging
Cornflour	18 months	
Crackers	6 months	
Flour, cake	6 months	
Flour, white	10–15 months	Opened in airtight container
Flour, whole wheat	6–8 months	Opened in refrigerator
Fruit, tinned	1 year	
Gelatine	12–18 months	
Herbs and spices, dried	6 months–1 year	Discard spices when their scent fades; store in airtight containers
Honey	1 year	
Infant formula	12–18 months	
Jam and preserves	1 year	Unopened in original packaging
Juice, tinned citrus	6 months	

Food item	Storage time	Packaging tips
Juice, tinned non-citrus	1 year	
Marshmallows	3 months	
Mayonnaise	4 months	Unopened in original packaging
Meat and poultry, tinned	12–18 months	
Milk, condensed	1 year	
Milk, non-fat dry	6 months	
Milk, sweetened condensed	1 year	
Molasses, unopened	1 year	Unopened
	6 months	Opened
Nuts, unshelled	8 months	
Oils (corn oil, vegetable oil)	18 months, 6–8 months	Unopened Opened Store in cool place
Oil, olive	9 months	
Olives	1 year	
Pancake mix	6 months	
Pasta, dried	2 years	Store opened pasta in sealed containers or airtight jars
Peanut butter	6–9 months	
Pickles	1 year	Commercially prepared, unopened in original packaging
Popcorn, unpopped kernels	1–2 years	
Potatoes, instant	18 months	
Pulses and peas, dried	18 months	
Pudding mixes	12–18 months	
Rice, brown	1 year	
Rice, mixes	6 months	
Rice, white	2 years	
Salad dressing	10 months	Unopened in original packaging

Food item	Storage time	Packaging tips
Salt	Indefinitely	
Sauces, condiments, and relishes	1 year	Unopened
Shortening	8 months 6 months	Unopened Opened
Soft drinks	3 months	Unopened in original packaging
Stuffing mix or croutons	6 months	
Sugar, brown	4 months	
Sugar, granulated	2 years	
Icing sugar	18 months	
Syrup	1 year	

Food item	Storage time	Packaging tips
Tea, bags	18 months	
Tea, instant	3 years	
Tea, loose	2 years	
Tomato ketchup, chilli sauce, barbeque sauce	1 year	
Tomato sauce or paste	12–18 months	
Vegetables, tinned	1 year	
Vinegar (balsamic, cider, rice, red wine, white, white wine)	Indefinitely	Store vinegar in original packaging or in glass containers; do not store in metal

How to store larder items

Select larder storage areas in cool locations; tinned food and larder items should be kept at 21°C (70°F) or below; don't store them in direct light. Newer packaged foods now include a use-by date as a guideline for product freshness. Where dates are unavailable, observe the food storage guidelines given here for best quality.

Product code dates: what do they mean?

■ **Sell-by date.** A sell-by date sets the last date of sale for perishable products, such as milk. A period for safe home use follows. Newer products often list both the sell-by date, after which the food should not be sold, and an expiry date, after which the food should not be eaten.

■ **Use-by date.** A use-by date is a guideline for best quality for foods with a longer shelf life. The use-by date is not a safety date. The food remains edible for some time after that date, but food quality will begin to decline.

■ **Expiry date.** Commonly used for highly perishable foods such as meats and dairy goods, the expiry date is the last date on which the product should be consumed. Discard foods that are past their expiry date.

■ **Pack date.** Pack dates for tinned goods and processed products indicate when they were packed. Use specific food storage recommendations to determine how long the food remains edible after packing.

Building a store cupboard on a budget

Investing in the store cupboard principle pays off in savings of time and money, but it does involve an up-front cost. Try these tips to spread the load:

■ **"Tithe" for the pantry.** Set aside a regular percentage of each week's food budget for store cupboard building.

■ **Buy on sale.** Take advantage of supermarket loss leaders – tuna, tomato sauce, tins of soup, and tinned beans – to stock up.

■ **Buy in bulk.** Bulk-buying for the larder really pays off. A 11-kg (25-lb) sack of bread flour at the warehouse store will be better value than the supermarket's pricier 2-kg (5-lb) bag. You'll save and stock up at the same time.

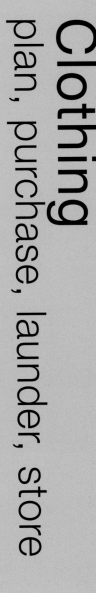
Clothing! For most of us, clothes are much more than something to cover our nakedness. Shopping for clothes, wearing clothes, and caring for clothes trawls through deep emotional shoals. Our wardrobes bulge with sartorial remnants of earlier selves – thinner, younger, with different interests and vocations.

In many homes, the cycle of clothing becomes bogged down. Mt. Washmore – a teetering tower of dirty garments – erupts in the laundry area with volcanic speed. Bulging drawers and overstuffed cupboards betray the presence of clothing clutter – and in the midst of it all, we stand and wail, "But I haven't a thing to wear!"

By observing the cycle of clothing – plan, purchase, launder, and store – we'll plan and shop carefully to maximize the family's clothing pounds. We'll free cupboards and drawers from the clutter of clothing that is out of style, out of season, or simply out of place. New laundry systems will keep clothing fresh, mended, and ready to wear, while well-planned storage will keep out-of-season clothing ready for use.

Planning
family wardrobes

What's the difference between clothing chaos and a working wardrobe? A wardrobe plan. A family wardrobe plan assesses clothing requirements for each family member, tracks existing garments, and identifies your new clothing needs – before you go shopping. Better still, a wardrobe plan encompasses style principles that help guide your clothing choices: colour, flexibility, and classics.

Children's clothing needs

Grandmother Betty had a very simple rule of thumb when it came to clothing her three children in the 1930s: "One to wear, one to wash, and one to have clean!"

Times, if not toddlers, have changed. Busy lives and lower clothing costs mean many families buy – and buy and buy and buy. Clothing stacks up and backs up and is often outgrown before it's outworn – or worn at all. Too much clothing clogs cupboards and drawers, and makes it harder for a child to keep his possessions tidy.

How many clothes do your children really need?

Let the laundry schedule be your guide. If you wash children's clothing once a week, seven to ten T-shirts and trousers will see them through with accidents to spare. If you wash more often, you can reduce that number to five to six outfits.

Double up on socks and underwear, especially for toddlers and preschool children. Accidents happen, and usually on the way to Grandmother's house.

Wardrobe plan basics

To create a simple family wardrobe plan, start with a piece of lined paper (or a free printable wardrobe planning form from OrganizedHome.Com) for each family member.

Focus on activities School and work, sports and play, worship and committee; the heart of any wardrobe plan is the activities the clothing must cover. For each family member, list the activities that require clothing: school, work, worship, sports, dance, or voluntary. Add an additional topic for basics: socks, underwear, nightclothes, coats, and rainwear.

Inventory clothes Next step: inventory the clothing you have, listing each item under the appropriate category. For growing children, check sizes; a growth spurt can see a child outgrow most of their wardrobe in just a few weeks.

As you build your list, you'll see who needs what quite quickly. In your wardrobe, jeans abound, but you've had trouble getting dressed for formal meetings. A young son has a plethora of T-shirts, but can't manage to button his smart trousers for going to formal parties or eating in a restaurant. A daughter has lots of pretty dresses, but needs tights, tops, and trousers for school outings.

Make a shopping list From the inventory sheets, make a running shopping list of family clothing needs. Your list will alert you to current clothing needs, and help control spending. Don't leave for the department store without it.

Wardrobe planning pointers

A good wardrobe plan requires every new item to pull its own weight in the clothes cupboard. No more unworn garments!

Consider colour Following a colour scheme can make the difference between a working wardrobe and nothing to wear (with a cupboard full of clothes). Yes, that pink blouse looks marvellous in the shop with its companion grey skirt, but it'll turn wallflower when paired with the beige-brown colours predominant in your wardrobe. Avoid colour mistakes and wardrobe orphans by developing a colour scheme as part of your wardrobe plan. For each family member, select a basic neutral colour and coordinate shoes, coats, belts, and handbags with it. Accent colours harmonize with the basic neutral: rely on them when selecting tops.

Reach for flexibility Look for flexible clothing that will do double-duty in the wardrobe: a summer T-shirt can take a turn in winter under a suit jacket, a child's simple shift dress doubles up in cooler weather with the addition of tights and a poloneck. The more uses the garment has, the better value it will give you for your money.

Rely on classic designs Sure, it's fun to splurge on the latest thing, but no one can build an efficient wardrobe by relying on hot trends. For big-ticket items, choose classic. The timeless look of a well-cut woman's suit will see you through meeting after meeting in style.

▼ **The right accent.** When it comes to choosing shirts, T-shirts, scarves, and sweaters, go for lighter, brighter accent colours.

Top tips buying guide:
how to spot quality clothing

Today, it's not possible to determine quality clothing from the price tag alone. Pricey designer garments can be shoddily made; modestly priced clothing can be of top quality. Quality clothing offers good fabric, appropriate styling, and proper construction and finishing – and can be found at every price point. Develop an eye for a buy. Try these tricks to tell the quality stuff from the tat.

1 Examine fibre content and care labels
Quality fabric has more natural fibre, and can endure normal laundering or cleaning processes.

2 Assess the overall appearance
Gathers or puckers at collar, cuffs, or waistband signal a poorly made item. Topstitching should be flat and even, zips should be hidden and smooth.

3 Check buttons, buttonholes, and fasteners
Bulging buttonholes are a bad sign; closures should be neat, tight, and adequately attached to the clothing. Check that buttons are firmly sewn.

4 Check hems
Unless a visible hem is part of the garment's design, hems should be invisible. A hem that rolls or twists is a warning that the fabric was cut off-grain – and the garment will follow.

5 Eyeball the seams
Look for straight, smooth seam lines and even stitching. Seams that are stretched, skipped, scanty, or bubbled will look even worse when worn.

◀ **Dress smart!** Buying quality clothing is a good investment, in financial terms and when it comes to your self-confidence. You're right ... if your clothes are right.

6 Finger the finishes

Flip up the hem and check seam and hem finishes. A well-finished seam won't unravel; a generous hem will allow alterations and will help a garment hang properly.

Save money on clothing

Clothing, like food, is an "elastic" expense in the family budget: it can be stretched or squandered. Save money and keep the family well-clothed with these tips:

1 Shop seasonally

Best buys on clothing occur at the end of each season, when clearance sales move out winter clothing to usher in spring styles. Retailing seasons are falling further and further out of sync with the real world, so pay attention! Shop for clothing bargains when retailers move from one season to the next.

2 Don't buy just to buy

Shopping for clothing can be part outing, part therapy, and part social event. Stick to your list, and if you don't find what you're looking for, don't buy something else just to buy something. That's a prescription for "14 white twinsets in the cupboard", all bought in desperation "because I can always use another twinset".

3 Know when to mend

Clothing in need of a stitch or two can be found at great prices, but be careful about taking on garments that need repairs. Know your sewing skill level and let it guide you. There is no point in buying trousers that need a new zip if you've never touched the zipper foot ... let alone the sewing machine!

4 Shop at charity or nearly-new shops

Quality "pre-owned" clothing may be purchased inexpensively at charity or nearly-new shops. A bonus is that the staff will check incoming clothing, and will reject stained or very worn garments.

Buying second-hand clothing

Garage sales, nearly-new shops, car-boot sales, and charity shops can all be good sources of inexpensive quality clothing. Try the following tips to help you shop smart for secondhand clothing:

- **Stick with reputable sellers.** When it comes to car-boot sales, do judge a book by the cover. A seller offering carefully hung clothing is probably offering higher-quality garments than one sitting next to a dusty jumble of rumpled garments.
- **Dress the part.** Car-boot sales do not offer fitting rooms, so slip into leggings and a slim-fit T-shirt before you leave. You'll be able to check the fit on the scene.
- **Follow your nose.** Give secondhand items a good sniff. If you can smell the previous owner's perfume (or worse), give it a miss.
- **Look for quality labels.** Brand-name labels can shortcut the search for good quality in pre-owned clothing.
- **Check all zips, buttons, and fastenings carefully.** Even if a garment passes muster, a broken zip or a missing button can move it from "deal" to "dud". Inspect all closures and zips for any signs of wear before buying.
- **Measure, measure, measure.** Take a tape measure with you, and use it to check garment dimensions. Size labels can be deceptive — or missing altogether. A quick check with the tape measure will give the true picture.
- **Don't get carried away.** In the heat of the chase, it's easy to fall for fashion mistakes when they offer a great label at a low price. Let your wardrobe plan be your guide to avoid clothing mistakes.

Declutter the **wardrobe**

Stacked, packed, and bulging, the clothes cupboard looms. When it takes too long to dress for a special occasion – or to find jeans and a T-shirt on Saturday morning – it's time to STOP clutter in the wardrobe.

The STOP clutter rules

In wardrobes, as in life, less is more. Specifically, the venerable 80–20 rule applies: we wear 20 per cent of our clothing 80 per cent of the time, while the remaining 80 per cent – impulse purchases, orphaned blouses, and the one-size-too-small brigade – represent the freeloaders of the wardrobe clan. Guiding principle: pare it down! Does each garment in your wardrobe pull its own weight? Apply these STOP clutter rules to determine whether to keep, throw out, sell, donate, or repair clothing.

Keep an item of clothing if:
■ It fits ... today. Not "4.5 kilos (10 pounds) from now" and not "last year after I had flu and lost all that weight". Today!
■ It's clean, unstained, and in good repair.
■ You've worn it within the last year.
■ You love it unconditionally.

Throw out any garment that is:
■ Worn, stained, or in need of major repairs such as broken zips, fabric tears, or shredded seams. Items eligible for the repair basket include those with falling hems, torn pockets, and opened seams.

Identify a candidate for the nearly-new shop if:
■ You haven't worn it in the last year.
■ It's out of fashion.
■ It's not your colour.
■ It doesn't fit, it's uncomfortable, or just unflattering.

before decluttering ▲

STOP clutter in the wardrobe

Gather your tools: timer, STOP declutter boxes (marked Put Away, Sell/Donate, and Storage), a rubbish bag for castoffs, and an extra box for Repair items. Set the timer for 20 minutes. Yes, I know that clothing consultants recommend trying on every single item with every other single item, culling the unacceptable, mending the ragged and tattered, and hanging the survivors in descending order according to colour. Yeah, right. Twenty-minute nibbles get the job done in controllable bites.

1 Sort
One garment at a time, make a decision using the STOP clutter rules. Start small: one shelf, 30cm (1ft) of hanging rail. Examine each garment and decide whether to keep, throw out, sell, repair, or store. If necessary, try on the garment to make the decision.

2 Throw out
If it's a keeper, hang it back on the rail or return it to the shelf. If not, put it in the appropriate box or throw it in the rubbish bag.

3 Organize
Misplaced items – sports equipment, fishing rods, hairbrushes, safety pins, the stapler you used for an emergency hem repair – go to the Put Away box. Arrange the remaining garments according to colour on the newly spacious hanging rail or cleared shelf.

4 Put away
When the timer rings, stop. The timer's bell is your friend, seeing to it that you don't bite off more clutter energy than you can chew. Empty the rubbish, take the Repair items to the sewing area, and go round the house with the Put Away box.

after decluttering ▲

Organizing
the clothes cupboard

You've weeded your wardrobe of the freeloaders, the ill-fitting, and the ugly. Time to think about the remaining clothing, and the word is cluster. Organizing your clothing into compatible groups that work together maximizes wardrobe options and versatility, and helps you get the most mileage from each garment.

Clothes declutter tips for **clutter personalities**

Check out the clothes cupboard to discover the owner's fashion personality – and their clutter personality, too:

■ **Hoarder.** In the hoarder's wardrobe, she'll stockpile new, unworn clothing anywhere and everywhere, while wearing only the old stuff. Foil hoarding instincts by recycling tattered T-shirts and nighties to make good cleaning rags, and open the door to new items.

Travel tip for hoarders (or anyone!): when underwear loses its bounce, collect it inside an empty suitcase. Next trip, pack it instead of new undies. You'll wear the stuff one last time, then discard it to make room for souvenirs on the trip home.

■ **Sentimentalist.** In the sentimentalist's wardrobe, clothes from other lives are alive and well – to the detriment of today's. To part with them feels as if you're tearing out your memories. To reclaim space, save a symbol of the treasured times represented by outgrown clothing. Snip a rose trim from the sixth-form ball dress, and add it to a scrapbook. Choose one cherished baby outfit and mount it in a box frame – then release the mass of clothing to a new life.

Guiding principle: store by cluster

A clothing "cluster" is a core group of five to eight clothing pieces that work together. A typical cluster might contain a woven wool jacket in tones of camel, red, and navy, a coordinating navy skirt, smart navy trousers, dark blue jeans, a red T-shirt, and an ivory blouse. Dress it up and you have a suit look with jacket, skirt, and blouse. Dress it down with the T-shirt and jeans, and throw the jacket over your shoulders for a casual outfit. Layer the blouse over the T-shirt and add the trousers for a committee meeting – you've mastered the art of the cluster!

Look at your culled wardrobe with an eye to forming several clusters from your existing clothes. The main organizing principle is colour, not season or style. Group similar-coloured garments together, and think, "What could I add to this group to form a cluster?" A stay-at-home mum might cluster her pale denim jeans and white T-shirts with a jeans jacket, a coordinating gilet, and a long red tunic dress/sweater.

Thinking "cluster" simplifies the process of buying clothes. No longer will you buy in terms of "outfit" – that's how you get in the position of having a wardrobe stuffed with clothes and nothing to wear. Adding another piece to a cluster means you can wear the garment several different ways, using the clothing already in the wardrobe.

Guiding principle: simplify storage

Let's face it. Many traditional methods of clothing storage just don't work. Drawers stick and squeak and are usually overloaded. Long hanging garments brush against shoes and wrinkle on the floor. Wire hangers grab one another with pointy metal edges, snagging delicate garments in their eagerness to spring apart. Shoes tumble over the floor, tripping the unwary. Try these tips to simplify your clothes storage:

■ **Make it easier to put away.** Liberate your thinking about clothing storage. There's a principle here, too: in storage, it should be easier to put something away than it is to get it out. With this principle in mind, put pants and bras in an open-topped plastic basket on a shelf, rather than confining them in a too-small lingerie drawer. Hang long nightgowns and dressing gowns from hooks and they'll be easy to find each bleary-eyed morning. Invest in one of the marvellous modern multi-level wardrobe systems, and your delicate blouses will never again catch on the hooks holding your skirts.

"In storage, it should be easier to put something away than it is to get it out!"

■ **Think cluster.** If possible, hang clothing in clusters, rather than segregating it by shirts and trousers and dresses. When the interesting multi-stripe shirt is hidden between two old jeans shirts, it's hard to remember how well it works with those stone chinos. Store clothes by cluster, and you simplify the process of getting dressed.
■ **Stay open.** Stack jeans, shorts, and T-shirts on open shelves, and you'll never again lose a favourite pair in the dark corners of an over-stuffed drawer. Socks deserve their own open basket; store tights by colour, with each colour confined to a separate large zipped food-storage bag.
■ **Hang it right.** Finally, invest in proper hangers for the life of your clothing (*see page 136*), and recycle those wire hangers at your local dry-cleaners.

▶ **If shoes** are stored in shoeboxes, use an instant or digital camera to snap a quick photo of the box contents. Staple the photos to the boxes so that you can see at a glance what's in each box.

Tips for organized wardrobes

If you can see it, you can find it … and wear it, too. Try these tips to get organized in the clothes cupboard:

■ **Boost storage with specialized organizers.** In the wardrobe, space is at a premium — yet many wardrobes teem with unused areas. Specialized organizers can tap that empty space. Double the room for shirts and blouses by hanging a second rail for twice the storage. Stackable shelves subdivide over-tall shelving and add a second layer of storage. Hanging-shelf storage units convert extra space into shelves for sweaters, handbags, or folded jeans.
■ **Round up shoes with shoe racks.** Shoe storage can cause even the most organized among us to stumble, so get shoes up and off the floor. Use shoe racks or shoe bags to store shoes in small spaces.

Tips for organizing for chests of drawers

Crammed drawers can lead to snagged hosiery, rumpled garments, and pinched fingers – so put the following tips to work if you want to declutter and organize clothing stored in chests of drawers:

■ **Declutter, declutter, declutter.** As storage devices, drawers function best when they have breathing room; when they are jammed and crowded, they damage clothing and make it hard to find garments. Keep drawer contents lean by decluttering them. Use the STOP clutter method (*see pages 20–3 and 130–1*) to throw out singleton socks and torn pants. Don't let clothing clutter bring drawer storage to a standstill!

■ **Labels point the way.** Keep the drawer contents tidy – and where they belong – with labels. Label drawers on chest-of-drawer fronts or on the upper edge of the drawer lip. Use labels with pictures on to help small children put away clothing in the proper drawer.

■ **Divide and conquer.** Drawer dividers keep pants neat, socks folded, and T-shirts in their stack. Use narrow strips of cardboard to subdivide drawers, or store lingerie and socks in shallow, flat-bottomed plastic baskets. Commercial drawer organizers can make a neat drawer out of a jumbled mess.

■ **On a roll!** For neat storage, roll garments instead of folding them. Mate socks, and then roll them together; they'll be easy to find, and you won't stretch elastic edges. Rolled T-shirts are simple to sort and store; no more flipping through folded piles to find a favourite. Rolled garments take up less room in the drawer; rolling lessens creases and rumpling.

■ **Turf it.** To pare down excess clothing in the chest of drawers, find alternative storage locations in less crowded areas. Throw rolled socks and tights into a flat-bottomed basket, and slide beneath the dressing table or a nearby bed. Bulky jeans can claim more than their fair share of drawer space; consider hanging them in the wardrobe instead. Don't hang sweaters, though; they should be stored flat to retain their shape.

◁ **Divvy it up.** Drawer dividers make it easy to find clothing you need quickly, and frustrate the tendency of small items to shift when drawers are opened and closed.

Clothes storage tips for **clutter personalities**

Try these tips for clutter personalities. They'll help sort out the cupboard clutter that holds you back:

■ **Perfectionist.** The perfectionist has the world's most organized clothes closet ... in her head. Because her dream of colour-coordinated storage systems is so lofty, she won't throw herself into the yawning void between what she has and what she imagines. In the meantime, she's diving beneath winter's fleece jackets to try to find the swimsuits.

The perfectionist needs to give herself a break! A "good enough" job is truly good enough. Keep in mind the 20–80 rule: 20 per cent of the effort to do any job will reap 80 per cent of the benefits.

■ **Deferrer.** The deferrer dreams of an organized clothes cupboard, too – but the job seems so overwhelming that she goes into a panic at the thought. Break the thrall of procrastination by making one tiny start. Declutter half a hanger rail or half a drawer. Tomorrow, do it again ... and again ... and again. The remedy of action is usually enough to get the deferrer going; taking many little steps will build a bridge to the goal: a clean and organized closet.

■ **Rebel.** Mum was a tyrant. She insisted that clothing be hung up or put away. Out on her own, the rebel continues the war, throwing clothing around with abandon. After a while, rummaging through piles on the floor to get dressed in the morning loses its appeal – but the rebel's behaviour pattern is entrenched.

To make peace with the internal rebel, remind yourself of the power of choice. "I choose to store my clothing in a way that protects it, and makes it easy for me to dress well", will send the rebel back into the past, where she belongs.

Storing
seasonal clothing

Unless your family lives in a balmy equatorial region, seasonal clothing must be rotated and stored between hot-weather and cold-weather seasons. Be alert for storage options that will keep out-of-season clothing safely and provide easy access for the next season's wardrobe changeover.

Before you store

Launder or dry-clean your clothing before storing it for the season — even if it looks clean. Hidden stains may not be evident now, but you'll see them in six months, after the stain has set. Body oils attract clothes moths and cause a deep-set odour if not removed from clothing before storage.

Remove dry-cleaned garments from plastic bags, as the bags trap moisture and encourage mildew. Cotton garment bags or old cotton sheets protect stored clothing from dust, while allowing air circulation.

Choose a storage location that is cool, dry, and well ventilated. Beware of the loft when storing winter clothing. Hot summer loft temperatures can cause fibre damage, while the heat will set any hidden stains. Avoid storing clothing in an area receiving direct sunlight; it can fade clothing.

Choosing hangers Select the right hangers when storing clothes for the season. Avoid storing clothing on thin wire hangers (*see page 138*). Store jackets and coats on padded hangers or wooden suit hangers. Hang trousers by the cuff or hem, hanging straight, to avoid creases. Hang skirts from waistbands using skirt hangers. Wooden or plastic hangers may be used for blouses or shirts. Dresses and skirts often include hanger loops designed to support the garment's weight; place them around the head of the hanger or on hanger hooks.

◀ **Bed them down.** Space beneath the bed works well for seasonal clothing storage. Use under-bed storage organizers, and if necessary raise the bed on blocks to make room for them.

Boxing clothes When boxing clothes for storage avoid boxes made from cardboard. Cardboard is acidic, and the glue it contains is attractive to pests and insects. Lidded plastic storage containers will hold clothing safely, without attracting pests or damaging fibres. Use labels or a permanent marker to label containers to help you identify the contents later.

Clothes moths In areas where moths are prevalent, mothballs can help protect clothes made from natural fibres, but treat them with extreme respect. Mothballs kill moth larvae with chemical fumes, so they should be used only in sealed containers. Do not place mothballs directly on stored clothing.

The fumes are hazardous to humans, so do not wear clothing immediately if it has been stored with mothballs. Clean clothing or air it in a well-ventilated location for at least a day before wearing. Always keep mothballs away from children and pets.

Cedar blocks, shavings, or cedar oil offers less toxic protection against moths when storing clothing. Like mothballs, clothing must be stored in a closed container when using cedar, so that the fumes will deter moths.

Where to store out-of-season clothes?
Try these tips to store seasonal clothing out of the way when not in use.

■ **Rack them up.** Wheeled hanging rails are sturdy, and make seasonal wardrobe changeovers easy. Wheel the rail to the wardrobe, and load it up with winter jackets, suits, and trousers. Add a canvas hanging-shelf storage unit to provide shelf space on the rail. When you have finished, wheel the rail to an alternative storage location; cover it with a cotton sheet to protect the clothing from dust.

■ **Suitcase solution.** Suitcases are ideal containers for transporting clothing – and for storing it, too. During the off-season, tuck seasonal clothing inside suitcases. A label or post-it note affixed to the outside identifies clothing inside.

■ **Aim high.** If you're blessed with a very tall cupboard, tap that empty space for seasonal storage. Add a hanging rail near the top and store out-of-season clothes up there for safe, accessible storage.

Create a kids' clothing archive

Families with growing children face additional clothes-storage challenges. In multi-child families, it makes financial sense to retain baby clothes and hand-me-down clothing for subsequent children. Frugal parents "buy up", purchasing sale clothing in the next size up for children's use as they grow; garage-sale addicts can collect an entire quality wardrobe of children's clothing as they go round the garage sales.

The problem is, most children's bedrooms have a difficult time storing clothing in active use, much less an added cache of "grow-into" clothes. Solution: set up a simple children's clothing archive to sort, store, and organize kids' clothes.

Ready to wear
To create a kids' clothing archive, collect or purchase eight to ten lidded plastic storage containers. Containers should be clean, dry, and stack easily.

Sort clothing by gender – boy or girl – and then by size or age. Assign each pile to a box, and label accordingly: Boy–Age 6; Girl–Age 8. Stack boxes in an accessible storage area in the garage or loft, arranging them by gender and size.

Did you find a great bargain on toddler dungarees? Stash them away in the "Boy – Toddler" box until the baby is ready to cruise the house. When daughter's dresses are all too short, check the "Girl–Age 6" archive box before you shop for new clothes; add her outgrown dresses in good condition to the "Girl–Age 4" archive for use next year by her younger sister.

Clothing
care and maintenance

Whether you love your clothes – or simply hate to shop – it makes sense to maintain clothing properly. Clothing represents a substantial investment of money, time, and energy, and no one likes to see the premature demise of a favourite garment. Good care prolongs the life of your clothing and keeps it looking good longer.

Here are basic pointers to protect your clothing investment:

■ **Air clothing before wearing it.** Wait! Don't put that expensive suit or pretty dress back into the wardrobe right away. When you've worn a garment, hang it up to air outside the wardrobe overnight before putting it away. An airing will smooth out wrinkles. By removing moisture and odours, it also reduces the need for costly dry-cleaning.

■ **Kiss wire hangers good-bye.** Dry-cleaning freebies are hard on good clothes. Hanger ends poke into blouse sleeves, stressing the fabric, while rough wire edges snag a fabric's delicate weave. Skinny wires cut into shoulder pads and don't support heavier garments. For advice on which type of hanger to use for which type of garment, see page 136 and the caption below. Earth-friendly tip: many dry-cleaners will recycle wire hangers; check with your cleaners to see if they will accept surplus wire hangers for re-use.

■ **Dress dry.** Deodorants, body lotions, and perfumes are a treat for your body but hard on your clothes. Chemicals used

"An airing will smooth out wrinkles and reduce the need for costly dry-cleaning."

◀ **Happy hang-ups.** Use sturdy, shaped wooden hangers to support the weight of jackets and coats; slender wood or plastic hangers keep blouses wrinkle-free and ready to wear.

in cosmetics can harm clothing fibres, so get dry before you get dressed. After you apply them, allow deodorants, sprays and cologne to dry thoroughly before donning clothing – and never apply perfumes or lotions directly to your clothes.

■ **Treat stains quickly.** Stains are harder – or impossible – to remove once they have set. Launder stained garments, or deliver stained clothing to the dry-cleaners as soon as possible after the stain occurs. You'll stand the best chance of erasing the mishap if you move quickly.

"It's an old home truth: 'A stitch in time saves nine.'"

■ **Dust … your clothing?** Dust and lint are more than just unsightly on your clothes; these abrasive particles can damage fibres. Use a lint roller and a clothes brush to remove dust and lint from clothing regularly.

■ **Mend your ways.** It's an old home truth: "A stitch in time saves nine." Mend small tears or rips quickly, before they become big ones. A quick stitch to a sagging hem will prevent an embarrassing downfall further down the line.

■ **Keep order in the cupboard.** Crowded cupboards are more than just inconvenient – they damage clothing, as well. Crushed too tightly together, clothes wrinkle unnecessarily, and moisture and odours are trapped in the fabric. Give your clothing breathing room in the wardrobe to preserve it.

■ **Go for the Gobi … wardrobe.** In humid climates, wardrobe storage can get downright funky. Moisture in the air settles on clothing and encourages mould and mildew; the enclosed space magnifies the destructive effect. Result: musty smells and damaged clothing. Investigate dehumidifier products to dry cupboard interiors and preserve your wardrobe. These plastic containers hold moisture-attracting crystals and can be placed in a corner where they'll absorb excess humidity.

■ **Repel pests.** Moths and carpet beetles love the confines of the clothes cupboard, where they attack natural fibres like wool and cotton. Keep them out safely with environmentally friendly cedar blocks. Hung from hangers or clothes rails, cedar's essential oils repel pests. When the scent fades, restore it by lightly sanding the blocks to expose a new surface.

Dry-cleaning do's and don'ts

Professional dry-cleaning is a valuable tool for preserving the life of your clothing, but it helps to be in the know. Get the most out of your dry-cleaning with these tips.

■ **Dry-clean sparingly.** The dry-cleaning process is harsh and costly. Subject clothing to it only when absolutely necessary.

■ **Double or nothing.** Because dry-cleaning can fade or alter fabric colour, always dry-clean both pieces of a two-piece garment, not just one.

■ **Come clean with your cleaner.** When you take clothing to the dry-cleaner, point out stains and spots, and identify what caused them, if possible. If he or she has to guess, it's less likely that the cleaner will be able to remove the stain.

■ **Put a stop to staples.** Ask the cleaner to use a safety pin to attach cleaning tickets to your garment, not a staple. The stapler shreds garment fibres unnecessarily.

■ **Tap the cleaners' clothing-care talent.** Many dry-cleaners also offer clothing repair and alterations, shoe repair, and special treatments for bridal gowns, duvets, or leather. Ask them about any speciality services you may need; they are a great source of wardrobe talent.

■ **Pitch the plastic bags.** Once home, remove clothing from the dry-cleaner's plastic bags. Fumes from solvents used in the dry-cleaning process need air circulation to dissipate, while plastic bags hold in moisture that can harm clothing during storage.

■ **Recycler's tip.** Tie a knot in the bottom of the plastic bag, and use it to line a rubbish bin.

To mend
or not to mend?

Grandmother Betty was quick to pick up her needle as a young mother in the 1930s, but whether or not to repair clothing is a more complex question in today's world. Cheaper global labour has brought down the relative cost of clothing, while overall clothing quality has declined – and sewing skills are no longer part of an ordinary school curriculum. When is it worth your while to mend or alter clothing?

Mastering mending basics

Growing up in the home of a hobby seamstress, my son was fascinated by sewing machines from an early age. By the time he turned eight, son Ryan had learned to machine-sew most of the seams of his favourite brightly coloured cotton shorts.

I was happy to encourage his interest, because everyone – male, female, fashionista, or fad-adverse – needs a set of basic mending skills. When he entered boot camp for the United States Marine Corps, Ryan came to agree with me as he watched fellow-recruits struggle with the simplest mending chores.

Here is a list of mending basics that everyone – even big, strong Marines – should know how to do. These simple sewing jobs require very few tools, and will keep clothing on the job and functional:

- Sew a button
- Mend a straight seam
- Patch a hole
- Take up a hem
- Darn a tear or a rip
- Replace hooks, eyes, and pop fasteners

These days, it's hard to know whether it's time or cost-effective to mend clothing. High repair charges versus lower clothing costs weigh against mending, lower-quality clothing is harder to mend, and we may not own the sewing tools – or possess the sewing skills – necessary to complete the job. Consider these questions to determine whether to mend or alter clothing:

- **Is the garment in good condition?** Repairing a slight tear in a new pair of child's cotton dungarees makes sense – but the identical repair will be hard to justify if the garment is worn and the fabric is thin. Mend garments only if they're in good condition, because worn fabric won't hold a repair for very long.
- **How extensive is the needed repair?** Taking up a frayed hem or reinforcing a split seam is a quick and easy job; removing and replacing a broken zip is difficult and time-consuming. Save major mending jobs for expensive clothing that will justify the effort.
- **Do I know how to make this repair?** Even a simple mending chore will weigh heavy if the task is above your skill level. Nothing can be more frustrating than struggling at sewing, so take a reality check when it comes to sewing skills. Some of us have them; some don't – so be honest with yourself about your sewing competence when you contemplate making repairs.
- **What tools will I need to repair this item?** A simple hem requires only needle and thread, but repairing a broken invisible zip may be impossible without a special adapter foot

for the sewing machine. Be sure to factor in the cost of any tools you will need for the job when you evaluate whether to mend an item of clothing.

■ **What would a professional charge for this repair?**
To get a true grasp of the economics of mending clothing, find out what a professional would charge to do the repair. Balance that amount against what the garment is worth for a good rule of thumb on the question of to mend, or not to mend?

"Even a simple mending chore will weigh heavy if the task is above your skill level."

Make a mending centre

The mending basket can be a black hole that swallows garments for years, giving them back only when time and styles have passed forever. Ease mending chores by creating a mending centre for your organized home. The centre's focus: a one-stop place to store garments in need of mending, and the tools to complete the repairs.

Locate a mending centre in or near the laundry room or laundry centre (*see pages 142–3*). A quick stitch to a sagging hem before washing makes sure the problem isn't exacerbated. Set aside a hanger area, or designate a basket or hamper to hold items in need of repair. Store mending tools in a basket or tote bag with a handle.

A basic kit should comprise:

■ Scissors
■ Needles and thread
■ Measuring tape
■ Thimble
■ Seam ripper

When a mending job needs more than a minute or two, the handled basket makes it easy to relocate to a comfortable chair with your sewing. Choose one with good light, and your eyes will thank you; make it near a television or radio, and you'll enjoy your sewing more.

Manage the mending basket

Let's face it: few of us look forward to mending clothes. As a to-do list item, "empty mending basket" ranks as a lower-than-low priority. Think again! Clothing that is already purchased but in need of repair represents a hidden asset in terms of time and money. To change your thinking (and free your clothes), try this method to keep mending within bounds.

■ **Get real.** If you're using the mending basket to avoid decisions (or even just stall ironing chores), you're misusing it. Use the tips on this page to be realistic about when and whether to mend.

■ **Shop at home first.** Before hitting the shops, check the mending. Often, those "new smart black trousers" on your list can be found in the basket – and it takes less time to shorten them than it does to drive to the shopping centre.

■ **Check when the seasons change.** Some garments bought at the end of a season never get as far as the wardrobe because they've been tucked into the mending basket for a quick alteration. Hunt them out when the seasons change and new wardrobe needs are fresh in your mind.

▲ **Basic sewing tools.** Needle, thimble, and thread are inexpensive allies in the fight to get the most use from your clothing. A basic sewing kit keeps clothing in good repair.

Laundry
activity centre

Where there's life, there are clothes – and where there are clothes, there's laundry! Does Mt. Washmore erupt and rise from the floor in your home on a regular basis? Laundry nerds may revel in the act of folding freshly dried sheets, but the rest of us need a laundry reality check. Stay on top of the laundry mountain with these tips.

Schedule laundry chores regularly

The equation is simple: you wear clothes? You wash clothes – and towels, sheets, and bedding, too. Put off the laundry side of the equation, and the job becomes much harder. In the laundry basket, stains and wrinkles have a chance to settle in and make themselves permanent. A load of wet laundry, left to itself in the washing machine, invites mildew. The dryer load, forgotten and unfolded, settles back into rumpled comfort once the heat dies down. As the laundry mountain grows, family members scrabble up its sides, looking for socks, jeans or underpants that are clean enough for a reprise wearing.

Solution: schedule laundry chores regularly. How often to do laundry will depend on your family's needs. Households with young children may have to launder multiple loads each day, while singletons can go for a week at a time between laundry sessions – as long as laundry operations are conducted regularly.

Create a laundry activity centre

A laundry activity centre combines the equipment, tools, and supplies needed to get in and get the job done – quickly. Establish a space to assemble, sort, wash, dry, fold, and return clean clothing and bedding.

■ **Location, location.** Look to the location of the washing machine (if you have one) to set up the laundry centre. Clear space around the machine; folding laundry is an active process, so you'll need as much clear counter space as you can create. A sink nearby will make it easier to treat stains and presoak soiled clothing.

■ **Let there be light!** Good lighting will help you find and identify stains, so supplement existing lighting if it's dark or dreary. Can you read the fine print on a garment label? If not, provide additional lamps or lighting fixtures.

■ **Find the upper reaches.** Store detergents and laundry products in an overhead cupboard, or mount a shelf unit on the wall above the washing machine. Households with small children will need to locate cleaning products up and away from little hands, but within reach of pre-teens and up, to make it easy for growing youngsters to take over their own laundry chores.

■ **Get hung-up.** Install a clothes rail in the laundry centre to hang non-iron garments. If cupboards permit, an expandable shower-curtain rail will hold clean shirts and extra hangers in smaller spaces.

■ **Fold and retract.** If space permits, add a retractable clothes line or folding drying rack to the laundry centre. Even if the house has an automatic dryer, a clothes line or rack makes it a quick matter to dry sweaters and underwear that should not be placed in the dryer.

■ **Colour-matching.** Code laundry baskets with a different colour for each family member – and place baskets in every bedroom and bathroom. On laundry days, family members who can toddle can toddle their own baskets to the laundry centre, and return the clean and folded clothing to their own wardrobes at the end of the day.

▶ **A series of** plastic laundry baskets makes it easy to separate whites from coloureds from darks and to hold garments until there are enough items for a full washload.

Laundry
basics

Our grandmothers knew the drudgery of washing clothing by hand; they'd envy the wealth of laundry appliances and products available today – and the ease and speed we take for granted. Ready to tackle the family wash? Here's the fast track to clean clothes: sort and prepare, treat or mend, wash, dry, fold, and put away.

Sort and prepare

Skip the sort step before starting the wash, and you know what'll happen: red jumper plus white knickers equals pink panties (or worse, pink boxer shorts).

To sort laundry, start with colour. Separate clothing into white, light-coloured, bright, and dark piles to avoid dye transfer – the pink knickers problem. Wash white and light clothing separately to keep dye transfer at bay.

Separating synthetics (polyester, nylon, acrylic) from natural fibres (cotton, linen) can also cure dye transfer problems; synthetic fibres can be dye magnets, absorbing the cast-offs from dye-rich natural fibres.

Are you troubled by lint in the wash? Keep lint-generators (sweatshirts, towels, towelling and flannel fabrics) away from lint-attractors (nylon blouses, microfibres) in the laundry process.

For cleaner clothes, sort clothing by soil level. Jeans worn while planting out seedlings in the garden aren't good wash-mates for lightly soiled blouses. Fabric weight, too, should be considered; the heavy stitching, brads, and buttons on jeans are too rough-and-tumble to share a wash cycle with lighter-weight or delicate clothing.

Treat or mend

As you load the washing machine, check each item of clothing. Close zips, remove belts and ties, and check pockets for forgotten items that don't belong in the wash.

Examine each garment, searching for stains and treat them before you wash (*see pages 150–1*). Check if items need a quick mend (*see pages 140–1*). Keep the mending centre in or near the laundry area so that it's easy to make repairs.

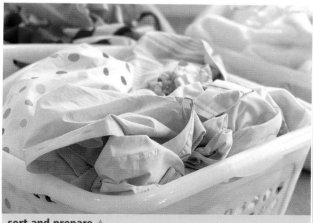

sort and prepare ▲

treat or mend ▲

Wash

You're ready to wash – but how well do you know your washing machine? Your machine's product manual has a wealth of information on how to get clothes clean effectively. Washing recommendations vary from machine to machine. For instance, filling a front-loading spin-cycle model fully gets clothes cleaner, but overloading a top-loader that uses an agitator will impede the cleaning process and could damage clothing.

Clothing loaded, add detergent. Detergent use is among those "know-your-machine" issues where it pays to be informed. Washing machines vary in capacity, and are designed to use

"Skip the sort step and you know what'll happen: red jumper plus white knickers equals ... pink boxer shorts."

differing amounts of detergent. Consult the washing machine's product manual first, then read the detergent box to determine how much detergent to add – and do measure carefully, using a measuring cup. You may need to use more detergent for large loads, very dirty clothing, or if you live in an area with hard water. Use a bit less detergent for soft water, small loads, or lightly soiled clothing.

Add any fabric additives or softener. Follow manufacturer's recommendations to use bleach, non-chlorine bleach, or fabric brighteners; these toxic products must be used with care and according to the directions on the label. Fabric softener should be added during the final rinse cycle.

Select the appropriate water temperature for the clothes in the washing machine (*see pages 148–9*). Start the machine.

Dry

When the washing machine cycle has finished, it's time to dry. Place clothing in a tumble dryer, and select the appropriate heat level and cycle duration. Give twisted items a good shake as you load them; you'll give them a head start to dry smooth and wrinkle-free. Hang delicate clothing from hangers, a dryer rack, or from a clothesline to air-dry. (*For more information on drying, see pages 148–9 and 151.*)

Fold and put away

Make sure that you fold or hang clothing quickly after removing it from the dryer; the last bit of heat in the garment will help to smooth out wrinkles (and prevent the need to iron). Watch out for metal buttons or zips. They can be very hot after a tumble in the dryer.

Using colour-coded baskets, place each family member's clothing in a separate basket as you fold. You'll make it easy for everyone to put away their own clothing if they only have to grab a basket and go.

wash and dry ▲

fold and put away ▲

When clothing was costly and appliances few, laundry was done only when truly necessary. However, with easy access to automatic washing machines, tumble dryers, and modern laundry products, today's families can get careless about what goes into the laundry basket.

Picture the scene in a typical household: a stack of clean, dry clothing is delivered to a bedroom. Ignored, it falls to the floor at bedtime, and a day or so later, is scarcely recognizable as clean ... so the room's occupant short-circuits the job of folding and putting it away by dumping it into the laundry basket. Again.

Rewashing clothing is costly and wasteful of water, detergent – and time! Apply a common-sense sanction: whoever seeks to rewash rather than fold gets to experience the laundry process first-hand.

Put the offenders to work in the laundry room to close the laundry loophole.

Clothing care for
different fabrics

New advances in fibre technology have created garments that are more functional than ever before, but caring for them can be confusing. Clothing care labels offer a dazzling array of choices. Hand wash. Delicate cycle. Line-dry. No iron. Read the labels – then follow these guidelines to care for the fabrics in your closet.

Acetate

Acetate is a man-made fibre, often found blended with other fibres to create beautiful, easy-to-drape clothing. Acetate and acetate blends clean up well, but can be very sensitive to dye transfer. Check the care label, and then wash garments containing acetate fibres in cold water.

Acetate is a weak fibre, and can be damaged by twisting, wringing, or heat. Hand-wash acetate blends, or use the gentle cycle of the washing machine for machine-washable garments.

Iron garments containing acetate using a low-heat setting. Press on the wrong side and use a press cloth to avoid shine and preserve the beauty of the fabric.

Cotton

Cotton is a worldwide favourite for comfortable, versatile clothing. A natural fibre, cotton can be found in garments as casual as a T-shirt or as elaborate as a ball gown.

Cotton fibres will shrink unless the fabric has been pre-shrunk or processed, so start with the care label. "Cold water only" may signal that your ankle-length cotton trousers will convert themselves into pedal pushers if not washed correctly.

Cotton items that are pre-shrunk may be washed in hot, warm, or cold water, depending on the colour of the garment and care label recommendations.

If care labels agree, add chlorine bleach to white cotton wash loads to remove stains; coloured cottons may be brightened by non-chlorine bleach formulated for coloured clothing. Cold-water washing will protect the deep colour of cotton jeans, and preserve the pep of brightly coloured shirts.

Over-drying cotton will encourage shrinkage; dry cotton garments at a lower heat and remove them from the tumble dryer while still fairly cool.

> **"'Cold water only' may signal that your ankle-length trousers will convert into pedal pushers if not washed correctly!"**

Linen

Linen is a natural fibre, made from the flax plant. Check care labels on linen garments to determine whether the garment must be dry-cleaned. If machine-washable, wash according to label instructions, using water appropriate to the garment's colour. Linen absorbs more water than other fibres, so don't overcrowd the washing machine and dryer. Iron linen from the inside out, using steam at a hot iron setting.

Polyester

The last century's "wonder fibre", polyester creates colourful, durable, easy-care garments. Most polyester fabrics may be machine-washed using warm water, but check care labels first.

Tumble-dry polyester garments on low heat. Remove them from the dryer while still slightly damp to prevent wrinkles and avoid a static build-up. If ironing is required, use a low heat: polyester will melt beneath a hot iron.

Silk

Supple, strong, and lustrous, this natural fibre is among the world's oldest clothing materials. While silk fibre itself is washable, many weave patterns used for silk fabric will tighten or pucker if washed, and deep dye tones may not be colour-fast.

Let garment labels guide you when cleaning silk garments. "Dry Clean Only" signals a fabric or construction that will not survive washing. Launder washable silk garments using products formulated for hand-washing or delicate fabrics. Mild baby shampoo (without conditioning additives that may add wax or oils) is a good choice for hand-washable silk fabrics. It will clean the natural protein and revitalize the fibre.

Never tumble silk in the tumble dryer. Instead, roll the item in a towel to press out moisture, and then hang to dry. Press silk garments with a warm iron.

Spandex

A touch of stretch makes clothing fit and feel better. Enter spandex, an elastic fibre now incorporated in small amounts in many types of fabric to add stretch and comfort. While spandex is hand- or machine-washable, avoid hot water and chlorine bleach. Both will damage the spandex fibres. Unless care labels indicate otherwise, hang spandex garments to dry, and avoid machine drying.

The heat of the dryer can cause some spandex-blends to pucker or bubble. If ironing is necessary, press the item quickly with a warm iron.

Wool

Sheep love it, and we do, too: the soft, warm fibre made from wool. Naturally insulating and easy to dye, wool fabric runs the gamut from rugged tweeds to floating wool challis.

In the natural state, wool is washable, but because many wool garments incorporate construction methods that cannot be washed, dry-clean wool clothing where the label specifies this. If washable, use a gentle detergent and hand- or machine-wash as directed by the clothing care label.

A tip from a venerable Shetland Islands' knitter: wash and rinse wool fibres in lukewarm water. Using cold water to rinse can cause shrinkage when it comes to wool.

FABRIC WASH AND DRY GUIDELINES

Fabric type	WASH				DRY			
	Hand	Cool	Warm	Boil	Dry naturally	Tumble cool	Tumble warm	Tumble hot
Acetate	●				●			
Cotton				●			●	
Linen		●			●	●		
Polyester		●			●	●	●	
Rayon			●		●			
Silk	●	●			●	●		
Nylon				●	●	●		
Spandex	●				●			
Wool	●				●			

Out, out, **damned spot!**

Life is like an ice cream cone: it's cool, it's sweet – but there are always going to be a few drips. When they land on your clothes, will you know how to handle them? Prompt and proper stain treatment will keep clothing looking new longer; delay or the wrong response can make the stain a permanent addition.

Pretreat promptly. As you sort laundry, be on the lookout for stained items; pretreating is the best and easiest way to remove stains. A trip through the washing machine and dryer can turn a dribble of salad dressing into a permanent addition to a blouse if it's not treated first.

Pretreat properly. When it lands on your trousers and must be removed, sauce for the goose isn't always sauce for the gander. Different stains require different pretreatment methods. Here are some of the most common stain problems and how to pretreat them:

■ **Oily stains.** Salad dressing, lipstick, and car grease create oily stains on clothing – and so does your neck on the inside of a shirt collar. To treat collar rings and oily stains, apply liquid detergent directly to the stained area. Allow the item to stand for 15 minutes before laundering. The detergent will loosen and dissolve the stain so that it can be lifted away in the wash.

■ **Protein stains.** When Baby spits up on your shoulder, you've got a protein stain. Blood, milk, and dairy products, and most body soil contain organic matter that will harden and set over time or when exposed to hot water. Soak protein stains in cold water for at least 30 minutes before laundering. A tip from the nursing profession: stubborn, dried-on blood stains may be removed by applying a 3 per cent hydrogen peroxide solution (sold in chemists for wound care) to the stain, but pretest fabric for colour-fastness, first.

■ **Tannin stains.** Tannin puts the pucker in your tea – and permanent colour on your clothing if you spill it. Wine, coffee, tea, soft drinks, fruits, and fruit juices commonly cause tannin

▲ **Easy does it.** Treating stains is one time when a light touch is best. Rubbing or scrubbing at stained fabric can harm fibres or lighten dye. Blot stains for best results.

stains. Pretreat them by soaking in cold water, then wash in the hottest temperature appropriate for the garment.

■ **Dye stains.** Loll on the grass some summer afternoon, and you're apt to get up with a grass-green dye stain, compliments of the lovely turf. Foods with strong colours, such as blueberries or mustard, create dye stains. So does direct transfer from fabric or leather, such as the blue cast rubbed off on white undergarments worn beneath new jeans. Pretreat dye stains with direct application of detergent to the stained area, then wash in the hottest water appropriate for the fabric.

Keeping a family in clean clothes isn't just a never-ending task; it's a major consumer of energy and natural resources in the household. Focus on these strategies to stay clean and green in the laundry area.

Using the washing machine

As an energy user, the washing machine is a household front-runner. Rein in the beast's use of water and power with these energy-saving tips:

■ **Chill out.** Heating water for household use is a costly proposition, so turn down the thermostat on the hot water heater. For most households, a setting of 49°C (120°F) is adequate – and lower hot-water temperatures make scald injuries much less likely to occur. By turning down the thermostat, you'll save energy whenever you launder with heated water.

■ **Stay cool.** Wash in cold water whenever possible. New detergent formulations for cold-water washing dissolve well and get clothes clean at lower temperatures. Even when heavy soil or fabric type requires washing in hot or warm water, a cold-water rinse saves energy. A bonus: cold-water washing preserves fabric colours.

■ **Fill it up.** Wash full loads of laundry – you'll use proportionately less water and energy than doing several partial loads.

■ **Cycle down.** Make good use of the washing machine's alternative cycles for best energy savings. Permanent press or delicate cycles are shorter, and agitate and spin less than "heavy wash" ones. Use them for lighter-weight or lightly soiled garments.

■ **Measure twice, wash once.** In the laundry area, more isn't better when it comes to the amount of detergent or other laundry additives you use, so measure carefully. Too much detergent won't clean clothing any better and will be hard to rinse away.

Chlorine bleach eats away fibres if over-used. Too much fabric softener can stain clothing; rewash to remove spotting.

■ **Clean and green.** A green hint: use a cup of white vinegar instead of commercial fabric softeners. Vinegar cuts detergent residue, softens clothing, and removes odour – and at a price point far less than commercial products.

Drying clothes

When drying laundry, convenience costs! Duck high power bills with these tips for efficient dryer use:

■ **Let the sun shine.** Sunlight and fresh air dry clothing for free – and the warm scent of sun-dried clothes is a sensory bonus. When possible, hang laundry outdoors to dry.

■ **Hang loose.** Don't over-fill the tumble dryer. Crowded with clothing, the dryer will have to work much too hard, and leave clothing with wrinkles that can require ironing. Let clothes tumble freely for most efficient dryer use.

■ **Enough is enough!** When using a tumble dryer, don't over-dry clothing. "Auto" settings sense the moisture levels and temperature inside the dryer, so use them when possible. Over-drying clothing can cause shrinkage and fabric damage, so save your clothes and the environment by removing dried clothing promptly.

■ **Free the filter.** Clean the dryer's lint filter with every load. A lint build-up impedes air circulation and forces the dryer to work longer and hotter. Every month, rinse the filter; you'll be amazed at the volume of lint that you'll remove.

■ **Vent it.** Check the dryer's vent hoses and outlet hood for lint build-up or obstruction. If the hood cover won't open freely, replace it. Proper ventilation is necessary for efficient drying and will save energy.

Energy-saving tips and tricks

TREATING STAINS

For this stain	use this product	and this method
Adhesive tape, chewing gum	Prewash stain remover	Rub the stained area with ice to harden the gummy residue; gently remove as much as possible with a dull knife. Saturate the stain with prewash stain remover. Rinse thoroughly before laundering.
Baby formula	Enzyme-based laundry presoak	Soak the stained item in a solution of enzyme-based presoak and water for 30 minutes to several hours.
Blood and bodily fluids	Enzyme-based laundry presoak; chlorine, non-chlorine or oxygen bleach product; hydrogen peroxide (3 percent solution, sold in drugstores for wound care)	Soak fresh stains in cold water for 30 minutes or until the blood is gone. For dried stains, presoak the garment in a solution of enzyme-based presoak and water, then launder. If the stain remains, launder the garment using non-chlorine bleach, chlorine bleach, or oxygen bleach, as appropriate for the fabric type. To remove set stains on a colourfast garment, apply hydrogen peroxide to the stained area using an eyedropper. Reapply until the stain is dissolved, then rinse and launder the garment. [Note: as hydrogen peroxide is a bleach, test the garment for colour-fastness first.]
Coffee, tea, soft drinks	Prewash stain remover or liquid detergent; non-chlorine bleach	Use prewash stain remover or liquid detergent; soak garments with fresh stains in cold water before laundering. For set-in stains, apply a prewash stain remover or liquid detergent; allow to stand for 15 minutes before laundering. Wash the garment using non-chlorine bleach where appropriate for the fabric type.
Candle wax, crayon marks	Paper towels and iron; chlorine or non-chlorine bleach	Apply ice to the stain to harden it, then remove as much wax as possible with a dull knife. Place the stained fabric between two layers of paper towels, and iron with a warm iron to remove wax. Repeat with fresh paper towels until the wax is removed. Launder, using chlorine or non-chlorine bleach where appropriate for the fabric type.
Chocolate	Enzyme-based laundry presoak	Presoak in an enzyme-based laundry presoak before laundering as usual.
Dye transfer	Colour-remover laundry additive	Use commercial colour-remover laundry additives as directed to remove dye transfer stains from light-coloured or dye-magnet fabrics, such as light-coloured garments and synthetics.
Eggs	Enzyme-based laundry presoak	Presoak egg stains in an enzyme-based laundry presoak for 30 minutes to several hours. Launder as usual.
Fruit or fruit juices	Prewash stain remover or liquid detergent; chlorine or non-chlorine bleach	Soak fresh stains in cold water before laundering. For set-in stains, apply a prewash stain remover or liquid detergent directly to the stained area; allow to stand 15 minutes before laundering. Wash garment using chlorine or non-chlorine bleach where appropriate for fabric type.
Grass	Enzyme-based laundry presoak	Presoak grass-stained items in an enzyme-based laundry presoak for 30 minutes to several hours. Launder as usual.

For this stain	use this product	and this method
Grease or oil	Prewash stain remover or liquid detergent	Apply a prewash stain remover or liquid detergent directly to stained area. Allow to sit for 15 minutes, and then launder in the hottest water appropriate for the fabric type.
Mildew	Chlorine or non-chlorine bleach.	Launder mildewed garments in the hottest water appropriate for the fabric type, using the bleach product safe for that fabric. Mildew stains may be permanent.
Milk and dairy products	Enzyme-based laundry presoak	Presoak stained garments in an enzyme-based laundry presoak for 30 minutes to several hours. Launder as usual.
Mustard	Prewash stain remover	Pretreat mustard stains with a prewash stain remover; launder as usual.
Perfume	Prewash stain remover or liquid detergent	Apply a prewash stain remover or liquid detergent directly to the stained area. Allow the item sit for 15 minutes, and then wash as usual.
Rust or iron stains	Commercial iron remover	Treat rust or iron stains with a commercial iron remover, according to package directions. Do not use chlorine bleach to try to remove iron stains, since bleach will set them permanently.
Sauces (tomato ketchup, tomato sauce, barbeque sauce)	Prewash stain remover or liquid detergent; chlorine or non-chlorine bleach	Apply a prewash stain remover or liquid detergent directly to the stained area; allow to stand 15 minutes before laundering. Wash the garment using chlorine or non-chlorine bleach where appropriate for the fabric type.
Tobacco	Enzyme-based laundry presoak	Presoak in an enzyme-based laundry presoak before laundering as usual.

Treating stains on the run

In a perfect life, spots and stains would occur right there in the laundry area, where the means to treat them was close at hand. In reality, stains love life on the fly: while travelling, eating out, or away from home. Try these ideas to deal with stains on the run:

■ **Duck them!** Simple as it sounds, avoiding stains prevents the need to treat them. Sit down to eat, when possible, instead of juggling drippy burgers behind the wheel (and wearing the catsup for the rest of the day). Tuck napkins into children's T-shirts to soak up the inevitable restaurant spills.

■ **Carry a first-aid kit for stains.** Whether it's car travel or just the daily commute, tuck an emergency stain kit into the car. Fold a few paper towels into the bottom of a plastic food storage bag; they'll help you soak up spills and blot fresh stains with cool water. Add a disposable plastic knife for scraping away solid materials. Some prepacked stain-removal towelettes will also come in handy.

■ **Be ready for holiday mishaps.** Pack a travel-sized bottle of liquid detergent or pre-packed stain-removal towelettes so that you can treat a stain on the spot. In an emergency, try using talcum powder from your washbag to treat an oily stain. Cover the stain with a layer of powder, then leave it for at least half an hour for the powder to absorb the oil. Brush the powder away with a clean, dry washcloth — if there's still some staining, repeat the procedure until the mark has gone.

Press on!
top tips for easy ironing

The tools: iron, ironing board, spray bottle, and starch. The job: remove wrinkles from clothing. The goal: get the job done, fast and smoothly. The problem: wilting resolve behind the ironing board. Speed household ironing chores by knowing what to press and how to press it. Try these tips to take the heat out of ironing.

1 I iron, ergo I am

Proper ergonomic alignment speeds the ironing process and avoids backache. Adjust the ironing board to hip level; when holding the iron, your elbow should be bent at a 90-degree angle and your shoulder should move freely.

2 Clean the scene

Before turning on the heat, check the iron's soleplate for built-up residue. Remove any deposits before ironing: scorch or dirt is a drag on the soleplate, and can be transferred to clean clothing.

3 Know your clothes

Read clothing care labels and match iron temperatures to the garment's fibre content. If in doubt about a garment's fibre content, set the iron on the low side of the temperature dial.

4 Duck a dirty job

Never press stained or dirty clothing. The iron's heat will set stains and body sweat, and intensify odours in the fabric. Heat plus dirt equals a fine mess, so keep clothing sweet by washing or dry-cleaning before you press.

◀ **Buying an iron.** When replacing an iron, new choices enhance safety and usability. Look for automatic shutoff features, labelled heat settings, roomy water reservoirs, and built-in sprays.

5 Into the mist

Keep a spray bottle filled with water close to hand. A quick spritz of water releases any accidental creases and makes pressing chores fly. For a scent-ual touch, fill the ironing spray bottle with linen water: water infused with non-staining fragrances. Find linen water at bath-and-bedding shops.

6 Go with the grain

Just as you sand a wooden table, iron with the grain, not against it. Ironing across thread diagonals causes fabric to buckle and stretch.

7 A pressing matter

The press cloth is your friend! Use this rectangle of tightly woven cotton cloth as an intermediary between the iron and the garment to guard against shine when pressing on the right side of wool or delicate fabrics.

8 Keep it moving, keep it light

Keep the iron moving and the pressure light. Pressing too hard flattens fibre nap and stresses reinforced areas such as pockets, while a slow iron is more apt to scorch or burn fabric.

9 Keep them wrinkle-free

When you've finished pressing, hang the garment immediately. Freshly ironed clothing is vulnerable to wrinkling in the first several hours. Allow clothing to cool and dry completely before placing them in a wardrobe or in a drawer.

A heaped-up laundry basket is nobody's cup of tea, so head off ironing chores with these suggestions:

■ **Buy smart.** When shopping for clothes, look for labels that promise "no-iron" or "permanent press" fabric finishes; they're your ticket to ironing freedom.

■ **Enlist the aid of the washing machine.** Special washing machine cycles for permanent-press clothing use cool rinse temperatures to encourage clothing to shed wrinkles – so use them!

■ **Shake it, baby, shake it.** Shake out each garment before adding it to the washing machine. Untwist spirals of trouser leg, and unwind clumps of bathrobe ties, long socks, and tights.

■ **Stay cool.** Over-drying clothing in the tumble dryer shrinks seams and sets wrinkles, so stop the dryer when clothing is just dry and not yet hot. Barely damp clothing will release wrinkles as it hangs, avoiding the need for touch-ups.

■ **Dance attendance on the dryer.** Remove clothing from the dryer promptly, and hang immediately. As you remove clothing, smooth collars and cuffs, and stretch seams for a smooth look.

TEMPERATURE GUIDELINES									
Fabric type	Acetate	Acrylic	Cotton	Linen	Nylon	Polyester	Rayon	Silk	Wool
Iron setting	Cool	Cool	Medium to high heat with steam	Medium to high heat with steam	Low	Low to medium heat	Low to medium heat (iron inside out)	Low heat (iron inside out)	Medium heat with steam

Today's homes are a treat for the senses. Rich rugs glow atop gleaming wood floors. Chrome fixtures reflect the sheen of ceramic sinks and granite countertops. Plush chenille pillows contrast with sleek, cushy leather sofas, while wood furniture invites the eye with the depth and richness of wood grain.

Beneath the surface lie a home's systems: the powerful friends that keep us cool in summer, warm in winter, and supplied with water and power year-round.

In this section, we maintain the surfaces and systems that make a home. Walls and windows, floors and ceilings – we'll discover easy ways to keep surfaces clean and well cared for. We'll share strategies to preserve furniture and fixtures, and learn to manage and maintain household systems.

Finally, we'll focus on safety, adopting simple checklists to keep the home a safe place to live. A household emergency plan will ensure that family members are prepared and informed in the face of fire, flood, or disaster.

Cleaning
walls and wallpaper

Soft with paint or bright with wallpaper, walls frame the life of the household –
but too often, they also wear it! Daily living tends to deposit smudges, smears, and
fingermarks (especially if there are small children in the household), marring the
beauty of walls and woodwork. Painted or papered, keep walls clean and gleaming
with these tips for wall cleaning and maintenance.

How to clean painted walls

On your mark, get set, prep! Cleaning painted walls is a big
job, so be prepared. Push furniture to the centre of the room,
and lay down old sheets or dust sheets to catch soapy drips.
Avoid plastic tarpaulins; they don't absorb water and become
slippery when wet. To protect your hands and to remind you
where pictures belong, cover picture nails with a chunk of
household sponge.

Assemble your wall-washing tools: lambswool duster,
white cleaning cloths, a natural sponge (avoid coloured
sponges, since they can deposit dyes on light-coloured walls),
and two buckets: one filled with cleaning solution (*see below*)
and one filled with clear water for rinsing. Rubber gloves
protect your hands; be sure to turn up glove cuffs to help
contain drips. A small stepladder makes it easier to get to the
high reaches for easy cleaning; tools with handles keep wall
cleaning sessions safe.

Ready to clean In one bucket, mix a wall-cleaning solution.
For normal dirt levels, try a mild detergent solution to clean walls
that consists of:

- 4 litres (1 gallon) warm water, to which you add
- a good squeeze of washing-up liquid

◀ **Take it easy.** A soft approach is best when cleaning walls and
mouldings. Harsh cleaners, abrasives, or an oversupply of elbow
grease can mar painted surfaces or damage delicate wallpaper.

For more heavily soiled walls, you'll need a stronger alkali solution – but spot-test any cleaning mixture first to ensure it won't remove or lighten paint. Add all of the following to your bucket and give it a good stir before you start:

- 4 litres (1 gallon) warm water
- 250ml (8fl oz) clear non-foaming ammonia
- 250ml (8fl oz) white vinegar
- 250g (8oz) washing soda

The second bucket should hold clean water, to be used for rinsing. Change the water if it starts to look very dirty as you work around the room.

Ditch the dust Dust is always easier to remove than mud, so remove any loose dust before bringing moisture into the mix. Circle the room with the lambswool duster, wiping walls and woodwork from the top down. Take the duster outside and spin the handle between your palms to release the dust.

Alternatively, use a vacuum cleaner's extension wand and bristle brush head (used for upholstery) to remove dust and cobwebs from the walls and the woodwork.

Bottoms up Drips are inevitable when washing walls. Should they run down dry, dirty surfaces, they'll dry – and create long muddy stains. Avoid drip issues by washing walls from the bottom up. Yes, you'll drip onto already-cleaned areas, but the solution will be a quick swipe with a sponge, not a tough cleaning job. Dip the natural sponge into the bucket of cleaning solution, and rub the wall gently to avoid removing paint. Work in small areas, washing, and then using the sponge to rinse the area with clear water. Finally, blot excess moisture with white cleaning cloths.

Take it to the end When washing walls, always wash the entire wall, bottom to top and side-to-side. If you need a breather, take it between walls, not in the middle. Stopping the job before you finish the entire wall can cause "wash marks": a wave effect caused by stop-and-go wall washing. Avoid this by washing an entire wall in a single session, using the same type and strength of cleaning solution.

Wallpaper-cleaning tips and tricks

Wallpaper's bright colours and varied textures enliven any room – but that same colour and texture can cause problems when it's time to clean. Try these techniques to clean wallpaper safely:

- **Check manufacturer's guidelines.** Because wallpapers differ in content and coating, follow the manufacturer's advice for appropriate cleaning methods.
- **Dust carefully.** Use a lambswool duster, or tie a dry cleaning cloth over a broom to dust the walls before cleaning.
- **Older, non-coated wallpaper.** Use a specialist dry cleaning sponge made of natural rubber (also known as a soot or smoke sponge) to lift and remove surface dirt without moisture. Rub it lightly against the surface in long strokes to remove dirt.
- **Scrubbable or washable wallpaper.** Use a natural sponge lightly dampened with a solution of warm water and a small amount of washing-up liquid. Before cleaning, test the solution in an inconspicuous corner to be sure it won't remove paper or coating. Don't scrub too hard or allow the paper to get too wet to avoid damage. Use cleaning cloths to absorb extra moisture after rinsing.
- **Fingermarks or smudges.** Remove by rubbing them gently with a soft putty rubber. Use a light touch to avoid damaging the area. Commercial wallpaper cleaners may also be used to lift the small stuff.
- **Cleaners to avoid.** Never use abrasive cleaners – scouring powder or cream cleaner – to clean wallpaper. The abrasive granules which they contain can scratch the wallpaper's coating.

Caring for
special surfaces

Marble floors, tile worktops, brick fireplaces, or granite surfaces bring a unique feel to any home, but require special care and cleaning methods. Preserve the appeal of special surfaces with these maintenance tips.

Marble

This stone is soft, porous, and relatively weak. Marble will scratch easily, absorb standing stains, and must be treated with care. For routine cleaning, dust, then buff with a barely damp cleaning cloth to restore the shine.

When more intense cleaning is required, pour a little clear non-foaming ammonia onto a cleaning cloth, wipe the marble surface, and buff dry. When finished, use a commercial marble polish to restore the shine.

Never use abrasive cleaners on marble surfaces; deep scratches should be referred to a professional for repair. Avoid acid-based cleaning solutions, such as products containing white vinegar; acids can dull or etch bright finishes.

Commercial marble sealing products will help protect marble from wear and abrasion; check with the manufacturer for recommended formulations.

Ceramic tile

Tiles come in two types: glazed and unglazed. Smooth glazed tiles are tough, but brittle and easily scratched, while the surface of unglazed tiles can absorb cleaning products. Finally, grout, used to set tiles in place, is porous and traps moisture, mould, and mildew.

For regular cleaning of glazed ceramic tiles – the shiny tiles most commonly used in kitchens and bathrooms – use a non-abrasive spray cleaner. Spray window cleaner leaves a nice finish, but avoid heavily coloured commercial sprays, as the bright-coloured cleaning solution can discolour porous grout.

Heavily soiled glazed ceramic tiles requires bigger guns: a cream cleaner or scouring powder. For a seriously stained kitchen worktop or grimy shower wall, apply a thin paste of cleaner containing a bleaching agent and water, and allow to stand for 15 minutes to several hours before wiping it away. Rinse the area well with water, then wipe dry.

Clean unglazed ceramic tiles with a natural sponge lightly dampened with a solution of water and non-soap detergent or commercial tile cleaner.

Avoid using acid-based cleaners, such as white vinegar, on tiled areas. Acid attacks the grout, causing it to crumble. Stay away from steel wool. It will scratch the surface of ceramic tiles.

Brick

Made from clay, brick is porous with open pores that can trap dust and dirt. Use a vacuum extension wand with a long-bristled upholstery brush to remove dust and dirt from interior brick on a regular basis.

Granite

While strong and durable, this natural stone product needs special care to maintain its characteristic high-gloss finish.

Prevention is key with granite worktops. Mop up spills as soon as possible, before they can penetrate the surface. Use coasters under beverages, since acids common in soft drinks and fruit juices can etch and dull granite surfaces. Clean granite with a solution of warm water and a few drops of washing-up liquid. Use a wrung-out cleaning cloth to clean the surface, then rinse with a cleaning cloth soaked in clear water. Special cleaners for granite are available to disinfect surfaces in the kitchen. Avoid cleaning products containing acid, such as white vinegar, since they can etch or dull the surface.

How to clean windows

When it comes to cleaning windows, nothing beats the professional cleaner's tool of choice: the squeegee. You'll also need a squeegee wet cover (or a cleaning cloth attached with elastic bands) and dry cleaning cloths. Have your preferred window-cleaning solution ready in a large bucket.

1 Dunk the squeegee with the wet cover or attached cleaning cloth into the bucket, then smear the cleaning solution over the entire surface of the window. Don't worry about drips; we'll catch up with them at the end.

2 Remove the wet cover or cleaning cloth from the squeegee. Working from top to bottom, draw the squeegee across the window, skimming the cleaning solution and dirt from the glass. Curve the squeegee downwards at the end of each stroke.

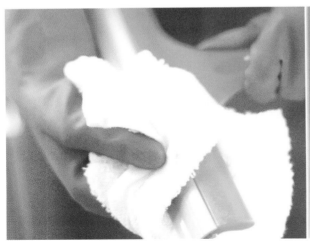

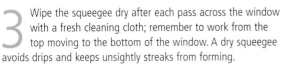

3 Wipe the squeegee dry after each pass across the window with a fresh cleaning cloth; remember to work from the top moving to the bottom of the window. A dry squeegee avoids drips and keeps unsightly streaks from forming.

4 Finished with the squeegee? Run the cleaning cloth along the "wet" side of the window to dry the drips left behind. Move to the window sill and soak up any puddled cleaning solution. Polish the sill dry with a fresh cleaning cloth – and let the light shine.

Floor care is like weeding: a little work at the right time prevents a jungle of problems from growing. A daily floor-care routine removes dirt and soil quickly, before it bonds with the floor. Passive resistance can play a role, too. Use these no-work ideas to keep floors clean without trying.

■ **Mats matter.** Placed both inside and outside household doors, entrance mats remove 80–85 per cent of the dirt coming into the home. Look for mats with a raised, ridged surface that cannot be compressed easily and has non-slip backing.

■ **Shoes off – but socks rule.** Worn outside, shoes become covered with tiny bits of grit and dirt that grind into flooring with each step. Spike heels can dimple hardwoods, puncture vinyl flooring, and pierce carpet backing. Even bare feet leave a film of body oils that attract dirt. Be kind to your flooring and wear socks or soft-soled slippers.

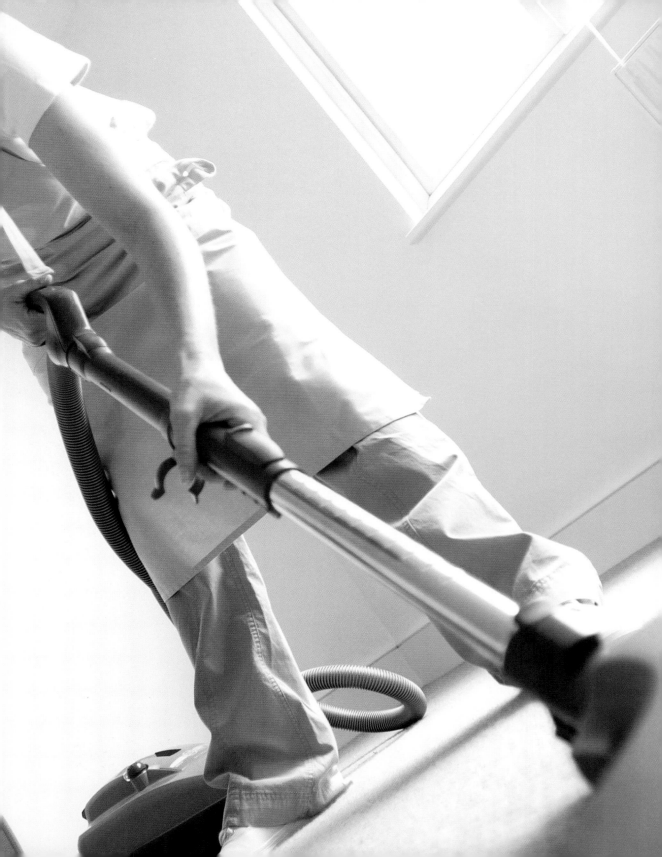

Fresh underfoot:
caring for floors

Dirt on the floor isn't just unsightly; it's the prime cause of premature wear on floor materials. Dust and grit scratch smooth floor finishes, remove wax and protective coatings, and crush carpet fibres and backings. The solution: simple daily care routines that keep them clean – and avoid the need for elbow grease down the road.

Caring for carpets

The three keys for clean and healthy carpets? Vacuum regularly, treat spills and stains promptly, and have carpets deep cleaned once a year. First rule of carpet care: vacuum regularly, even if the carpet doesn't look dirty. The vacuum delivers a one-two punch: combining suction, which pulls free dust inside the vacuum bag or dirt bin, with agitation from a beater bar, which fans carpet fibres, raising them and releasing dirt and debris. For high-traffic living areas, daily vacuuming keeps carpet dirt under control; less-used rooms, such as guest rooms, still need weekly or bi-weekly attention. Here's how to vacuum carpet for best results:

■ **Inspect the area to be vacuumed.** Remove any small objects that could be sucked into the vacuum.
■ **Check the vacuum.** Straighten kinked hoses, and empty the dirt bin or vacuum bag if needed.
■ **Plug in the vacuum, and go to it!** To save your back, vacuum in short strokes, moving forwards across the room. Overlap strokes for even coverage of the carpet.
■ **Work in alternating directions.** For best cleaning and to raise carpet nap, make passes across the room in alternating directions. After covering the carpet, turn 90-degrees and vacuum again in a perpendicular direction.
■ **Finish with skirting boards and wall edges.** Use an extension wand and crevice tool to clean dust from these areas.

◄ **Household carpets** look lovely on the surface, but in the course of daily life, they collect dust, dirt, skin flakes, and pet dander, so it is essential to vacuum them on a regular basis.

Speed is of the essence when removing spills and stains from carpeting. The longer stains stand, the more chance that the substance will soak through the carpet backing and pool up in the carpet pad beneath.

To treat liquid spills and stains:
■ **Blot up as much of a liquid spill** as possible. Use clean white cleaning cloths or white kitchen roll to avoid dye transfer. Continue to blot gently, using fresh cloths, until no more liquid can be absorbed.
■ **Don't scrub** or brush the stain.
■ **Apply an appropriate carpet spot-remover.** Spot-test the product in an inconspicuous place before using.

For solid or semi-solid spills:
■ **Use a spoon or spatula** to scrape up as much of the spilled material as possible. Don't use a knife, even a blunt one, as it can harm carpet fibres.
■ **Allow the spill to dry,** then brush gently to release it from carpet fibres. Vacuum up as much of the spilled material as possible.
■ **Treat any remaining stain** with an appropriate spot-remover.

Treating spills and stains

Carpet deep-cleaning Carpets will keep their beauty longest if deep cleaned at least once a year – but this job is one where it pays to bring in the professionals. You can deep-clean your own carpets if you know what you're doing – but it's a big, dirty job, and one where home methods and machinery don't yet match the cleaning firepower available to the professionals. Should finances or circumstances require home deep cleaning of carpets, observe these cautions:

- **Know your carpet.** Be sure you understand the type of cleaning method recommended by your carpet's manufacturers.
- **Stick to steamers, not shampooers.** When you buy or rent a carpet cleaner, choose a carpet steamer. Older "carpet shampoo" units use rotary agitators to apply detergent solution and may overwet carpets. The shampoo film can be difficult to remove, causing resoiling.
- **Vacuum first.** Dirt plus water equals mud, which is almost impossible to remove. Before cleaning the carpet, vacuum thoroughly to remove as much loose dirt as possible.
- **Buy the right cleaners.** Stick with cleaning products designed specifically for home carpet cleaning, and follow package directions to mix cleaning solutions.
- **Pretreat.** Use a traffic-lane cleaner or pre-spray to treat areas of high soiling before cleaning.
- **Keep it dry.** Over-saturated carpets aren't cleaner, just wetter. After extracting, make a second dry pass over the carpet to remove as much moisture as possible. Keep traffic off freshly cleaned carpeting until it is dry.

Hard-surface floors

As with carpets, routine cleaning is the best way to maintain the beauty of hard-surface flooring. Daily sweeping, vacuuming, or dust-mopping removes abrasive grit and dust from the floor. Establishing a "shoes-off" policy and using door mats helps prevent dirt from the street from entering the home and being trodden into floors.

When it's time to clean, clean with a light hand. Hard-surface floors look best when clean and clear, but detergent use or cleaner build-up can create a hazy film that dulls floors – and attracts and holds more dirt. Rely on these cleaning tips to keep hard-surface floors looking clean and beautiful:

Vinyl and linoleum floors To care for vinyl and linoleum, sweep, vacuum, or dust-mop daily to remove surface grit. Damp-mop with clear water to remove dirt and restore shine. For more heavily soiled floors, vacuum first, then wet-mop floors using a very light solution of about 1–2 teaspoons washing-up liquid per 4 litres (1 gallon) of warm water. Rinse the floor with clean water before drying it with white cleaning cloths.

If there are depressions in the floor, use a household sponge to loosen any dirt in these areas as you clean, then rinse with fresh clear water.

Hardwood floors These floors are susceptible to abrasion, are easily dented, and can be damaged by moisture or incorrect cleaning methods. Remove dust and surface dirt from hardwoods daily, preferably with a large-headed microfibre dust mop. Alternatively, hardwood floors may be vacuumed, but be sure to turn the beater bars off to avoid scratching the floor. When necessary, damp-mop with plain water to pick up dirt, using a barely-wet mop. Avoid any drips or standing water; the mop head or terry mop cover should be wrung until nearly dry before it touches the floor. A solution of white vinegar and water will up the cleaning ante, so try it for stubborn dirt.

More intense cleaning will require a cleaning product formulated for the floor's specific finish.

Ceramic tile floors Keep ceramic tile floors looking their best with daily sweeping or vacuuming to remove surface grit. If using a vacuum, set the beater bar to the off position to vacuum.

Every week or so, damp mop with a solution of 2 tablespoons washing-up liquid to 4 litres (1 gallon) of warm water. Use a cleaning toothbrush to scrub stained or dirty grout. Rinse with clear water. Buff the tiles with a clean, dry towel to remove any water spots. Never apply wax to ceramic tile floors; it can be difficult to remove, can cause slip-and-fall injuries, and may interfere with resealing grout.

Do not use bleach or cleaners containing bleach to clean stained grout. Also avoid cleaners that contain coloured dyes. For advice on cleaning heavily stained grout, see pages 192–3.

▶ **Ceramic tile floors** are tough – if brittle – and are easy to keep clean with a daily sweep plus a damp-mop once a week.

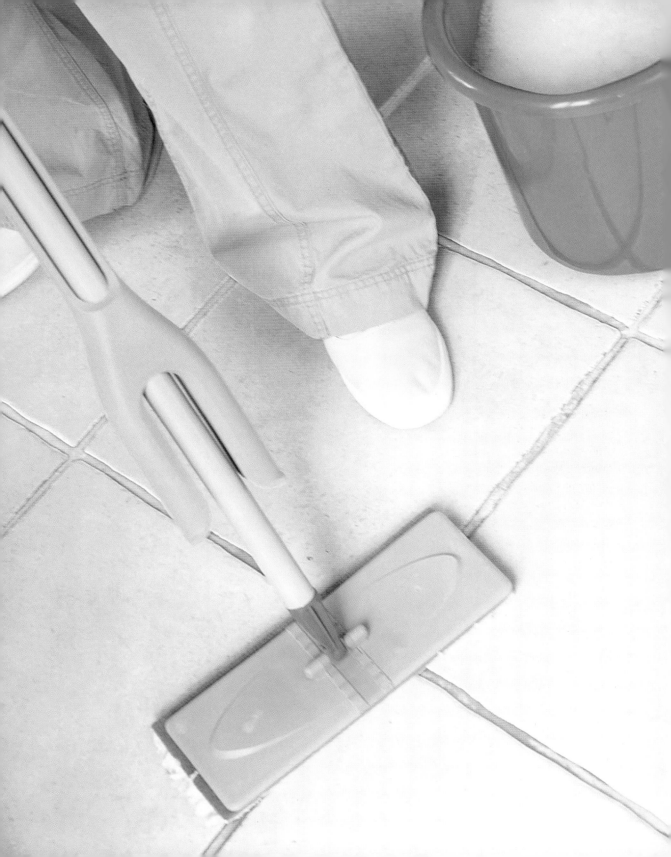

Sitting pretty:
caring for furniture

Fine wood furniture is a treasured possession in any home, and with good care, it can last for generations. Upholstered furniture provides us with comfort, colour, and texture. Maintained properly, upholstered pieces will give long furniture life.

Caring for leather furniture

Leather upholstery can last for many years if looked after correctly. Follow these tips to take good care of leather furnishings:

- **Keep away from heat and light.** Leather furniture is very sensitive to heat and sun damage. Position it away from windows, and from heat sources such as fireplaces, radiators, or central heating vents.
- **Uncoated leathers.** Furniture made from uncoated leathers should be dusted frequently. A soft putty rubber may remove some stains or deposits safely, but do not use leather creams, conditioners, or saddle soap on uncoated leather, since these products can change the colour or appearance of the leather.
- **Coated leathers.** Check with the manufacturer for recommended cleaning methods. Vacuum regularly to remove surface soil. Commonly, leather creams or conditioners may be used to clean coated leather once or twice or year. Test leather cleaners in an inconspicuous spot before using.
- **Avoid unsuitable products.** Never use oil, furniture polish, dusting sprays, or ordinary stain removers on leather furniture.

Fine wood furniture

Care for fine furniture with these recommendations:

- **Avoid heat and light.** In a natural state, wood contains a surprising amount of moisture. Preserving appropriate moisture levels is key to the preservation of fine furniture. Accordingly, position fine wood furniture away from radiators, heating vents, or fireplaces. Don't store fine furniture in lofts, where temperature and humidity levels vary widely from summer to winter, and from day and night. Avoid placing furniture in areas where it will sit in direct sunlight, which can fade fine furniture; use curtains, sheers, or protective window films to guard against the sun's rays.
- **Protect from damage.** Everyday life can be hard on wood furniture. Moisture from sweating beverage glasses leaves round rings in the finish, while the heat from a hot dish can ruin the wood finish beneath. Provide cork- or felt-bottomed coasters if you will set glasses or mugs on fine wood, and always use trivets to support hot serving dishes. Place mats, tablecloths, or padded table covers protect dining room tables from spills or scrapes.
- **Clean safely.** Dust frequently (*see page 171*). Occasionally, wood furniture will require heavier cleaning. To remove greasy stains or the film from cigarette smoke, use a furniture balm as instructed on the bottle. Apply a little balm to a clean soft cotton cloth and gently stroke the furniture, in the direction of the grain, to loosen the dirt. If the balm leaves an oily residue (for example, if the furniture has a French polish finish), wipe off any excess with fresh cleaning cloths.

Note: seek professional advice before cleaning if the wood is in poor condition or the item of furniture is an antique.

Polish or wax? Both wax and furniture polish are applied to fine wood furniture to protect the surface – but you'll need to pick one or the other. Don't try to combine these products or you'll create a gummy mess. Make sure that you have selected the appropriate treatment for the piece's finish. Check with the manufacturer for recommended polish or wax options.

Which to choose? Wax is a semi-solid product; it requires elbow grease to apply, but it creates a long-lasting coat. Furniture polish is easier to apply than wax; it is made using petroleum distillates (a solvent), and evaporates fairly quickly. Most people overuse polish to restore a fresh finish. Layers of polish build-up, combined with body oils and dirt, create a sticky, dull film over the surface. If you use polish, use it with restraint.

The same applies to furniture sprays. They contain silicone oil, which is inert and which does not evaporate like furniture polish. Use them sparingly, and buff the sprayed area well with a clean cloth. Buff it again to raise the shine.

Apply wax or polish to furniture about once every six months; treat with furniture balm first if required (*see Clean safely, opposite*). Follow package directions, and have plenty of clean white cleaning cloths available.

Note: seek professional advice for the care of antique furniture, or if the wood is in poor condition.

Upholstered furniture

Dust and dirt act like sandpaper on furniture fabric, so remove it frequently. Vacuum upholstered furniture weekly; lift cushions, and use the crevice tool to remove hidden crumbs beneath. Keep upholstered furniture looking new with these tips:

■ **Flip, swap, and rearrange.** Being territorial creatures, most humans gravitate to their favourite places – but when it's the same seat on a long sofa day after day, that preference will start to show. Flip loose cushions regularly, and rotate them on a multi-cushion unit. Similarly, rearrange upholstered furniture once or twice a year to distribute wear more evenly. Switch the position of a chaise longue and a sofa, or swap the positions of a set of chairs as the seasons change.

■ **Arm caps.** Places where bare skin or hair come to rest – armrests, chair backs, seat cushions – are subjected to higher levels of dirt and abrasion. Protect high-contact areas of

▲ **Wax adds shine** and provides the best protection against scratches and damage. It'll remain on the piece longer than furniture polish, and needs less frequent maintenance.

upholstered furniture with arm caps tailored to fit snugly over chair and sofa arms. Made from the same upholstery fabric, they're all but indistinguishable as they protect fabric from wear.

■ **Slipcovers.** In areas with hot summer weather, consider washable slip covers. Traditionally applied to furniture during the warm season, slipcovers protect against sweat, suntan oil, and other summer hazards.

■ **Fabric protection.** Spray-on fabric protectors coat fibres and protect upholstery from spills and stains. Fabric protectors can be applied at the mill as the fabric is processed, by the furniture retailer, or at home using commercial spray products. If you apply fabric protection yourself, read the product instructions and observe safety procedures carefully.

Dust is everywhere, but no one wants to see it film fine wood furniture. Keep your cherished pieces glowing with these dusting tips:

■ **Clean safely.** Dust fine furniture often with a lambswool duster or barely damp white cotton cleaning cloth. Microfibre cloths do a good job of attracting and removing fine blown-in dust and dirt. Avoid using a feather duster, as a broken quill can scratch and damage delicate finishes.

■ **Dust damp.** Dusting with a dry cloth can scratch, so lightly spritz your cleaning cloth with water, a spray dusting agent, or wood polish. Never spray furniture directly, as overspray can leave a difficult-to-remove film. Follow the grain of the wood as you dust to avoid cross-grain scratches.

■ **Dust often.** Frequent dusting removes dirt before it has a chance to settle in and make itself at home. Dusting often keeps an oily build-up from forming on wood furniture.

Caring for
beds and mattresses

A good night's sleep starts with a good bed. How does yours stack up? Since we spend one-third of our lives in them, beds and mattresses deserve proper care. They'll repay us with a clean, healthy place to sleep. Whether heaped with pillows or minimally spare, beds and bedding will stay in top shape with these tips.

The Pea Princess' guide to mattress care

While the fairy tale "The Princess and the Pea" was meant to show the delicacy of the true princess, in reality, it showed up her future mother-in-law's housekeeping habits. Keep your castle's bedding in top shape with these tips for mattress care:

■ **Frame it right.** Just as our bodies need the support of a good mattress, so mattresses need a proper place to rest. Purchase mattress and base as a set to make sure that the two pieces will work together harmoniously. Check the bed frame; larger mattress sizes – queen- or king-sized beds – require centre support or full-width slats to span the wider width.

■ **Take a seasonal spin.** Unless the manufacturer advises otherwise, rotate mattresses from heel to toe when the seasons change. To rotate, revolve the end of the mattress nearest the headboard towards the foot of the bed, then nudge the mattress back into place on the base. Rotating mattresses helps prevent the formation of sleeping "wallows," caused by the same body in the same spot every night.

■ **Flip it.** Some mattresses should also be flipped when the seasons change. While pillow-top mattresses should not be flipped, other mattresses wear more evenly when the bottom surface nearest the base is flipped over to the top of the bed during a seasonal rotation. Check with your manufacturer for specific recommendations for your model.

■ **Ban bouncing.** Kids enjoy bouncing on the bed, but the poor mattresses loathe the practice. Discourage these child gymnasts. Jumping on beds can damage mattresses and base, and fracture bed frames.

■ **Use protection.** Sweet dreams are the goal, but accidents happen. Protect mattresses from messy mishaps with mattress pads. They'll absorb moisture and spills before they soak through to the mattress.

■ **Suck it up.** Regular vacuuming will keep mattresses clean and fresh. Remove all bedding from the mattress, then use the upholstery brush to vacuum the top surface and sides of the mattress. Vacuuming removes dust, skin flakes, and the dust mites that feed upon body waste. Vacuum mattresses thoroughly when rotating them seasonally.

■ **Clean stains safely.** If a stain does occur, use an upholstery shampoo as directed to remove it. An alternative cleaner, recommended by manufacturers for use on mattresses, is called "dry suds". Create them by placing about 125ml (¼ cup) of washing-up liquid in a small mixer bowl. Turn the mixer on,

"Rotating mattresses helps prevent the formation of sleeping 'wallows.'"

and add a few teaspoons of water, a teaspoon at a time. Stand back! The bowl will quickly fill with foam. Scrape the top layer of foam into a small bowl, and take it to the mattress. Rub the stained area gently with the foam, using a sponge or a soft brush, being sure not to wet the padding beneath. Leave the mattress exposed until it is thoroughly dry before replacing the bedding.

Controlling allergens in the bedroom

We share our sleeping quarters with more than family pets or beloved teddy bears. Carpet, window treatments, and mattresses collect dust and dander and provide a happy playground for dust mites. Found anywhere there are humans, humidity, and warm temperatures, dust mites are a major cause of allergic symptoms in the home. More correctly, it's their faeces and dead body parts that cause allergic reactions – and their food source is us! Dust mites feed on discarded skin flakes, making bedding and bedrooms prime dust-mite sites.

Over the years, they'll multiply inside mattresses to the point where it's estimated that 50 per cent of the weight of a 10-year-old mattress is caused by dust mites and their leavings. If family members wake each morning with puffy eyes and sneezing noses, it's time to control allergens in the bedroom. Fight back against dust mites, dander, dust, and pollen with these tips:

■ **Cover mattresses.** Use vinyl covers designed to form a barrier between mites and the mattress.

■ **Replace down products.** Pillows, duvets, and other items should be made from synthetic fibres. Encase pillows in vinyl covers for added protection.

■ **Clean well and often.** Regular cleaning is the best defence against allergens and dust mites.

■ **Send the dog to other quarters.** Bed down household pets in an area outside the bedroom if allergies are a problem. Pet dander is an allergen for many, and pets shed fur and skin cells, too, promoting dust mite populations. Banish the dog from the bedroom at night, and make it up to him with extra walkies in the morning – after a good night's sleep.

■ **Keep humidity levels low.** Dust mites die back when there's insufficient moisture in the air. In humid climates, use a portable or whole-house dehumidifier to reduce in-house humidity levels to between 30 per cent and 50 per cent.

■ **Keep cool.** Mites thrive in warm weather, so keep household temperatures on the low side in the bedroom.

▶ **Fresh and free.** Surprising amounts of dust and dirt filter down onto mattresses through sheets and mattress pads. Regular vacuuming reduces dust and allergens and promotes sound sleep.

■ **Fight back with spring-cleaning.** Because mites grow best in warm, humid weather, take advantage of early spring to clean the house. Vacuuming and dusting will remove the mites who've wintered over before they can run riot in spring.

■ **Kiss Teddy good-bye.** Stuffed toys are a comfort for children of all ages, but harbour dust mites just as mattresses do. Replace the teddy bear with a plastic model for a healthier night's sleep.

■ **Wash bedding often, in hot water.** Temperatures of 54°C (130°F) are required to kill mites; mites can survive cold-water washing. Wash sheets and pillowcases weekly, and give pillows, duvets, and blankets a trip to the washer every month to six weeks.

■ **Pitch the houseplants.** They are lovely to look at, but plants bring pollen, insects, dust, and microbes into the bedroom. For best rest, restrict them to other rooms.

Blowing hot and cold:
heating and cooling systems

Gas or oil boilers, heat pumps or forced air, heating and cooling systems are essential components of home comfort and safety. Treat them well to keep them blowing hot and cold. Your comfort, your power bill – and your household's safety in inclement weather – depend upon good care and proper maintenance.

Safety tips for fireplaces

Improper burning practices can encourage formation of creosote – a highly combustible coating that is deposited inside chimneys during fireplace use. Creosote build-up creates a risk of chimney fires. Use these safe-burning practices to lessen the danger:

- **Burn only dry, seasoned wood.** "Green" wood contains moisture that encourages the creation of creosote. Season green wood at least six months before burning.
- **Avoid burning rubbish.** Do not put newspaper, gift-wrap, cardboard boxes, Christmas trees, or any other kind of rubbish on an open fire or in a wood-burning stove.
- **Build small, hot fires.** These will burn completely, as opposed to large cool fires. The lower temperatures slow smoke release and form more creosote than hot fires.
- **Give fires adequate air circulation.** Closing stove or fireplace doors too tightly slows the release of smoke, making it more likely that creosote will form.
- **Inspect and clean.** Have chimneys professionally inspected and cleaned regularly, at least once a year.

Add these maintenance routines to your schedule to keep hard-working heating and cooling systems happy on the job:

- **Safety, reliability, and efficiency.** If you have gas central heating, make sure you know how to shut off the gas supply at the meter. If you smell gas or suspect a gas leak, open doors and windows, turn off the gas at the meter, and call the gas utility emergency line. Do not operate light switches or any other electrical items, including doorbells. Do not smoke, light a match, or use a naked flame.
- **Change filters regularly.** If you have a forced air heating or cooling system, make sure air filters are not clogged. They reduce airflow and make heating and cooling systems work longer and harder, consuming more energy and causing premature wear. Check system manuals, and change disposable filters regularly to keep air flowing freely. Changed once a month, disposable filters clean the air of dirt, mould spores, and pollen before it settles as dust on household surfaces.
- **Keep compressors free and clear.** Central air conditioning and heat pump systems rely on outdoor compressor units to exchange hot air for cold. To do the job, these units need unobstructed surroundings. Each spring and autumn, check the area around compressors for obstructions. Prune or trim any encroaching shrubs or plants. Remove leaves and debris from the sides and base of the unit.
- **Schedule service calls early.** Heating and air conditioning systems require regular professional maintenance. Don't wait for the first chilly night or hot day. Schedule tune-ups before the weather changes. You'll have the service technician's full

attention if he's not hopping to respond to emergency calls after the first hard freeze. Gas appliances and oil boilers should be serviced annually by a qualified engineer. Your engineer can also service your heating system and advice you on efficient use. Unserviced gas appliances can and do kill, so fit a carbon monoxide detector in any room with a gas appliance and check it regularly. Serviced appliances run more efficiently and save you money.

■ **Ask for advice**. While he's on the premises, ask the engineer for advice about your heating and cooling systems. Most techs love talking about their job, and are happy to give pointers on how to keep your unit running efficiently.

■ **Fine-tune thermostats.** If your household has a programmable thermostat, turn down the heat at night, or when the family is out during the day, then raise the settings for the morning and evening hours. Try to keep thermostat temperatures steady for best comfort and energy savings.

Fire it up!

Who can resist the lure of a crackling fire? Know how to use fires safely for warm good nights by following these tips:

■ **Maintain wood-burning stoves.** Wood-burning stoves can be freestanding or designed as inserts to existing fireplaces. They increase energy efficiency when burning wood as a heat source. Make sure that household wood-burning stoves are installed properly, and use them according to instructions. You'll need to know how to properly load wood, empty ash pits, and clean a household wood-burning stove unit; the product manual, manufacturer, or stove installer should provide instructions for safe and efficient use.

■ **Dispose of ashes safely.** Ashes generated by wood-burning stoves or fireplaces may appear to be cool – but many a house fire has been started by improper disposal of fireplace ashes. Ashes retain their ability to kindle fire for several days,

> ## "Try to keep thermostat temperatures steady for best comfort and energy savings."

so use great care when disposing of them. When cleaning a fireplace, place the ashes in a metal container, moisten them, and cover the container with a metal lid. Never use a paper bag to store or dispose of fireplace ashes. Use only a dustpan and brush to collect ashes from the fireplace – never use the vacuum cleaner around ashes. Keep the discarded ashes in the metal container, tightly covered, for at least four days.

When selecting a disposal site, avoid wooded areas. If disposing of ashes in a garden or flower bed, make sure you remove all leaves or dry vegetation from the disposal area, and ensure that the site is located well away from wooden fences or furniture. Tilling ashes into the top layer of soil will decrease the danger and increase the benefit to garden plants.

◀ **Know your systems.** A breakdown is no time to try to get acquainted with household heating or cooling systems. Learn how your system works and where it's located before trouble strikes.

Plumb perfect: maintenance tips
for plumbing systems

Plumbing. It's been with us since Roman times, but today's homes have a lavish supply of hot and cold water on demand, thanks to modern plumbing systems. The principles are simple – pressure and valves – but if they fail, the household may be faced with a soggy mess. When this happens, act quickly to avert major problems.

Smart householders know how to spot and resolve small plumbing problems before they become major issues at home. Help your plumbing stay dry and happy with these tips:

■ **Keep an eye out for trouble.** When it comes to plumbing, little leaks can lead to big problems. Be alert to signs of impending plumbing failures; leaking taps, damp cupboards, rocking toilets, or dripping refrigerators all signal problems that need prompt attention.

"When it comes to plumbing, little leaks can lead to big problems."

■ **Repair problems early.** A leaking tap isn't just annoying; the moisture it releases puts wear on sink fixtures and can encourage the growth of mould and mildew. Stay on top of problems to keep the household clean and dry.

■ **Know where to go when trouble happens.** Should plumbing fail, will you know how to stop the flood? Make sure that you know where the stop valve for the mains water supply is located. If it's fitted internally, it is may be situated under the kitchen sink, but if it's in a dark, hidden, or hard-to-reach place, make sure you have a torch standing nearby. Alternatively, you may find that the stop valve for the mains water supply is located externally, under a cover in your garden or main path.

■ **Shutting off appliances.** Similarly, know how to shut off the water supply to sinks, toilets, washing machines, and water-using appliances such as the refrigerator's icemaker. Should they misbehave, knowing the location of the relevant stop valve will save the day – and a lot of wet clear up.

■ **Learn how to tackle small problems.** With a few tools and a little knowledge, most of us can handle small plumbing emergencies. If your tool kit includes a plunger, a pipe wrench, and a drain augur, you'll be able to take care of small problems like clogged drains, blocked toilets, stuck valves, and dripping taps. How-to books, home improvement shops, and adult education classes can pay for themselves when it's time to call the plumber.

Cold snap: keep plumbing safe in cold weather

In hard-winter climates, freezing pipes can create a sudden household emergency. Frozen water expands, cracking pipes; when the area thaws, the cracks vent a flood. Plumbing help can be hard to find in a weather crisis, so try these tips:

■ **Prevent frozen pipes before they start.** The best defence is insulation. Insulate exposed pipes in the loft or in the garage with easy-to-install foam insulation. Before winter comes, remove exterior hoses and turn off supplies to outside taps.

■ **When extreme cold weather strikes, go into action.** Open the cupboards beneath sinks and bathroom fixtures; warmer household air will help prevent the pipes inside from freezing. Opening taps to a bare trickle keeps water flowing and avoids a frozen blockage.

■ **If pipes do freeze, don't panic.** First, turn off the mains water supply to the house, then open a tap near the blocked area to vent pressure from the frozen water. If you suspect that pipes in the hot water system are frozen, turn off the hot water system to avoid the risk of an explosion. Either apply hot water bottles or use a hair dryer to warm the frozen pipe (never use an open flame to thaw a pipe), starting at the end of the pipe nearest to the tap. (Don't use a hair dryer in areas of standing water.) You'll know the pipe has begun to thaw when water begins to trickle from the open tap. When the flow is restored, check the plumbing carefully for cracks or leaks. Call a licensed plumber if your efforts are unsuccessful.

■ **If the pipes burst, don't panic.** Turn off all the stop valves in the house, and if this doesn't control the water flow immediately, open all the cold water taps to help the system

"With a few tools and a little knowledge, most of us can handle small plumbing emergencies."

drain quickly. It is important not to turn on the hot water taps, and you should turn off all heating systems. Call a licensed plumber as soon as possible.

Maintaining water conditioning systems

In hard-water areas, water softeners condition water to remove unwanted minerals. Softened water uses less soap, prevents mineral build-in pipes, and extends the life of appliances and hot water heaters.

Keep water softeners on the job with proper maintenance. Most models use a salt-exchange method that depends on a supply of salt pellets or nuggets. You should use the type of salt recommended by your manufacturer for best results. Check the brine tank regularly to be sure salt levels are adequate (about once a month). The salt should sit above the water line. "Salt bridging" occurs when a crust of salt forms over the top of the water in the brine tank; break it up by

▲ **Clean and flowing.** Plumbing systems are relatively simple, so don't be intimidated by small repairs. Simple maintenance routines and easy plumbing repairs keep the water flowing.

adding hot water to the tank or by poking the crust with a broomstick if it occurs.

After a period of use, water softeners will need to regenerate or recharge: the unit will flush collection areas of accumulated mineral particles pulled from hard water. If your unit offers an automatic regeneration scheduling, use it – you'll have soft water automatically. If your unit requires manual recharging, stick carefully to the manufacturer's recommended time intervals.

Power play:
electrical safety at home

It's a true miracle: the electrical power that infuses your home. Your electrical system keeps the lights on and the household humming, and illuminates every aspect of life. Power has its price, however. Treat your electrical system with respect: learn these simple safety routines and schedule maintenance jobs.

Follow these guidelines to maintain your home's electrical system and keep the lights on and the power flowing:

■ **Be alert for problems.** Keep a careful eye out for electrical hazards at home. A flickering lamp or crimped extension cable could cause a short — or worse, a fire. Be on the lookout for frayed or bent leads, hot plugs or sockets, or a shock or tingling when you touch an appliance.

■ **Repair quickly.** If an appliance appears to have an electrical problem, take it out of active use until it is repaired. Don't pass the trouble on to others by donating or selling the item. Have the appliance repaired if possible; if not, dispose of it to keep every home safe.

■ **Know your fuse box.** Most homes have a central fuse box or breaker panel. This service box controls delivery of power to different areas of the home. At the fuse box, you can cut power to any — or all — areas of the home.

■ **Take time to get familiar with your fuse box.** If it uses fuses, lay in a supply of extra fuses for emergencies. Work as a team with another family member to label each circuit; labels will make it easier to cut the power in the right place if an emergency arises.

■ **Test RCDs monthly.** Residual current devices, known as RCDs, have a sensor that detects fluctuations in electrical current; when current surges, they shut down to protect against shock. RCDs have small coloured buttons or switches that permit you to reset a tripped circuit. The T "test" button allows you to test the RCD. Test RCDs once a month, and after any thunderstorms, to be sure their protective function continues

to work. Replace them if they no longer trip when the "test" button is pressed.

Use electricity safely

Prevent shock hazards and system outages by observing these safety rules:

■ **Water and electricity.** Don't use hair dryers or any other electrical equipment in the bathroom; keep all electrical appliances away from water.

■ **Take the right precautions.** Unplug appliances before you clean them, and never carry a small appliance by the cord.

■ **Avoid overloading.** Don't overload sockets with multiple plugs. Avoid the use of "multiplugs", and if a plug or cable feels warm, unplug it immediately. A multi-socket trailing adaptor is preferable to a block adaptor that plugs straight into the sock. Don't plug adaptors into adaptors; use one socket per adaptor.

■ **Avoid extension cable hazards.** Don't run extension cables under rugs, under carpets, or across doorways. They're a potential trip hazard, and they can wear through.

■ **Keep electric blankets safe.** Electric blankets are a common cause of fires. Have them serviced every 3 years.

■ **Childproof electrical sockets.** Install childproof socket caps on electrical sockets in households with young children.

■ **Check light bulbs.** Make sure that light bulbs have the correct wattage for the lamp in which they'll be used. Don't use bulbs with a higher wattage than that specified by the fixture. This can overheat the bulb, and may cause a fire. Tighten light bulbs securely; loose bulbs can also overheat.

Checklist for household systems

Household systems work hard to keep us comfortable and safe. Keep them running smoothly with this maintenance list (see also pages 174–5):

Every month:

■ Check bathrooms, kitchens, and utility rooms for leaking taps or signs of water damage. If the refrigerator has an ice dispenser, include it in the inspection.
■ If you have a forced air heating or cooling system, change the filters. Clean air filtration devices as recommended by the manufacturer.
■ Test smoke detectors.
■ Test remote alarm systems according to the instructions of the monitoring service.

Every 3 months:

■ Make an inventory of first aid supplies. Replace any missing items. (Print a free first aid kit inventory checklist at Organized Home.Com; see also page 181.)
■ Hold a family fire drill, and review the family disaster plan with all household residents.
■ Remove and replace or clean kitchen extractor filters. Most can be washed in the dishwasher to remove grease build-up (check the product manual for instructions). Alternatively, spray washable filters with a degreaser, and then rinse. Dry them before replacing.

Every 6 months:

■ Replace batteries in smoke and carbon monoxide detectors.
■ Check fire extinguishers to make sure they're charged and ready for use.
■ Clean the ashes from the fireplace or a wood-burning stove, and empty the ash pit (do more frequently if required).
■ Check the hoses installed on washing machines, and replace them if they show signs of wear, or every two years.
■ Vacuum refrigerator coils to remove dust.
■ Check refrigerator gaskets with the "bank note" test: insert a bank note between the door and the refrigerator. If you can pull it out easily, the refrigerator gaskets are loose and they should be replaced.

Pre-holiday checklist

Nothing spoils a good holiday quicker than discovering that a problem cropped up at home while you were gone. Before you leave, put the house to bed with this pre-holiday checklist:

■ **Turn off hot water heaters.** As big tanks of hot water stored under high pressure, unattended water heaters present a real hazard in an empty house. Ask your plumber to show you how to power them down properly, cut off the water supply, and depressurize the tank. Instructions will vary depending on whether the water heater is gas or electric.

■ **Shut down optional plumbing features.** To avoid sudden leaks, shut off the water to refrigerator icemakers, humidifiers, or in-sink water heaters before you leave.

■ **Unplug telephones and electronic devices.** Summer thunderstorms or disruptions to the power supply can damage televisions, computers, and audio equipment, even when surge protectors are in place. Before travelling, unplug electronic devices from power sources and phone lines. Since voltage surges can travel along telephone connections, unplug all telephones except the one with the answering machine.

■ **Set thermostats to a maintenance setting.** Where possible, turn off central heating and cooling systems, but if travelling at the height of summer or dead of winter, your home will need some protection against temperature extremes. Set thermostats to a maintenance setting for safety: 13°C (55°F) in winter, 30°C (85°F) in summer. These settings will protect the house and its contents.

Be prepared with a
family disaster plan

Life happens – and so does fire, flood, and natural disaster. Will your family know what to do if disaster strikes? Just as schoolchildren practice fire drills, family members need to prepare for the unexpected. A family disaster plan teaches everyone what to do and where to go when an emergency arises.

Make a family disaster plan

Does your family know what to do in the event of fire, earthquake, or severe weather? A simple family disaster plan will help all family members deal with natural disasters on the home front. If you live in a high risk area for natural hazards – for example forest fires or floods – emergency management agencies will advice you on what you will need for an emergency kit, and what action to take in the event of an emergency. Your local council may also be able to provide help and advice.

To create a family disaster plan, follow this advice from the British Red Cross (for advice in other countries, contact your local Red Cross office):

Practical advice for emergencies

The following practical guidelines provide advice on how to prepare for and deal with emergencies:

Preparing for an emergency:
- Keep all family and friends' home and work phone numbers with you. Select someone living away to be your contact point. If anything happens contact them.
- Pack an emergency bag and keep it handy:
  - ✳ Bottled water
  - ✳ High-energy food
  - ✳ Radio with spare batteries
  - ✳ Torch with spare batteries
  - ✳ Essential medication
  - ✳ First aid kit

- Ensure your mains electrical, gas, and water valves/switches are well marked and you can turn them on and off.
- Go on a two-hour Red Cross "Save a life" course
- If you can't go an a Red Cross course, the British Red Cross produce a first aid CD-ROM.

If an emergency strikes:
- Listen to local radio. Follow the advice of the emergency services.
- Check for immediate dangers like smoke, water, unsafe buildings.
- Assist vulnerable people near you.
- Give first aid and get help.
- Prepare to evacuate yourself, family, vulnerable neighbours, and pets.
- If you have time and it is safe to do so, take your emergency bag with you.
- Follow your personal contact plan.

Be safe checklist

In addition to the guidelines above, complete the following checklist:
- Post emergency telephone numbers by the phones: Fire Police, Ambulance
- Teach children how and when to call the emergency services for emergency help.
- Check if you have adequate insurance coverage.
- Install smoke detectors on each level of your home, especially near bedrooms.

- Conduct a home-hazard hunt.
- Determine the best escape routes from your home. Find two ways out of each room.
- Find the safe places in your home for each type of disaster.

Practise and maintain your plan:
- Quiz your kids every six months or so.
- Conduct fire and emergency evacuations.
- Replace any stored water and stored food every six months (see also Setting up a store cupboard on pages 120–1).
- Test and recharge your fire extinguisher(s) according to the manufacturer's instructions.
- Test your smoke detectors monthly and change the batteries at least once a year.
- Check and update emergency numbers on telephone lists and mobile phones.

The first aid kit
The following list covers the contents of a basic first aid kit. In addition, you may want to include a first aid manual and a torch and extra batteries for emergency use. Keep the kit out of reach of children.

- Antiseptic wipes
- Tweezers
- Antiseptic ointment
- Antiseptic solution
- Assorted plasters
- Sterile gauze
- Adhesive tape
- Selection of bandages
- Sharp scissors
- Safety pins
- Plastic gloves
- Painkillers (paracetamol and ibuprofen)
- Diarrhoea medication
- Insect repellant
- Thermometer
- Instant cold packs

Fire, weather disaster, or earthquake can happen any time, anywhere. When the unexpected disrupts life at home, keep these points in mind to stay safe:

- Remain calm and patient. Put your plan into action.
- Check for injuries.
- Give first aid and get help for seriously injured people.
- Listen to your battery-powered radio for news and instructions.

Check for damage in your home
- Use torches. Do not light matches or turn on electrical switches, if you suspect damage.
- Sniff for gas leaks, starting at the water heater. If you smell gas or suspect a leak, turn off the gas supply at the meter, open windows, and get everyone outside quickly.
- Shut off any other damaged utilities. (You will need a professional to turn gas back on.)
- Clean up spilled medicines, bleaches, petrol, and other flammable liquids immediately.

Remember to ...
- Confine or secure your pets.
- Call your family contact – do not use the telephone again unless it is a life-threatening emergency.
- Check on your neighbours, especially elderly or disabled individuals.
- Make sure you have an adequate water supply in case the service is cut off.
- Stay away from downed power lines.

Room by room around the house, clutter can stage a seemingly never-ending battle for space and place. While the principles for clearing clutter and regaining calm remain the same, specific tactics are needed for the distinct types of clutter challenges posed by the rooms in your home.

Private areas, such as bedrooms and bathrooms, may suffer from function overload, expected to do too many jobs in the same space. Public areas are afflicted with "too many generals" issues; in these shared spaces, fighting chaos is a team effort, and requires coordination with, and cooperation from, all members of the household.

In this section, we'll move through each area of the home to cut clutter, get organized, and clean the house. We'll apply the STOP clutter methods to fight disorder from the master bedroom to children's play spaces, entry hall to family room. We'll declutter books and magazine, entertainment areas, and create order among the arts and crafts supplies.

Fighting clutter room by room:
where does the shoe pinch?

Room by room, clutter and chaos take hold, complicating even simple everyday actions – but not all clutter is created equal. Where does your clutter shoe pinch? Pile-ups of "stuff" give valuable clues to where life isn't working. Let the clutter lead the way, and solve the biggest problems first.

Observe clutter clues A heaped-up dining room table, covered with mail and paperwork, signals a need for a household paper management centre (*see pages 226–7*). Piles of rucksacks, shoes, school projects, and jackets at the back door indicate an informal – and messy – attempt to create a family Launch Pad (*see pages 186–7*). Bathroom surfaces heaped with cosmetics bottles and grooming products tell you that better organization – and a morning schedule – are needed to cut clutter in the bathroom.

Keep clutter magnets clear In every home, some "clutter magnet" areas attract clutter faster than black trousers attract lint. A convenient surface or a table near the front door can't seem to shake off a constant influx of mail, newspapers, car keys, discarded toys, and loose change.

Because clutter breeds faster than rabbits, identify the clutter magnets, and build time into each day's schedule to clear them. A daily sort will prevent them from mushrooming into clutter mountains when your back is turned.

▲ **Clean.** Around the house, each area presents different challenges. Kitchens and bathrooms require more cleaning.

▲ **Declutter.** Shared living areas tend to inherit clutter from every family member. Decluttering is a team effort.

▲ **Organize.** Storage areas, such as linen cupboards or shelves, must be organized to make good use of space.

Clutter, like beauty, is in the eye of the beholder. A level of clutter that's cozy to one person will seem sterile and bare to someone with a higher tolerance level. Find your tolerance level with this quiz, and shape solutions that are right for you.

1   There are monthly bills to pay. How do you tackle the job?

A   I shove aside the breakfast dishes, dig out the plastic bag holding the bills, and write the cheques – who cares about a few toast crumbs?

B   I turn on the TV, pull up a lap desk, and tear into the envelopes during commercial breaks. Hey, it's good exercise to get up and go hunt for the bills!

C   I stack the bills neatly on the desktop, get out the calculator, and arrange the pens in the pen holder before I begin.

2   Time for bed. What's your routine?

A   I remove the cat from the pillow, sweep a few crumpled tissues onto the floor, and plop down amidst the magazines – it's been a long day!

B   I shake out the sheets (it was a busy morning!), plump the pillow, and move a few things to make a spot for my water glass on the bedside table.

C   I turn down the fresh bedding and frown at the wrinkle that developed in the pillowcase during the day. I arrange my water glass, bedtime book, reading glasses, and emergency flashlight neatly on the bedside table.

3   Stand on the front step or entrance to your home. Based on what you see – decorations, shoes, and clothing – what season is it?

A   Christmas. Actually, it's Christmas two years ago, if you really want to know – but I think it would be wonderful if every day were Christmas. Also, I see a few Halloween decorations in the corner, over there, next to the flippers from last week's trip to the sea.

B   Goodness, I've been meaning to take down the sign from John's birthday party last month; think I'll do it right now, thanks for reminding me.

C   Aside from the holiday season, I don't believe in decorating the front door. Even then, I think a simple evergreen wreath makes just the right statement, don't you?

4   First thing in the morning, you enjoy reading the newspapers. What does the table look like afterwards?

A   Table? What table? I read the papers whenever I can … I think the supplement is still in the bathroom, and last I saw, the children had the comics in the family area.

B   OK, I admit it: I just toss them in a pile on top of the table and hope the Newspaper Elves come and put them in the recycling bin.

C   I read the newspapers front to back, and when I'm finished with them, I fold them neatly for the next person. Doesn't everyone?

If you answered mostly A, congratulations! You have a high tolerance for daily clutter. You'll get the job done even in disorganized surroundings – but you do admit that life would improve if you didn't spend so much time looking for lost items.

If you answered mostly B, you're a happy medium. You tolerate some clutter in your life, but take active steps to keep the clutter level down. Since you become stressed when life gets too chaotic, focus on building daily routines that bring life back to centre.

If you answered mostly C, why are you reading this book? You have a very low tolerance for visual clutter, and know that life runs most smoothly – and you are happiest – when you keep possessions under control and disorder at bay.

Decluttering
the hallway

It's the portal of passage between home and the outer world: the hallway. For the family, it's the place from which they launch themselves each day and get out the door; for guests and visitors, it's the place where they form their first impression of the house or flat that lies behind that front door.

A clutter-free, organized hallway makes life easier on all fronts – and creates a beautiful entrance to your family's home. Try these tips to organize door areas and hallways:

■ **Focus on floors.** In the hallway, the outside meets the inside – and brings plenty of mud and moisture with it. Place door mats on both sides of the door to trap tracked-in dirt and rainwater before it hits your clean house.

■ **Clear clutter regularly.** Family comings and goings tend to deposit post, paperwork, newspapers, magazines, library books, broken items, and extra clothing at the door. Schedule regular STOP clutter sessions in the hallway.

■ **Climb the walls.** Make the most of wall space for storage. Hang a key rack near the door for easy access. Pegs and hooks hold rain gear, jackets, and summer hats.

■ **Use the door.** Hang or attach a shoe organizer on the back of the door or on a wall close by. Roomy pockets hold gloves and scarves, sunglasses and suntan oil, pet leashes, and garden gloves and shoes where they're accessible but not in the way.

■ **Contain it.** Provide a mixture of open and closed storage to house hallway contents: shelf units to hold baskets or plastic bins used as family Launch Pads (*see right*). Add a low storage bench for seating when changing shoes or putting on boots. Label containers to help family members remember to use them.

◀ **Transition zone.** The hallway brings the outside in – along with boots, umbrellas, and overcoats. Plan storage for outerwear and rainwear near the front door for an organized home.

Mission Control: family Launch Pads

Just as a spaceship must have a dedicated structure to support liftoff, so family members need a Launch Pad to stabilize them as they blast out the door in the morning. What is a Launch Pad? It's a dedicated space – perhaps on a bookcase shelf – to contain all the "out-the-door" essentials for each person.

"Handbags, car keys, and return videos – or homework and lunchboxes – can all live in personal Launch Pads."

■ **First principle: contain, contain, contain.** So you've cleared a shelf on that bookcase? Give each family member a different-coloured plastic bin for their Launch Pad, and nobody's field trip permission slip will walk to school with the wrong sibling – or disappear behind the shelf.

■ **Second principle: make putting away easy.** Child comes home from school, tosses homework and lunch menus in her container. Dad comes home and tosses keys, wallet, receipts, and pocket change into his. There things stay, safe and segregated, until they are needed next morning.

■ **Third principle: think creatively.** A Launch Pad need not be a space on shelf or table. In one family, each child has a rucksack that lives on the back of its owner's dining chair. Lunches, papers, and gym clothes go directly to the sacks.

Decluttering
a bathroom

The scene: a master bathroom in any location. It's home to grooming rituals and heir to all sorts of oddments and obsessions. To cut the clutter here can be a journey into the heart of darkness.

before decluttering ▲

Bathrooms are dedicated areas set aside for grooming, health, and hygiene, but have an unacknowledged purpose, too — as a repository for inner hopes, dreams, and insecurities. Follow these tips to loosen the ties that bind you to bathroom clutter:

■ **If you don't use it, lose it.** In any bathroom cupboard, you'll find products that Simply Don't Work. The "rotary hair straightener" built around a power screwdriver — that pulled your hair straight out from the roots. The brush-on nail treatment, guaranteed to grow long, strong nails in just seven days, that peeled like sun-damaged skin. Wonder products are sold on the basis of hope; if there's no hope for those in your cupboard, take their message to the landfill.

■ **If you won't lose it, use it!** Pricey salons know when we're ripe for a sale; tantalized by the lovely new look in the mirror, we can be suckers for expensive cosmetics. Once home, these products migrate to the recesses of the medicine chest, but memories of the high price charge keeps us from decluttering them. Fine — you may keep the luxury shower gel — but on one condition: that you use it.

■ **Knock down the number.** Every bathroom-dweller has a secret grooming product obsession; they buy multiples of their fetish item. When faced with more than three of anything in the bathroom, invoke the Law of Numbers: keep two favorites, declutter the rest.

■ **Time to throw it out.** Allow cosmetics languish too long, and bacterial growth can pose a danger to health. Throw away items that are past their safe storage life (*see also page 190*).

STOP clutter in the bathroom

In an average bathroom, expect to devote two to three STOP clutter sessions to the task. Start at the bathroom sink area, and then move to nearby cupboards or drawers. Finish with the shower/bathtub area. Assemble your tools: timer, Put Away box, Storage box, Sell/Donate box and a black bin bag. Set the timer for 15 minutes.

1 Sort
Starting at the bathroom sink, sort items that belong into like piles. Place items that belong elsewhere in the Put Away box, and tuck any items for storage in the Storage box. Surplus items that are still useful go to Sell/Donate.

2 Throw out
Throw out any rubbish, broken, or valueless items into the bin bag. This being a bathroom, you'll find lots of the following: dried strings of dental floss, crumpled tissues, grimy makeup applicators, dried-out bars of soap. Let dust be your guide: any bottle with a dusty coating goes into the bin bag! Ditto for broken items: combs with missing teeth, fraying toothbrushes, the perfume mister that's missing the spray bulb. Out!

3 Organize
Once the sink is cleared, organize the survivors in the cleared space. Shallow baskets, cosmetics organizer trays or bathroom carryalls bring order to surfaces. Then move on to the rest of the room.

4 Put away
When the timer bell rings, stop the session and put away the items in the Put Away box. Store the timer and boxes for the next STOP clutter session. Throw away the bin bag in the bin.

after decluttering ▲

The rules of
bathroom storage

Spartan or spacious, all bathrooms have one thing in common: there's never enough storage space. Plumbing fixtures take centre stage, leaving precious little room for lotions and potions. Add to this the problem of family members competing for the same sink-and-mirror space, and you've got an organizational challenge.

Health facts
for the Hoarder

A hoarder's bathroom is a magpie's nest of scent bottles, sample packets, and throwaway cosmetics. A hoarder's personal-care cache grows with each visit to the cosmetic counter or appointment at the hairdresser's. No department store freebie or sample packet goes ungathered. Perfumes, cosmetics, and grooming potions deteriorate much as stored foods do – and using outdated cosmetics can be harmful to health. To help eliminate the pile-up, take to heart these issues of health and safety – and get decluttering!

- **Perfume loses** its potency after 3 years.
- **Liquids** can support bacterial growth. Liquid and cream foundations are fine to use for between 6 and 12 months, then throw them away.
- **Using stale eye-makeup** or mascara can cause serious eye infections. Once opened, never keep mascara for longer than 3 months. Liquid eyeliner lasts for about 6 months; powder eyeshadow is usually fine for between 14 months and 2 years.
- **Wax-based products** such as lipstick and lip balm harden and crumble if kept too long. Throw them away after a year.

Bathrooms, like other activity-intensive rooms such as kitchens, need a refined, systematic plan for storage. It's not enough just to stuff it all in there somewhere. Organize them according to the rules of bathroom storage, to make best use of that scarce domestic space.

1 "A" is for every day

Active, accessible, and meant for daily use – that's the definition of "A" storage areas. In a bathroom, the "A" areas get the toothbrush and the dental floss, the shampoo bottle and the razor.

"A" storage areas should be user-friendly. They should welcome the groping hand with no hidden hazards, even before the poor, blind shower-taker has inserted his or her contact lenses or found his or her glasses. The vanity units, the top drawer, a chrome mesh bucket, or hanging organizer in the shower area are all "A" storage areas.

2 "B" is for occasional

Items that are used weekly to monthly should be given homes in the "B" storage areas. The box of nifty, pore-unclogging strips, the collection of hair scrunchies for exercise-class ponytails, nail care equipment, and the battery-operated beard trimmer are all consigned to "B" areas.

"B" areas aren't so easy to reach. You'll stretch or bend to reach the middle drawer, the under-sink spaces, and the toilet-top storage cupboard. "B" also stands for "box;" candidates for "B" storage can often be accommodated in labelled boxes underneath or behind their more popular "A" companions.

3 "C" is for seldom

Storage areas that are designated "C"s are those that require excessive bending, stretching, or standing on tiptoe – and home to those items that are seldom used. They're where you keep the gold-flecked makeup for nights out, the foot-massager, and the upper-lip depilatory cream. If you use an item less than once a month but more than twice a year, it belongs in the lowly "C" category, so put it where the sun doesn't shine.

Personal care centres

One creative solution to bathroom traffic is to create "centres" for personal care items that will make it easier to outsource bathroom storage. Assign each member of the family a different-coloured plastic organizer or basket to hold cosmetics and toiletries. Each person's "centre" should hold it all – their toothbrush and toothpaste, shampoo and conditioner, shower gel or soap, and any other essential or often-used products – and be stored in that person's bedroom when not in use.

Hang lighted makeup mirrors in bedrooms belonging to teenage girls. Assigning each daughter her own makeup centre reduces early-morning squabbling and frees up space in the bathroom. Cosmetics benefit, too, because they stay fresh longer away from heat and steam.

Similarly, set up a health and first aid centre in an accessible area away from the bathroom. Storing prescription medicines, over-the-counter remedies, and vitamins elsewhere also protects them against the bathroom's harmful heat and moisture. Consider relocating hot water bottles, feminine hygiene products, and the first aid kit in a cool, dry storage location outside the bathroom. Laundry, too, can be outsourced in collection areas outside the bathroom. Dirty laundry can be collected in the laundry activity centre (*see pages 142–3*), or in individual baskets in family bedrooms.

▼ **Shower holdall.** Sharing bathrooms comes more easily if the room's users don't have to work around one another's gear. Handled plastic baskets make it easy to carry personal-care products.

Bathroom
cleaning challenges

Considering what we put them through each day, sinks, showers, baths, and toilets deserve special cleaning attention. Thankfully, modern plumbing fixtures are designed to make the job of bathroom cleaning as easy as possible. Keep your bathroom fixtures bright with these cleaning tips.

Sink

From toothpaste dribbles to overspray from hair products, the lowly sink endures a daily barrage of dirt and grime. Keep it sparkling back at you with regular cleaning.

> "Put the job off and deposits harden and ossify, and mildew and mould take up residence in dark corners."

■ **Right for the job.** Use all-purpose bathroom cleaner to remove light soil and film. For more hardened deposits, a scouring powder or cream cleaner may be used: they will be easy to rinse from ceramic (vitreous china) surface. Cleaners formulated with bleach will remove toothpaste dribbles and sanitize surfaces, too. Don't extend the cleaner past the sink rim or apply it to fixtures, however; the abrasive particles will scratch shiny finishes and be difficult to remove.
■ **On the edge.** Clean the rim and fixtures with a disinfecting spray glass cleaner or an all-purpose bathroom cleaner. Buff fixtures shiny and dry with a fresh cleaning cloth.

Shower and tub

Soap scum, bath oil, hair products, and body soil combine forces to assault the shining surface of the shower and bath, while bath rims, fixtures, and taps provide hiding places for moisture,

mould, and mildew. Put the job off and deposits harden and ossify, and mildew and mould take up residence in dark corners. Harness time and cleaning power to make short work of cleaning the shower and bath.

■ **Spray and stand.** Before cleaning the rest of the bathroom, spray the bath area with a generous layer of all-purpose bathroom cleaner, and allow the product to stand while you clean elsewhere. The standing time helps the cleaner to dissolve oils and soap scum, so you'll need less elbow grease to remove it.
■ **Get scrubbing.** Use a scrubbing sponge to remove bath rings or deposits on shower floors. Use a tile brush to scrub tile grout and reach into cracks and corners; the handle protects knuckles from accidental contact with the bath. A toothbrush does a quick job of removing build-up deposits around bath fixtures or taps
■ **Rinse clean.** A detachable showerhead allows you to rinse off cleaner quickly and cleanly. If you don't have one, stock your cleaning holdall with a removable rubber showerhead that attaches to the bath taps. Commonly used for shampooing hair or bathing pets, they're inexpensive and make it easier to rinse bath and shower walls after you clean.

Fibreglass showers and glass doors

These surfaces need special treatment. Clean them with a non-abrasive cleaner such as an all-purpose bathroom cleaner or baking soda. Avoid abrasive cleaners or abrasive sponges because they may scratch or dull the finish.

Cloudy glass shower doors may be cleaned with full-strength white vinegar or a commercial lime and scale remover. Use good ventilation and protect skin and clothing when using these products.

Toilet

Cleaning the toilet isn't most people's idea of a good time, but where would we be without it? I'll tell you: back in the outhouse. Try these ideas to keep it clean and inviting:

■ **Take your time.** Place granulated or liquid toilet bowl cleaner into the bowl, and let the cleaner go to work. Standing time is necessary to dissolve deposits and kill germs, so don't cut the time short.

■ **Brush up.** A good bowl brush is a must. If yours is flattened or mashed, replace it; you need those bristles bristling to do a good job. Curved bowl brushes reach up-and-under the toilet rim to scour away hidden deposits.

■ **Scrub up.** If the toilet develops a stubborn ring that regular cleaning won't cure, bring on the pumice stone. This natural stone is porous and crumbles. Rub the stone directly on the ring to remove the deposit.

■ **Disinfect.** Use a disinfecting spray cleaner or an all-purpose bathroom cleaner to spray toilet rims, seat and lid, tank and bowl exterior. Be sure to check the label for the recommended standing time; antibacterial cleaning products require a certain amount of wet exposure in order to kill germs. Wipe clean and dry with fresh cleaning cloths.

■ **Drips and dribbles.** These are a predictable hazard in a home containing boys – of any age – and can cause odour problems and floor damage if urine is allowed to stand at the base of the toilet. Use disinfecting cleaner and the cleaning toothbrush to remove stray dribbles – or assign the job to the manly offenders.

▷ **Working hard.** Bathroom cleaning products need time to soften dried-on soil (*top*). Allow them to stand for a few minutes before tackling scrubbing chores.

▷ **Stand and deliver.** Most disinfecting spray cleaners need to stand in order to kill bacteria and viruses (*below*). Follow the manufacturer's guidelines, then wipe clean with a cleaning cloth.

Decluttering the
linen area

What is the state of your linen cupboard? Is it crammed with clutter or neat and tidy? While it's tempting to use linen storage areas as a store-all for homeless items, resist the temptation!

Tossing broken appliances, seasonal decor items, or everyday clutter among the sheets and towels in the linen cupboard can introduce unwelcome dirt, insects, and odours into the family's linens. An organized linen cupboard extends the life of expensive bedding and towels. Properly folded and stored, linens are protected and ready for use – and far less likely to be appropriated for misadventures, such as washing the car or wiping down a muddy pet. Most of all, an organized linen cupboard is a delight for the eye – and for the nose! Honour your family's linens with a proper place to live.

Attention panic clutter

Cluttered linen cupboards can be found in the tidiest homes. Why? They're the natural place to store panic clutter. "Panic clutter" is born when the doorbell rings unexpectedly. Fearing drop-in guests, family members sweep up out-of-place items and look wildly for a door, any door that will shut them away from view. Enter the linen cupboard – the storage area most accessible and most amenable to depositing panic clutter.

As a result, expect that STOP clutter sessions in the linen cupboard will require about twice the normal time for the "put-away" step. You'll also find many more storage items than you would expect. Swept up into the linen cupboard, lost items find snug hiding spots among the jumbled towels.

Save-your-back tip: set up a portable table or clean another surface nearby when decluttering the linen cupboard. There will be a good deal of refolding to do, so make the process easier on your lower back with a good work area.

before decluttering ▲

STOP clutter in the linen area

Pick a cool day to begin linen cupboard decluttering; it's more pleasant to handle blankets and thick towels when you're fresh and cool. Ready to STOP clutter in the linen cupboard?

1 Sort
Set the timer for 20 minutes, grab your sorting boxes, and turn your attention to a single shelf, area, or drawer. Remove everything from the shelf – sheets, towels, lost toys – and sort into like piles. Linens to be returned to the cupboard can be placed on the portable table for refolding; out-of-place items are delivered to the appropriate boxes (Put Away, Sell/Donate, Storage).

2 Throw out
Assess your linens while you throw out rubbish. Ripped sheets, ragged towels, and stained tablecloths deserve an honourable retirement, offering new life if repurposed. Worn pillowcases, a hole snipped for a hanger, serve as dust covers for stored clothing; the household's car washer will prize shredded sheets for polishing chrome bumpers.

3 Organize
Once the space is clear, use spray cleaner to remove dust and dirt. Turn to the stacked linens on the temporary table. Refolding is probably a must, but fold smart (*for folding tips, see pages 197, 198–9*).

4 Put away
When the shelf is replaced or the timer rings, grab the Put Away box and go around the house, restoring items to their proper home. Tuck away the Storage and Sell/Donate boxes, and bin the cast-offs.

after decluttering ▲

Top tips for
the linen cupboard

Crisp sheets, fluffy towels, and colourful tablecloths represent gracious living and a happy home – and deserve proper storage to maintain your investment. Whether your household includes a formal linen cupboard, or you store linens on a shelf or in a chest of drawers, these tips will keep household fabrics looking their best.

Make your bed work. Tuck an extra set of pillowcases and sheets between the mattress and base of every bed. The weight of the mattress will keep linens smooth, and they'll be close at hand.

1 **Store clean and dry**
Keep the linen cupboard fresh and preserve pretty fabrics by storing only clean, dry linens. Even if a tablecloth looks clean, any hidden stains will harden and discolour during storage. Body odours trapped in blankets can cause musty odours, while moisture encourages mildew.

2 **Keep cool, dark, and dry**
The watchwords for proper linen storage: cool, dark, and dry. In humid areas, packaged de-humidifying granules will help keep the linen cupboard free from moisture and mildew.

3 **Take turns**
For best wear, ensure that you rotate linens. Place freshly washed towels at the bottom of the stack, or draw clean sheets from the bottom of the pile to use all your linens in rotation.

4 **Refold**
If linens aren't in active use, refold them once or twice a year. This will prevent creases becoming fixed and avoid fibre damage along the creases.

5 **Avoid cardboard**
They may seem a practical storage option, but don't store linens in cardboard boxes. Acids in the

cardboard transfer to the fabric, causing yellowing and damage, while the glue between the layers is attractive to pests – and when they're finished with the cardboard, they'll often start feeding on the fabrics.

6 Store sweet and fresh
Tuck fabric softener sheets into the linen cupboard – and your bedding and towels will come out smelling sweet and fresh.

7 Make bedding bundles
If you use sheets in sets, store them that way, in a "bedding bundle". Fold both sheets, and all but one pillowcase. Tuck the folded linens inside the remaining pillowcase and fold the "case" down around the linens into a tidy packet.

8 Use the shelf system
Sorting through different-sized bed sheets can be an exercise in frustration – just ask any parent who has had to change an ill child's bedding in the middle of the night. If space permits, store sheets on different shelves in the linen cupboard, or label cupboard shelves with sheet sizes.

9 Introduce a family colour strategy
Make it easy to get the right sheets on the right beds by designating a colour, pattern, or style of sheet for each size of bed: plain white sheets for the baby's cot, patterned sheets for children's beds, and solid colours for the parental double bed. That way, you will know at a glance which sheet belongs to which bed.

10 Make bath bundles
For easy storage and instant access, make bath bundles: sets each containing a bath towel, hand towel, and face flannel. Place the folded hand towel and face flannel in the centre of the folded bath towel, and roll the three towels together from the short end. Store the rolled bath bundles on their side, stacking them as needed.

Folding tips for household linen

The word "shambles" must have been invented to describe linen shelves after a late-night rummage for a warmer blanket. Carelessly folded linens invite the risk of an avalanche; they tumble and fall to the floor at the slightest provocation. Keep stored linens easy to find and easy to store with proper folding techniques. Think of it this way: better to fold the linens right just once, than to refold them poorly once each time you visit the shelf for a fresh towel.

- **Flat sheets.** Fold in half lengthways, quarter them, and then fold in half again. Depending on the size of the sheet, flip the remaining rectangle into halves or thirds to make a smooth fabric packet.
- **Pillowcases.** These look prettiest (and sleep best) when you avoid creating sharp centre creases as you fold. To fold, grab the pillowcase by the top corners and shake it smooth. Fold in half lengthwise, then in half again. You'll have a long, slender strip of pillowcase; fold gently in half, then in quarters to store.
- **Hand towels and face flannels.** Folding in quarters makes sense for hand towels, as they're used more often – and more quickly – throughout the day. To fold, hold the two upper corners of the towel's short side in your hands. Bring your hands together, being sure the right side of the towel is on the outside of the fold. Tuck the folded edge between chin and chest as you grasp the towel halfway down the length. Drop the top half over the bottom. Hang the towel or face flannel, or set aside for the linen cupboard.

Folding a fitted sheet

Hospital nurses, military recruits, and my 97-year-old grandmother can make a taut bed using only flat sheets, but the rest of us are grateful for the invention of fitted bottom sheets.

1 Fitted sheets are great on the bed, but can be tricky to fold. Here's how. Hold up the sheet, inside-out, and slip your hands inside the top two corners. The wrong side of the fabric should be facing you and the right side should be touching your hands.

2 Carefully lay the sheet down on a large, flat surface – such as a table, or the top of a bed – so it is spread out smoothly . Fold the sheet right side together, slipping the top corners gently inside the two bottom corners. Arrange the corners neatly.

3 Fold the sheet edges to the inside. The flaps of fabric that hug the mattress should be neatly folded down in line with the corners, making a large rectangle with all loose edges tucked in smoothly.

Folding a bath towel

Large towels should be folded in thirds, lengthways, and hung over a towel rack from the centre. This ensures that they will dry more quickly after use.

1 To fold a large bath towel, pick it up so that the front is facing you. Grasping it by the two upper corners, hold the towel up at shoulder height and stretch it out sideways so that it is smooth and flat.

2 Bring one corner towards the other to a point roughly two-thirds of the width of the towel. Hold it there as you fold the second corner of the towel over towards the first, creating three layers.

3 Pinch the folds between your fingers and shake the towel gently to distribute the folds. Tuck the towel between your chin and your chest to pin it down.

"If linens aren't in active use, refold them once or twice a year to avoid fibre damage along the creases."

4 Fold the sheet in half, stacking all four corners on top of one another and encasing the folded sheet sides. The curved edges should be tucked down to create a (more-or-less) smooth rectangle

5 Fold the sheet in half again to create a long, narrow strip. The tighter and smoother the folds, the less likely it is that the sheet will become wrinkled — or balloon to an enormous size in the linen cupboard.

6 Fold the strip in half, then (depending on the sheet size) in half or in thirds to make a compact — and wrinkle-free — rectangle. Match the fitted sheet with its flat partner (and any pillowcases), and tuck away neatly in the linen cupboard.

"For best wear, ensure that you rotate linens. Place freshly washed towels on the bottom of the stack."

4 Grasp the towel midpoint down its length, then lift your chin to allow the top half of the towel to drop down over the bottom half.

5 Lay the towel on a flat surface and fold it again in the middle to form a neat bundle, and store it. If the towel is to be used right away, it doesn't need as many folds; just hang it over a towel rack.

6 Having a different-coloured towel for each family member makes it easy for people to find the right fresh towel when needed. Let children pick the colour of their towel and they'll happily cooperate.

Sweet dreams in the
organized bedroom

Marriage counsellors and doctors who treat sleep disorders tell us that clean, uncluttered bedrooms make for happy homes and a good night's rest – but you wouldn't know it, judging by the clutter in a typical master bedroom, which for many families becomes a second-level storage area.

The theory seems to be that since the eyes are closed while sleeping, the mind won't notice the disorder. Tumbled laundry spills over fitness equipment, books and crafts projects compete for floor space, a motley gang of dirty dishes sends colonies of water glasses to new settlements under the bed and on top of the chest of drawers, and the bedroom television wears a rakish cap of piled post and unpaid bills.

A chaotic bedroom makes you feel wired and tired. If you want sweet (organized) dreams, it's time to get organized – but be prepared to devote several declutter sessions to get rid of chaos in the bedroom.

Get it tidy

Gather your declutter tools – timer, boxes, and bin bags – for a STOP clutter session in the bedroom. Because so many unauthorized items wander into the bedroom (or are thrust there, unwilling, at the sound of the doorbell), the Put Away box will do extra duty during a bedroom declutter.

■ **Sort.** Set the timer for 20 minutes, and start by tackling the bed area. Drag everything out from beneath it, and behind and inside the nightstand. Sort each item into one of the boxes: Put Away, for items that belong in other rooms; Sell/Donate for no-longer-needed items that are still in good repair; Storage, for items that belong in storage areas. Using the same

◀ **Calm oasis.** A bedroom is the home's most personal space. Time spent there should be devoted to rest and renewal. Clean and decluttered, the bedroom can be an oasis of calm and order.

strategy, move on to the chest of drawers and any dressing tables, and any clutter littering the floor. Work systematically around the space and, little by little, you'll reclaim the bedroom as the sanctuary it's intended to be.

■ **Throw out.** As you sort, consign broken items and litter straight to the bin bag.

■ **Organize.** The smart declutterer notes where the clutter is coming from, and then looks for ways to prevent the build-up in the future. As you declutter, pay attention to the cause of the problem. Scattered piles of dirty clothes signal a need for a laundry basket in a nearby spot. Linty piles of pocket change, train tickets, and crumpled receipts can be kept under control with a pretty bowl or wooden box designated for pocket-emptying at the end of the day. Stacks of unopened moving boxes, resident along the wall since you moved in, indicate a need for a household storage plan.

■ **Put away.** When the timer bell rings, stop the session. Circle the house with the Put Away box, put Sell/Donate items in the boot of the car for delivery to a charity shop. Add Storage items to loft, basement, or garage storage areas.

Keep it clean

If the bedroom is to be a calm and peaceful haven, it's not enough for it to be tidy — it must be clean, too. To achieve this, include it in the household cleaning schedule. The primary goal is to reduce and remove dust, dander, and other irritants.

Weekly vacuuming and dusting is a must in the bedroom. Pay particular attention to window treatments; vacuuming curtains and dusting lamp shades will help to keep air quality high. Skirting boards, too, need regular attention to keep dust build-ups away. If the room contains a television, computer, or entertainment centre, use an electrostatic dry cleaning cloth to collect dust weekly, since electronic equipment attracts dust.

Wash windows seasonally, and wipe down sills and window fittings to remove dust and dirt. A lambswool duster picks up any dusty residue on walls and snags cobwebs on ceilings or in corners; when necessary, wash the walls to remove smudges and stains. Seasonal cleaning should also include lamp shades and the light-diffusing bowls from overhead fixtures; you'll see clearly and cut the dust with clean lighting. Allergy sufferers may want to add a portable air filtration unit to improve air quality.

Tips for bedroom clutter personalities

Our bedrooms reveal more about us than our taste in bed linens; they offer bedrock evidence of clutter personality type. Expressing personal taste in the bedroom is one thing, but try to rein in clutter personality excess with these tips:

■ **Sentimentalist.** Visiting the sentimentalist's bedroom is like a trip in a time capsule. Too often, the room holds so many cherished symbols of the past that there's no room to move. Childhood teddies nestle next to sports equipment, the walls are papered with posters and portraits tracking earlier enthusiasms, and chests of drawers sprout a forest of athletic trophies.

If you're a bedroom sentimentalist, learn to celebrate the now! Cut the ties to sentimental clutter by saving a symbol and releasing the surplus. Deforest the chest of drawers of a trophy collection, for example, by choosing the most memorable award. Photograph it, and then write a brief description of the memory it provokes. Tuck the photograph and journal entry into a scrapbook — then donate the trophy collection to a youth organization for recycling.

■ **Rebel.** The bedroom can be the last refuge of a rebel clutter personality. While he or she may present a self-controlled face in the rest of the house, the riotous bedroom remains, strewn knee-deep in rumpled clothing and half-eaten sandwiches.

If you're a rebel, remind yourself that you're a big kid now! Big kids have better things to do in their bedrooms than relive a childhood power struggle. Give yourself permission to pursue your adult side, and create an atmosphere of relaxation, not rebellion, in this most intimate of all rooms.

Top tips for organizing
in the bedroom

Clutter conquered, it's time to get organized in the bedroom and stop clutter from creeping back. The bedroom is our most private and personal home sanctuary. Focus on the room's function – rest, relaxation, and renewal – with these ideas to arrange and organize bedrooms.

1 Light up your life!
Given the bedroom's function as a haven for rest and relaxation, harsh overhead lights have to go. Reading lamps and indirect lighting will enhance comfort and induce a sense of calm.

2 Furnish right
Arrange furnishings to support the activities you'll conduct. Add a row of hooks next to the treadmill to hold exercise clothing, pulse monitor, and towel. Set up a restful reading spot on the bookworm's side of the bed, with reading lamp, extra pillows, a basket for books and magazines and, on the nightstand, a coaster for his or her mug. Use hanging pegs and desktop organizers to create a cosmetics centre on top of a chest of drawers; hang jewellery, scarves, and hair accessories for a neat and pretty touch.

3 Avoid "suite syndrome"
Often, bedroom furniture is purchased as a suite of multiple pieces – and you'll find every blessed one of them crammed into many bedrooms, space notwithstanding. Pare down bedroom furniture and release living space by dispensing with the idea that a furniture suite cannot be separated. The extra tallboy or spare chest of drawers can do good service in the hallway, where it won't cramp your style – or your night's sleep. "Mix and match" works as well in the bedroom as in the wardrobe.

4 Tap under-bed areas
Commercial organizing products are available to slide neatly in the space beneath the bed, made from plastic and with a lid. Use them to store handbags, out-of-season clothing, bulky jumpers, or gift-wrap.

5 Safety counts!
Be sure the bedroom includes basic safety supplies: a nearby smoke detector, flashlight and batteries, and for upper-storey bedrooms, an escape ladder. Tuck safety supplies beneath the bed to avoid stumbling around in the dark next time there's a power cut. A tip from earthquake country: never retire for the night without placing robe and slippers near the bed.

6 Go for dual-duty
When selecting bedroom furnishings, look for double-duty solutions that will add storage space to the bedroom. A bed headboard that doubles as a bookcase keeps a bedtime reader's books close to hand. Toss a long cushion over a wooden chest, and you'll create a seating area and storage in one. Add a fabric skirt to a dressing table to conceal a small rolling drawer organizer.

▶ **Hidden storage.** Incorporate organizing products under the bed, beneath upholstered chairs, or supporting a night table to increase storage options in the bedroom.

Mitring a sheet

Taking a tip from woodworkers, who join wood pieces at a 45-degree angle, mitring a sheet bottom keeps it snug and sharp beneath the bed covers.

1 Centre the flat sheet on the bed, and tuck the bottom of the sheet underneath the mattress. Grab the trailing edge of the sheet, about 60cm (2ft) from the corner of the sheet, to make a 45-degree angle away from the mattress corner; pull it towards you.

2 Still holding on to the sheet, pull it up vertically to form a triangle (the sheet should fold at a 45-degree angle).

Putting on a duvet cover

This method of putting on a duvet cover beats crawling inside the cover while attempting to stuff the duvet in – and you won't feel as if you've been in a three-way wrestling match!

1 Try this method for putting on a duvet cover that I learned from a Swiss hotel maid. Standing, grab the top two corners of the duvet cover, fabric right side out, holding one corner in each hand.

2 Holding tightly to the corners, toss the duvet cover up and inside out, allowing it to fall over your arms. The upper corners of the duvet (with your hands inside them) should be visible.

3 Grab the corresponding corners of the duvet through the corners of the cover. Make sure you've got the duvet aligned properly, matching short and long sides.

"Designate a colour, pattern, or style of sheet for each bed, and you'll know at a glance which belongs to which."

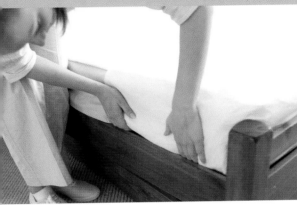

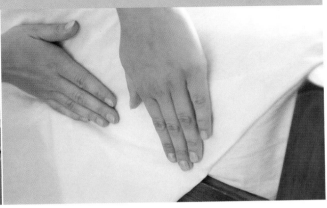

3 Lay the triangle of sheet onto the bed, then tuck the bottom part of the sheet under the mattress. Building in this tucked fabric is the secret to a well-mitred, taut-fitting sheet.

4 Drop the triangle of sheet down towards the floor, then tuck it under the mattress to form a mitred corner. Smooth the hanging sheet bottom underneath the mattress, all the way to head of the bed. Repeat on the other side of the bed.

"Tuck fabric softener sheets into the linen area – and your bedding will come out smelling sweet and fresh."

4 Hold on tight to the duvet-cover and shake. As you shake, the duvet cover will fall right side out, down and over the duvet itself.

5 Flip the newly covered, freshly fluffed duvet up and over the bed, and turn your attention to the cover's bottom. Some covers have sewn-in pockets; if so, tuck the duvet's remaining corners into place.

6 Fasten the bottom of the duvet cover; some makes have pop fasteners, others have buttons or ties. When you've finished fastening, give the duvet a final shake to distribute the down or filling. Bed made!

Bed-making battles! Once the preserve of parent and child, the debate has now entered the public domain: to make or not to make the bed each day? Designer offerings of artfully unmade beds give comfort to the "why bother?" contingent. There's no law (aside from Mother's) that says you must make the bed every day. On the other hand, a made bed protects sheets from dust and gives the room a feeling of cleanliness and order – and there's nothing more delightful than poking tired feet into a smooth bed at the end of a long day.

Those of us with a bit of the rebel on the issue of bed making can overcome it by looking into easier bedding options. A "made" bed is easier to achieve with a simple duvet: just shake and flip to bring the bed to rights each morning. A rule of thumb: if it takes more than 2 minutes to make the bed, the bed is over-dressed. Take away some of the frills and furbelows to achieve a neat look with less effort.

Decluttering a
child's room

"Clean your room!" It's the battle cry of millions of parents. Try these strategies to calm clutter and bring order to children's rooms.

Special challenge

It's a conundrum. Children's rooms are usually small, often shared, and may lack built-in storage. Yet these rooms are host to out-of-season and outgrown clothing, surplus toys, and even household overflow from other rooms. Children can't stay organized when the wardrobe is crammed, the drawers are stuffed, and playthings are strewn across the entire carpet area.

The solution: use the STOP clutter method to sort, store, and simplify children's belongings. Long sessions of "clean your room" are an ordeal for all concerned, but by working for a limited time with a defined method, kids and parents can come to terms with clutter.

Skills for life

For all but the youngest toddlers, resist the urge to wade into the mess alone, bin bags flying. Instead, look at the decluttering process as a learning activity, and put the focus on the child. In your role as organizational consultant, survey what's working, what's not, what's important to the child, what's causing the problems, and why the child wants to get organized. If they're involved in the effort, children are better able to understand the organizational logic and maintain the new, organized room.

It will take a number of STOP clutter sessions to clear a crowded child's room. Boost your patience with the process by remembering that you're not just clearing out the stuff — you're building skills that will stand the small fry in good stead for life.

Let's play the STOP clutter game

In addition to the usual STOP clutter tools — timer, boxes, and bin bag — you'll need a good selection of lidded plastic shoeboxes, other stackable containers, and a few floor level open containers. Set the timer, and show the child how to play the STOP clutter game.

1 Sort

Start with a small section of the little person's domain: a single shelf, a small area of floor, or one drawer. Grab each object and ask the question: is this something we want to keep, to put away, to give away, or to throw away? No, we can't put it down! We've got Magic Clutter Sticky on our hands, and we can't put it down until we make a decision!

2 Organize

STOP clutter for 15 minutes, and then begin to sort the keepers. Here's where the lidded storage containers earn their star billing. Toss small items such as all connecting blocks into one bin, dolly's clothing into another, tiny trucks and cars into a third. Playing "match the toy" is a good identification-and-labelling game for young children, and teaches them organizing skills.

Warning from an Old Mum: there will be resistance to the Give Away and Throw Away options. Try tactics such as Choose Three to break through the block: "Yes, you may keep the cuddly toys — but only three. Which are the most appealing?"

3 Throw out and put away

Finally, when the timer bell rings, throw out the rubbish and return Put away items to their homes in other rooms. Deliver Sell/Donate and Storage items to their storage locations, and stack and store the newly sorted kids' toys.

before decluttering ▲

after decluttering ▲

Top tips for organizing
children's rooms

Decluttering achieved, it's time to bring order to children's rooms and play areas. The trick is to take a child's eye view. Look at the space, storage, furniture, and possessions from his or her vantage point – and tailor organizing strategies to suit.

1 Think child-friendly

To organize a child's room, solutions must fit the child. Adult furniture and organizing systems don't translate well to children's needs. Sticky drawers are hard for small hands to manage. Folding wardrobe doors pinch fingers and jump their rails when pushed from the bottom. Wardrobe hanging rails are out of reach, while traditional toy boxes house a jumble of mixed and scattered toy parts.

For younger children, remove wardrobe doors entirely. Lower clothing rails and invest in child-sized hangers – adult versions don't fit children's clothing. Use floor-level open containers to hold toys, and open plastic baskets to store socks and underwear.

▼ **The smaller the child,** the lower you go. Organize children's rooms according to their eye level. For the smallest children, that means floor level. Open bins allow toddlers to play "put away" easily.

2 Hard to get out, easy to put away

The premier rule for efficient children's storage? Make it easier to put something away than it is to get it out. For example, store picture books as a flip-file, standing upright in a shallow plastic bin. The child flips through the books, makes his or her selection, and tosses the book in the front of the bin when he or she's done. It beats using a traditional bookcase, where little fingers can pull down a whole shelf faster than they can replace one book.

3 Organize bottom to top

Befitting a child's shorter stature, start the organizing process from the bottom of the room, and work to the top. Most-used toys and belongings should live on lower shelves, in lower drawers, or on the floor. Higher levels are designated for less-frequently-used possessions.

4 Label, label, label

Use a computer printer to make simple graphic labels for young children. Pictures of socks, shirts, dolls, or blocks help remind the child where these items belong. Enhance reading skills for older children by using large-type word labels. Slap labels everywhere: inside and outside of drawers, on shelf edges, on boxes and bookcases and filing cubes. Playing "match the label" can be fun – and turns toy pick-up time into a game.

5 Build a maintenance routine

The usual peaks-and-valleys approach to keeping a room in order can vex and frustrate children. Their room is clean and tidy, they play, and suddenly their room is back to messy normal. Help children stop the cycle by building maintenance routines into the family's day. "Morning Pick-up" straightens the quilt, returns the pillow to the bed, and gets yesterday's clothing to the laundry basket. Before dressing for bed, "Evening Pick-up" involves putting away the day's toys.

Storing children's artwork and school papers

The paper trail begins in nursery school, and follows kids along the years. Don't let it bury your organized home! Try these tips to display, declutter, and store children's artwork and school papers:

- **Refrigerator magnets** make it easy to show off a gold-star essay or a colourful drawing in that traditional children's art gallery space – the refrigerator door.
- **Some artworks** will show talent above and beyond everyday achievements. Ready-made frame and mat kits are inexpensive, and give a child's best work a professional presentation.
- **A large accordion file** provides handy storage for the artworks that accumulate over the school year. Use one slot for each month. After the art has had its season on display, tuck it inside. At the end of the year, select the best piece from each month for permanent storage. Use hanging file folders to hold the year's 12 representative masterpieces in the household files.
- **Surplus artwork** can be put to good use. Write thank-you notes to Granny on the back of a colourful drawing. Incorporate 12 paintings into a calendar for holiday giving. Wrap birthday gifts inside children's artwork for a cheerful way to recycle.
- **A brief pencilled notation** on the back of stored children's papers is something you will thank yourself for doing in later years. Include the name of the child, the year, the grade in school, and the teacher's name to refresh memories from the far reaches of an empty nest.

The paper tide begins with a toddler's first crayoned scrawls, and grows to a school age high by primary school: children's artwork. Displaying a child's artistic creations brings bright affirmation to their creative efforts.

Be equally creative when displaying, sharing, and storing art projects. Lightweight, inexpensive clotheslines – designed to take a traveller's drip-dries on the road – offer a great way to display the week's artistic triumphs. Mount these short lengths of cord behind a desk, and use the clips to hang paintings and papers. Alternatively, use clear acrylic frames to display artworks – they make it easy to switch pieces on an ongoing basis.

Share the wealth with others in your child's life. Regularly posting artworks to Granny not only celebrates family ties, but also gives her bragging rights at the bingo game or exercise class. Best of all, sharing children's artwork in this way helps introduce them to the delights of correspondence.

Family room
declutter

The family room: it's the centre of family life – and in too many homes, the cluster of activities we do there leads to an explosion of clutter.

Divide and conquer

Clutter is like chickenpox: it spreads from person to person with only casual contact. One person's ongoing craft project becomes authorization for the next person to spread his or her stuff out, too. How to control family room clutter? With a family STOP clutter session. The communal nature of the room means that any clutter solution will require everyone's cooperation. By agreeing to divide and conquer, a STOP clutter session can attack problem areas simultaneously.

Tips to organize family rooms

Try these tips to make the most of storage space in shared spaces and family rooms:

■ **Contain clutter.** Practise containment policies to keep clutter under control. Store the week's newspapers in a low-sided bin; a knitting project in a wicker basket.
■ **Practise "cart and carry".** Establish a policy that, while family members are welcome to do homework, work on crafts, or play with toys in the family room, their supplies must be carted and carried. Plastic laundry baskets, shopping bags, or shallow plastic bins can be used to bring out the playthings – and to collect them at the end of the evening, for return to the bedroom.
■ **Sweep it clean!** Take time during the day for a "sweep". During a pause in a television programme, announce that it's time for a sweep, and ask all family members to pick up out-of-place items and put them away. Quick! The programme will be back on the air in just minutes!

STOP clutter in the family room

Gather your tools: timer, STOP declutter boxes (marked Put Away, Sell/Donate, and Storage), and bin bags for rubbish. Set the timer for 20 minutes. To make it easier to do a group declutter, double or triple the number of boxes used for Put Away. Limit the STOP clutter session to 20 minutes to shortcut the potential for argument.

1 **Sort**
Start sorting. Assign each family member a small area to clear – a shelf, table, or corner – and a tight timeline to declutter it to make the job specific and short. Key targets: the choked video storage rack, the piles of old magazines, the scattering of toys all over the carpet. Give the children a Put Away box for far-flung toys, the family crafter another box to collect his or her paints for return to the craft corner.

2 **Throw out**
Disagreement is a potential hazard when diving into a group STOP clutter session. Mum may be perfectly happy to send a stack of old motocross magazines to recycling, but a teenage son objects. Limit potential disagreements by assigning the interested parties – the motocross enthusiast himself – to sort and decide. A second tactic: use black bin bags to collect rubbish. If the clutterers across the room can't see the contents, they're less likely to put up a fuss about the discards.

3 **Organize and put away**
When the timer bell rings, throw away the rubbish and return Put Away items to their homes in other rooms. Organize the remaining family-room residents – DVDs, videos, and game equipment – into flat-bottomed open containers for easy access.

before decluttering ▲

after decluttering ▲

Organizing
books and magazines

Every household is rich if it is home to books, but for some of us, there's such a thing as "too rich". When household reading materials have swelled past the point where they can reasonably be termed a library, it's time to prune the literary collection with a STOP clutter session.

STOP clutter in the library

Depending on the number of books you have, expect to devote two to three STOP clutter sessions to the task. Gather your tools: a timer and a STOP clutter box marked Sell/Donate (you may need more than one Sell/Donate box!). Set the timer for 20 minutes. To help focus the STOP clutter decision-making process in the library, ask yourself these questions:

- When was the last time I read this book?
- Will I read it again?
- If a reference book, is it current? If so, have I consulted it in the last year?
- If it's a cookbook, do I use it? Hint: the presence of food stains indicates a keeper.
- Is this a textbook from my old school days?
- Is the book a classic?
- Does the book have intrinsic value – is it a signed copy, first or collectible edition?
- Is the book out-of-print or hard to replace?
- Is this a book I've borrowed and need to return?

The answers to the above will point you to a decision. Books that have never been read don't belong in an active library; release virgin books so that another reader may love them. Similarly, you should pass along any read-it-once titles; there's nothing so stale as reopening a whodunit when you already know who did.

Cookbooks and reference works are the gym rats of any library, and should be kept only if they are exercised regularly.

Similarly, old school textbooks are dead weight on household bookshelves; find a more endearing souvenir of university days to cherish, and free space on the shelves for titles that don't bring the agony of calculus to mind.

> "Cookbooks and reference works are the gym rats of any library, and should be kept only if they are exercised regularly."

Be cautious in your approach to classic works; far too many families spend literal generations dusting old matched sets of "great books" for their imagined cachet. If you read the classics for enjoyment, hold on to them – but dead paper does nothing to promote knowledge or culture if it is simply sitting there as a status symbol. Pass unwanted classics on to a library or school, where the great minds can reach out and touch a rising generation.

Finally, don't focus too closely on value when deciding whether to keep a book. A signed copy of a friend's cookbook is a keeper, but a "first edition" of a widely distributed "Sex Among The Cavemen" bodice-ripper has negligible intrinsic value. Online auction sites are a great way to get a quick valuation of most books and can help you decide whether to keep so-called "valuable" titles.

Organizing a home library

Even pared down, the household library needs to be organized so that you can find the book you want when you need it. Think like a library, and sort your books by collection.

Children's titles belong in the children's room or on a low bookshelf in a family room where they're convenient and accessible for little readers (see also page 211). Computer users or work-at-home professionals need their reference works shelved close to hand. Don't make the household's computer geek go too far from the keyboard to find his or her guide to Linux operating systems, and shelve work titles in the home office area. Keep cookbooks on a handy kitchen shelf where everyone knows where to find them.

Just as a library has a reference section, it's best to group dictionaries, encyclopedias, and reference works together. If you house them on shelves in a family area, they'll be easy to consult for questions over homework or arguments over the Scrabble board.

Separate novels and non-fiction titles to make it easier to find a good read on a rainy night. The library shelves novels alphabetically by author, and while that treatment causes those of the decorating persuasion to shudder, you'll get a hearty thumbs-up from the literati among us if you follow this system.

Non-fiction titles work best grouped by subject matter. Sorting books into history, politics, biography, travels, and foreign language sections make it easy to prepare for a holiday abraod or to check your French spelling.

"To find the book you want when you need it, think like a library, and sort your books by collection."

Shelving books according to size or colour is a dead giveaway of books bought to accessorize a model home, but shelving limitations may require a separate section for oversized books. Stack them on their sides so that they fit more easily on bookshelves.

Pare the library down with these ideas to declutter reading material:

- **Assess magazine subscriptions.** Issues that are devoured within a day of arriving in the post are fine, but cancel subscriptions to periodicals that you don't really read.
- **Set limits.** When a new catalogue arrives, recycle any older offerings from the same firm. Store magazines in magazine holders. When the holder is full, recycle the oldest issue to make room for the newest one. A roomy (but not too roomy) basket provides active storage for current magazines. Place unread issues in the basket; when it's full, weed it of older editions.
- **Store where useful.** Issues of sewing magazines are most usefully housed in the sewing area, while those on car mechanics can be assigned to the garage.
- **Say no to catalogues.** In the US, register with the Direct Mail Marketing Association's Mail Preference Service to remove your address from mailing lists (for further information, visit http://dmaconsumers.org). In the UK, contact the Direct Marketing Association's Preference Services department at http://www.dma.org.uk. Alternatively, call the catalogue company direct and ask to be removed from their mailing list.
- **Borrow, not buy.** Reduce book clutter the old-fashioned way: borrow reading materials from the local library.
- **Sell online.** Use online sales sites to recoup your investment in hot titles that you've already read – somebody out there will pay a respectable price to read that blockbuster, so sell it after you've read it!

Declutter tips for **reading materials**

Declutter
entertainment systems

Recent decades have seen an explosion in at-home entertainment options – matched by an equal explosion of entertainment clutter. Where a single television set once stood, we now have towering stacks of video and DVD players and audio equipment, not to mention teetering DVD disks and dusty piles of videocassettes.

Entertainment clutter is uniquely different from garden-variety clutter such as stacked newspapers or kitchen tinned goods. First, it's mobile: videocassettes, audio CDs, and DVDs are prone to wander through the house – and even into the car.

Second, it tends to accrete. When the family buys a new DVD player, they don't discard the old VCR, they just add a new system – and layer of clutter – on top of the old.

Finally, entertainment clutter falls apart easily. DVD disks part company with their protective cases; remote controls slide between sofa cushions or cower under the ottoman.

STOP electronic clutter

To counter these slippery tendencies, begin a STOP clutter session with a treasure hunt. Give family members lightweight baskets and send them out to scour the house for CDs, DVDs, videos, video game cartridges – and every bit of electronics packaging and every accessory they can find.

Bring it all together, and play match-and-sort. Restore disks and cassettes to original packaging where possible, and sort DVDs from videos from computer software from CDs. Now work through the pile in 20-minute timer bites. To help you decide whether to toss, put away, or store, ask these questions:

■ When did we last watch, listen to, or play with this item?
■ Will we want to see/hear/play it again?

◀ **Protect digital media.** Small and slim, CDs and DVDs are easy to use – and lose. Protect and organize digital media to protect your investment. Disk storage binders keep disks safe and accessible.

■ Do we have the same film or music in another format?
■ Have family members outgrown this title?
■ Is the item in good condition?

Candidates for donation or sale include stretched videotapes, outgrown children's titles, duplicate copies, and any film, music, or computer game that is not likely to be used again.

Stay organized

When the session is over, try these tips to organize the survivors for efficient family fun:

■ **Protect.** Digital media is delicate and easily ruined. Store videocassettes in their original sleeves, or in replacement boxes. CDs and DVDs can be stored in their original cases, or slipped into the slots of special organizers.

A tip for families with young children: protect the family DVD collection with a disk changer. It will hold and store DVDs, allowing them to be watched with the touch of a finger, but protecting them from handling.

■ **Contain.** Commercial storage organizers and shelf units get the film collection off the floor efficiently. Shallow adjustable shelves store all audio and video materials neatly.

■ **Categorize.** As with books, sorting media into categories makes it easy to find what you're looking for.

■ **Centralize.** For most efficient storage, keep all computer software in a single location.

■ **List.** Keep track of items with a simple running inventory. Knowing which seasons of a favourite TV series are already on the shelves will keep you from buying duplicates.

Declutter
crafts and hobbies

Few collections of objects provide as much clutter potential as craft materials and hobby supplies. The sewer's fabric store reproduces stealthily until wardrobes and containers overflow. For the painter, model train builder, or scrapbook maker, supplies multiply like a population of rabbits. Add the tools required by each activity, and even the most organized home is overwhelmed.

Storage solutions

How do you meet the space-gobbling demands of all the materials and supplies, tools and gizmos involved in the family's craft activities and hobbies? The answer is to get creative: check out these pointers to keep the necessities under control and maximize storage in your crafting area.

Wallspace Look up and down the walls to find storage possibilities in the work area. Empty space above and below workstations can be tapped to store most-needed tools and equipment. Wall-mounted organizers keep tools and equipment close to hand. Thread racks, pegboards, and shelves inserted in the desk's kneehole area contain small items and store manuals and idea books for easy reference.

In the clear Clear-view organizers are a crafter's best friends. Their see-through property allows crafters to locate needed items quickly without opening the box. Use mid-sized storage towers with clear drawers to sort and store rubber stamps, embellishments, paints, and adhesives.

Because these larger units roll easily beneath tables or desks, they offer an added bonus: they provide handy access to much-used tools while crafting, then allow you to remove supplies from sight when you have finished with them.

◁ **Recycle craft supplies.** To control clutter in craft areas, recycle scraps for other purposes, rather than storing them away. Leftover fabrics are easy to stitch into bags or gift pouches.

Smaller clear storage containers may be used to house eyelets and brads, beads, and sequins. Because their contents are easily visible, the busy crafter can quickly pinpoint just the right tiny embellishment, tool, or fastener.

Off the peg Old-fashioned pegboards are always handy. Fabric and craft stores use pegboards to organize and display notions. So should you. Construct pegboards on top of 2.5cm (1in) wide spacers, and trim them with moulding for a finished, built-in look. Prowl through the ironmonger's to find special hooks to add to the traditional selection of small, straight, and curved hooks.

Use pegboards to store scissors and tools, hang hanks of yarn, or keep quilting supplies in view. Hang instruction sheets from a document clip suspended from a spare hook to keep directions in front of your eyes but out of your way.

Baskets and containers Flat-bottomed plastic storage baskets have many uses in the crafts room. Use them to create flip-file pattern storage, in which items are stored upright for easy access. Organized by category, you can find that special blouse pattern in record time.

Plastic storage containers with lids stack neatly beneath desks or tables. Load them up with works-in-progress. Pile them in unused corners or on closet floors; they're neat, light, and easy to locate.

Count on wardrobes Make the most of wardrobes to store crafts materials. Using commercial organizers, install shelf units to maximize usable space where clothing once hung.

Short or long, fabric lengths can be hung from clothing rails in the wardrobe. So can rotary cutting mats, if you pinch the mat into a hanger designed for holding skirts or trousers.

Still more room on the clothing rail? Take some clean plastic shopping bags and slip both handles over the rail. The plastic bags will hold light, bulky items such as batting, cushion pads, or yarn.

Add rolling drawer towers to wardrobes for maximum use of wardrobe space. See-through drawers sort tools and notions. Stackable units let you squeeze out every available bit of crafting storage space.

STOP clutter questions

For many of us, love of our craft transmutes into an obsessive tendency to collect the materials it uses. The problem is, after a certain point, the clutter interferes with our ability to pursue our hobby. Consider these questions when deciding whether to declutter crafting supplies:

- **Is the item high quality?** Is a fabric length a pure, natural fibre – or a stiff, low-quality blend or synthetic? Did that hank of yarn fray when used for plastic canvas? Crafting time is too precious to spend it frustrated with low-quality materials.
- **Is the item dated?** Craft projects, like fashions, come in waves. One year, needlepoint is the crafter's choice, the next, knitting needles flash from every corner. Give dated craft kits and out-of-fashion materials to a crafter more in tune with retro styling.
- **Is the skill level appropriate?** You're a beginner at cross-stitch? No matter how beautiful it is, find a new home for the kit marked "Advanced Stitchers Only". Attempting a crafts project outside your skill level can bring a new hobby to a quick end. Pass it along to the neighbour with the flashing needles, and find a simpler project.
- **Do I love this item?** Last and best test for decluttering craft supplies: the love affair. Yes, when you bought it, every item in the crafts cache tugged at your heart in some way. But as with old lovers, has the magic moved on? Recycle everything that doesn't make your heart pound and your fingers itch to start crafting. Why waste precious time and energy working with something you don't absolutely love?

The rules
of household storage

In most homes, storing and retrieving household items involves a pitched battle. In one corner, we have family members who want only to find holiday decorations or seasonal clothing when they need it. In the opposite corner, crammed cabinets, cluttered basements, and inaccessible attics bursting with bags and boxes.

For most of us, an efficient household storage system seems like an impossible dream. The answer? A household storage plan. Follow this battle plan to conquer storage clutter:

- **Assess**
- **Box and banish**
- **Contain and control**

With a storage plan, you'll find the kids' summer clothes while it is yet summer. You'll save money by using stored goods, instead of buying new (because you are able to find that box of sprinkler-system parts you bought last year). You'll know what you have, where it is, and how to find it.

1 Assess

Grab a notepad and pen and start with List One: Storage. Walk the house from attic to cellar, and list every potential storage area, large or small. The hard-to-reach top shelves in children's closet, the skinny space beneath the master bed, the attic, the storage shed in the back garden.

Now for the second part of your assessment: Stuff. Make a quick list of the items you need to retain. These will include: out-of-season clothing; seasonal decorations; personal documents; keepsakes; tools and hardware; and original packaging for electronic equipment that is still under warranty.

The other half of your "stuff" list is stored clutter that may need to be banished. Good candidates for banishment include ugly knick-knacks, unused small appliances, and building and decorating leftovers. Look over your list and circle Banishment Candidates with a big red pen.

Within the Stuff List there's another category: the "let's negotiate" group. These are stored items that might appear to be worthy of banishment, but which belong to another family member. This tricky category includes: collections of LPs and a grown child's childhood possessions; sentimental overload, such as every school paper ever brought home by each child; and tool-o-holic indulgences – unused tools and sewing and craft supplies.

For "let's negotiate" items, a discussion is in order with the interested party. Goal: eliminate, reduce, or accept the necessity of storing each class of item.

2 Banish and box

This is the working phase of setting up efficient household storage. Shelf-by-shelf, room-by-room, rout out your storage areas. One at a time, pull out currently stored stuff, sort it out, banish the rejects, and box everything that belongs elsewhere. Only then put away the designated stored items. Banished items can be donated to charity, sold in a car-boot sale, or hauled to the rubbish dump.

3 Contain and control

Now that your storage plan is largely in place, buy, scrounge, or make storage containers necessary to hold what's left. Last step? Take a brief inventory of your completed, contained storage areas. As with your assessment lists, your Inventory Control list comes from a top-to-bottom walk through your home. This exercise should make you feel good – and provide your family a road map to stored items.

A storage plan is only the starting point; putting it into effect can seem daunting. Take the process step-by-step, and try these tips to make the changeover easier:

■ **Keep your assessment list in view.** Know exactly what items are assigned to the top-most shelf in your daughter's closet: boxes containing out-of-season clothing. With your plan in the forefront of your mind (and eyes), you won't be tempted to redistribute extra toys or bed linens to that space.

■ **Work one shelf at a time.** Never tear apart way more storage than can be reassembled in a single sorting session. Keep the effort small and sustained, and you'll win the storage battle. Spread your energies too thin and you'll merely muddle the battlefield.

■ **Box it, box it, box it** – unless you banish it. You're sorting out the top shelf in a utility room cupboard. You've decided that party supplies should live there, but right now, the shelf is a jumble of old vases, rejected knick-knacks, extra cleaning supplies, and board games. Drag the rubbish bin, a box marked "Donate" or "Car-boot Sale," and two or three extra boxes to the utility room. Item by item, pick it up and assign it to a box (or sentence it to Banishment). Cleaning supplies go in a box destined for the kitchen. Toss the vases into the "car-boot sale" box. Husband wants to keep his Mum's old china shepherdess, so wrap and place her into a box marked "U" for Ugly and Unwanted. Board games go into another box. Repeat until the shelf is empty.

■ **Shift boxes to their new storage site.** After you've cleared your shelf and wiped it down, deliver the contents of each surviving box to the new site according to your assessment list. Board games go to the family room shelves. Store the "U" box in the loft, where you'll add to it when you clear the next shelf. Car-boot sale boxes live along a garage wall waiting for the next car-boot sale.

■ **Plan your put-away.** Like STOP clutter sessions, clearing storage is best done in little 20-minute bites. Clear storage into boxes until the timer rings, then spend the remaining time moving boxed items to their proper place. You'll never get caught with a clean shelf and a chaotic house if you make put-away part of the process.

■ **Divide or conquer?** Only you can determine whether delegation and family involvement are appropriate as you put your storage plan into place. Struggling with a messy spouse? It may be best to work alone and spare him the stress of boxing his treasures. Is a tidy husband cheering you on? Harness that energy with a family garage clean-out day. Weigh the benefits of family participation against the potential stress or distraction it may bring.

■ **Slow and steady wins the storage race.** Keep at it! When motivation flags, return to the spaces you've cleared and sorted. Admire them. Pat yourself on the back. Take the day off, but return to that hall cupboard the next day. Remember, your home didn't get into this state overnight, so you can't expect to undo it overnight, either.

■ **Consider outsourcing household storage.** Life changes can bring storage issues in their wake. An empty nest isn't quite so empty when the nestlings leave their childhood possessions behind. A parent's estate can bring a whole new generation of possessions to declutter and store. When sudden storage problems arise, consider outsourcing. Small storage lockers or units can be rented quickly to handle the overflow while you sort out a parent's belongings. To clear adult kid-clutter, next holiday season give the grown children notice that their stuff must be collected before the unit's lease expires.

Easy storage guidelines

Do you know where your tax records are? Chances are, they're swimming in a stack of paper … somewhere.

Rafts of paper flood into the average home each day. The post brings letters and bills and bank statements. Briefcases explode with professional journals, pay slips, and calendars. School rucksacks unload the children's artwork, meeting notices, and sports schedules.

Paper clutter costs money and time, and causes stress. A missing permission slip derails the entire family on the way out the door. Hide-and-seek bills lead to late payment fees. Lose the team roster, and it's back to the telephone directory each time you need to contact the car run for football.

Without a plan for paper management, a household can drown in a rising tide of paper. In this section, we'll establish a centre for household paper handling, cut paper clutter, learn the 1–2–3s of household files, and create a home inventory.

Information Central:
create a centre for paper

No business would ask a secretary or a bookkeeper to handle paperwork tasks without an appropriate workspace. Just as in an office, every home needs a centre for paper handling: Information Central, a designated location for post handling, paying bills, filing jobs, business, and social correspondence.

Information Central's focus is all aspects of your household paper handling: bills to budgets, grocery lists to tax preparation. The specified location of Information Central will vary according to your family's needs, but all home information centres need to have access to:

- Telephone
- Household Notebook (*see pages 84–7*)
- Address book
- Calendar
- Calculator
- Filing trolley or filing cabinet
- Action file or in-and-out tray

A designated desk is ideal; it provides appropriate workspace and storage for the jobs handled at Information Central. If the family owns a computer, add it to the centre or locate it in a nearby spot. A document shredder is a smart addition. Use it to shred bank records, junk post, and credit card applications to help protect against financial loss and identity theft.

In tight quarters, one end of a kitchen table can serve as Information Central, with supplies stored in a nearby drawer and paperwork kept in a filing trolley beneath the table.

"Just as in an office, every home needs a centre for paper handling."

Finally, Information Central requires these tools and supplies for quick and easy paper handling:

- Supply of extra file folders
- Extra hanging files
- Stapler
- Cellophane tape
- Paper clips
- Post-it notes
- Pens
- Highlighters
- Stationery or letterhead
- Greeting cards
- Stamps
- Post supplies
- Scissors

Use Information Central to handle all your paperwork at home. Clip and file coupons. Balance the chequebook. Pay the bills. File your tax information and insurance forms. Answer your correspondence and send greeting cards. Post a letter. Information Central is the one-stop location to tackle paper chores, filing, and financial tasks.

Finally, make it comfortable. A supportive chair and good lighting make Information Central a pleasant place to work.

▶ **Bright ideas.** Colourful storage options for paper and desk supplies brighten any office area. Who says office supplies have to be dull? Fill your office space with colour and style.

Top tips for
speed paperwork at home

Paying the bills, filing tax returns, hunting down receipts, and dealing with correspondence all take time. Digging the documents you need out from stacks, piles, and bags of papers stored deep within wardrobes can take much longer. Try these tips to speed and organize paper chores. Get the job done fast!

1 Do it now
Throughout the day, paper-handling jobs pop up regularly. If the job can be completed in two minutes or less, you should do it now! Clip special offers from Sunday's newspaper, dash off a thank-you note to a friend, or file a receipt for tax purposes as soon as the newspaper, gift, or receipt comes into your hands. Since it takes at least two minutes to retrieve postponed items, doing short jobs on the run makes sense – and it saves you time.

2 Put paperwork in its place
Information Central features an in-and-out tray or action file, so use it! Whenever paperwork comes to hand – whether it's upon returning from work or when you're bringing in the post – put the paperwork in its place. This way, you'll always know exactly where to find the bills when it's time to pay them.

3 Throw out the junk
Dispose of any unneeded paper immediately. Ditch junk mail and unwanted catalogues as you sort through the day's post, throw out supermarket flyers and unneeded receipts as you remove them from a handbag, and get rid of extra memos as you empty a briefcase. The sooner stray paper hits the bottom of the bin, the better. Remember to shred any post that is information sensitive, such as unsolicited credit card applications with your name and address ready printed.

4 Tag it
Post-it notes light the way when paper-related issues cannot be resolved right away. If a catalogue company sends a broken item, use a post-it note to track telephone calls to the company and other actions taken to resolve the matter. The post-it reminds you of the current status as you work out the problem.

5 File it fast, file it right
A "To File" folder is an invitation to chaos; week-by-week, the folder's contents swell out of all proportion, leading to a long, weary session of catch-up filing. Stay on top of filing chores and file receipts, pay slips, insurance paperwork, and tax records the first time you handle them. The extra second won't be noticed at that end, and will prevent a filing jam.

6 Stay stocked up on stationery and postal supplies
Make sure that you are well stocked up with stationery and postal supplies – because nothing is more frustrating that having to end a bill-paying session with an unplanned trip to the post office. Buy books of stamps, and if you have the storage space available, buy stationery in bulk. Keep a list of the supplies you use regularly (along the same lines as the shopping list, see page 94) and check through the list before you go to the stationers.

7 **Schedule paper-handling chores regularly**
Schedule banking, bill paying, and tax chores to keep them from overwhelming you – or costing money in the form of late payment charges. Set aside a weekend day early in the year to assemble tax information and prepare tax forms. Waiting until the last minute costs money, time, and stress.

8 **Create a Chuck-it Bucket**
A quick and dirty way to help with filing paperwork is to create a Chuck-it Bucket. Designate a single cardboard box for records to receive any paper that you know should be thrown out, but which gives your hoarding anxiety meter a good shove. Dump all-of-the-above into the Chuck-it Bucket as you file. Six weeks from now, throw the contents of the box into the bin. No looking, no sorting, no peeking. If you haven't needed that catalogue in a month or so, you'll never need it again – so toss the whole mess out.

9 **Buy an electronic labeller**
For a quick way to label files, invest in an electronic labeller. These small keyboard-driven machines print neat, perfect labels one at a time, and they're a boon to anyone who wants to have easy-to-find files. Make a mistake on a file label? It's easy – just print a new one. Need to re-label a file? It's as simple as type, print, and stick.

10 **Make friends with your files**
Filing is the bedraggled stepchild of home office chores – yet doing it promptly pays off a hundred-fold when it comes time to find the dog's vet records or a receipt for a returned gift. Bulging "To File" folders are the enemies of an organized home office, so complete each session of paper chores with a brief filing session. Tuck receipts, pay slips, utility bills, and credit card statements into their respective file folders. Filing "to the back", placing each new paper behind previous ones, makes it easy to drop new items into their proper place.

Paperwork tips for **clutter personalities**

Time and money! Rock-bottom issues run deep, and can reveal the clutterer within. Try these ideas to tame desktop chaos:

■ **Hoarder.** If you're a hoarder, nothing can be as anxiety-producing as decluttering your paperwork and files. What if you need that catalogue, letter, receipt, or circular at some time in the future?

The chances are you won't need it, and this is where the Chuck-it Bucket (*see Tip 8*) comes in. The Chuck-it Bucket creates a cooling-off zone for surplus papers when the thought of throwing them away raises welts on the Hoarding psyche. Knowing that these papers will have a temporary home – just in case – puts the Hoarding fears on ice. If you do happen to need them, they're there, but by taking up residence in the Chuck-it Bucket, they're easier to dispose of after time has passed and your Hoarding attachment to them has waned.

■ **Perfectionist.** Where everyone else considers it a job well done to get the papers in the files, the Perfectionist goes a step further. He or she must have Perfect Files – labelled and arranged in an orderly manner.

Perfectionists tend to worry about such matters as whether the file folders are the same colour, or if a new file will be out of alignment with the old ones' crosscut scheme. Each peek in the file drawer will irritate a Perfectionist if the files don't meet his or her outlandish standards.

Silly as it sounds, such things matter to us (Oops! The author's clutter personality stands revealed!). Get past the whole problem by buying yourself a simple tool to create uniform, nice-looking labels – an electronic labeler (*see Tip 9*) – and get back to filing.

An Action File makes quick work of daily paper management. When it's time to handle weekly deskwork, you'll find it all in the Action File.

■ **Use a small tabletop file** holder and add to it hanging folders labelled "To Pay", "To Do", and "To File".

■ **Include separate folders** in each one for every member of your family, and for projects, sports, or school activities.

■ **Sort and drop** incoming paperwork each day into the appropriate file.

■ **Bills go into** the "To Pay" folder, while medical insurance papers and other important paperwork should be assigned to the "To File" folder.

■ **File things** that need doing, such as permission slips that have to be signed, correspondence that requires a reply, and reminders to schedule the children's dental check-ups, in the "To Do" folder.

Free yourself
from paper clutter

Despite our best efforts, paper mounts up around the house. Stacks of bills breed in corners, while the week's post spills across the kitchen table. Leave paper free to migrate, and each session of bill-paying will take twice as long. Keep paper in its place! Try the following tips to cut down on paper clutter.

Decide to decide

What force lies at the bottom of paper pile-ups? Like all clutter problems, the culprit is deferred decision-making. It's fun to go through the day's post at the kitchen table, but if it's left there to moulder, it'll have to be sorted again later. Chances are, important items will go missing.

Instead, decide what to do with each piece of paper the first time you handle it. Ask yourself, "Will this item need to be paid, answered, or filed?" then drop the paper into the appropriate folder of your Action File. An immediate sort-and-store operation heads off paper clutter at the source.

Keep it or toss it?

Desktop efficiency experts tell us that the 20/80 Rule is alive, well, and running amok amongst the filing cabinets. Specifically, we'll need only 20 per cent of the papers that are entrusted to any filing system; the remaining 80 per cent are never seen, consulted, or handled again.

When adding to your household files, always keep the 20/80 Rule in mind in order to cut down on clutter in the filing cabinet. Resolve to limit the contents of your filing cabinet to that important 20 per cent; discard any item that won't be needed again.

▲ **Day to day.** Establish a home for incoming paper, and use it daily to contain the incoming tide. You'll always know where to find the week's bills, post, and announcements.

▲ **Store it away.** Don't consign completed paperwork to the messy mountain known as "To File". Filing records promptly means you'll always be able to find the information you need quickly.

Take back your space with these simple tips to pull the plug on paper clutter:

■ **Children's artwork.** When you can't see the refrigerator, it's time to stem the flow of children's artwork. Sort each day's papers into an "artwork" folder in the Action File (*see page 231*). Each week, select the best work to display as "Refrigerator Art of the Week", and consign last week's entry to a basic file marked with the child's name. At the end of the year, tuck the collection of the year's best works into a large envelope, mark it with the year, and add it to the household's classic files. Share extra art projects by writing letters to family members on the reverse side.

■ **Calendars, menus, and phone lists.** Save telephone time by putting calendars, schedules, takeaway menus, and phone lists into clear page protectors in the Household Notebook (*see pages 84–7*). Flip through the Household Notebook to quickly check meeting dates or find phone numbers.

■ **Cards and correspondence.** Birthdays, celebrations, and events are a regular part of life – so why dash to the card shop for each occasion? Once a year, purchase an assortment of greeting cards, sympathy notes, and stationery items. Stored together with stamps and pens, they'll handle social correspondence without stress.

■ **Daily post.** Sort each day's post over the recycling bin to make quick work of unwanted catalogues, flyers, or promotional offers. For safety, shred or destroy credit card applications and financial solicitations before recycling.

■ **Junk mail.** Bar the door to junk mail, depositing it straight into the bin. Where it can't be avoided, as when it's enclosed in bill envelopes, put the problem where it belongs: remove any identifying information from the application and post it back to the offending company inside the postage-paid envelope with a quick note saying, "No, thanks!" You'll support the postal service and help discourage junk mailers.

■ **Manuals and warranties.** Three-ring binders and a supply of clear plastic page protectors make it easy to file and find product manuals and appliance warranties. Once a year or so, flip through the binder and remove any paperwork concerning items that you no longer own.

■ **Newspapers and magazines.** Forget placing fanned-out magazines or neatly stacked newspapers on table surfaces. Low-sided baskets or trays use the principle of "controlled clutter" to display readable items without permitting them to overrun the family room at will.

■ **Receipts.** When business expenses or tax considerations require that you save receipts, designate a quick-drop hanging file folder in the Action File (*see page 231*) to receive them. Discard other receipts – from the supermarket, florist, or service station – as soon as you get them.

children's artwork ▲ see also pages 210–11, 212-13

Set up a
household filing system

Create a household filing system as easy as 1, 2, 3. What's the purpose of a household filing system? It's the place where we store papers against the time we'll need them again. Set up properly, a household filing system will allow users to find documents easily, and maintain and retrieve important papers in the future.

Efficient paper management can be as easy as 1, 2, 3. Simply incorporate the following three key elements into your household filing system:

1 An Action File.
A tabletop file used for daily, short-term filing chores. Use your Action File to hold bills for payment, to set aside correspondence and other papers that require response, and to provide short-term storage paperwork and other information that must be filed (*see also pages 231 and 232–3*).

2 Basic Files.
These are a household's working file system. Kept in a filing trolley, cabinet, or desk drawer, your basic files should hold medical insurance records, credit card statements, rent receipts, and bank statements. Use your basic files for routine activities such as paying bills, tax files, medical information, and home maintenance.

3 Classic Files.
Archive files used for papers that need to be stored for the long term. What files belong in classic files? Most families save copies of income tax returns, cancelled cheques, property documents and receipts, insurance policies, car documents and warranties, and credit card statements. Use filing cabinets or box files to protect these items for long-term storage. Note: original documents such as insurance policies, legal documents, or tax records should be stored in a secure place, such as a home safe or a bank safe deposit box.

"Efficient paper management can be as easy as 1, 2, 3."

File it right: setting up a filing system

To set up your own household filing system according to the 1, 2, 3 plan, follow these three steps.

Step 1 Gather paperwork and records. To set up your filing system, scour the house and collect the family paperwork. Look for these types of documents and files:

- **Car:** Car titles, car insurance policies, car repair records, tyre warranties, owners' manuals, and car loan documents.
- **Banking:** Bank statements, cancelled cheques, cheque registers, safe deposit box numbers and keys, money market accounts, and certificates of deposit.
- **Bills and loans:** Credit card statements, receipts from utilities, cable and phone companies, loan documents, furniture loans, and department store accounts.
- **Health and healthcare:** Medical records, doctor and dentist information, prescriptions, medical bills, health insurance policies, and insurance handbooks.

▶ **Smart storage.** Away with boring beige and olive drab! Paperwork files and storage containers can be decorative as well as organized. Look for new colours and design options.

SAMPLE RETENTION SCHEDULE

Document	How long to keep it
■ Bank statements	6 years
■ Birth certificates	Forever
■ Cancelled cheques	6 years
■ Contracts	Until updated
■ Credit card account numbers	Until updated
■ Divorce Papers	Forever
■ Home purchase and improvement records	As long as you own the property or are rolling over profits from it into new property
■ Household inventory	Until updated
■ Insurance, life	Forever
■ Insurance, car, home, or property	Until updated
■ Investment records	6 years after tax deadline for year of sale
■ Investment certificates, stocks and bonds	Until cashed or sold
■ Loan agreements	Until updated
■ Military service records	Forever
■ National insurance card	Forever
■ Real estate deeds	As long as you own the property
■ Receipts for large purchases	Until the item is sold or discarded
■ Service contracts and warranties	Until the item is sold or discarded
■ Tax returns	6 years from filing date
■ Vehicle titles	Until sold or disposed of
■ Will	Until updated

■ **Housing:** Mortgage statements or rent receipts, house title, surveyor's report, floor plans, deeds, land surveys, insurance policies, and property tax assessments.

■ **Insurance:** Insurance policies, policy amendments, and declarations sheets.

■ **Legal:** Marriage certificates, birth certificates and adoption papers, estate files and wills, powers of attorney, medical powers of attorney (living wills), military service and discharge papers, and passport.

■ **Retirement:** Pension documents, annuities.

■ **Valuables:** Appraisals, inventories and photographs of art, antiques, jewellry, rare books, silver, china, or crystal. Keep these in a secure place.

Step 2 Give each record a home. Good filing systems are like snowflakes: each family's system is unique. While prefab filing schemes (which often require filing documents according to numbers or numero-alphabetic codes) seem as though they might be easy to use, a filing system won't work for your family unless your family understands what's in it and where every record belongs. Make your filing system make sense – to you. Label file folders in everyday language, using terms that will help you remember what's inside each file folder. If more than one family member handles household paperwork, make sure everyone agrees on file headings. What's "bills" to one partner may be "payments" to another, so come to terms. Commonly used options for file labels include:

■ **Car:** Label files for car records descriptively, such as Car or by car model.

■ **Banking:** Use folder names like Bank, Savings,or the name of the bank.

■ **Bills and loans:** File by name of payee, or by type of bill (Utilities, Telephone).

■ **Health and healthcare:** Include files for Medical Bills, Insurance Records, Prescription Drugs, and by family member's name (Michael – medical records).

■ **Housing:** File labels can include House, Mortgage, Repairs, or can be listed by address (3310 Threadneedle Road).

■ **Insurance:** Set up files by insurer or by policy type: Homeowners, Life, and Car.

■ **Legal:** Sort family members' personal records in separate files (John, Mary, Alice), and set aside folders for specific legal issues (Grandmother's Estate, 2004 Car Accident)

■ **Retirement:** Label file folders descriptively, such as Inland Revenue, Benefits, Pension.

■ **Valuables:** Choose folder labels that make it easy to find information: Art, Books, Jewellry, and Antiques.

As you set up folders and sort paperwork into them, set aside original documents that must be stored securely. Legal documents, birth and marriage certificates, titles to cars and deeds to property, stocks and financial instruments all should be stored in a safe place, such as a home safe; alternatively, keep important papers in a safe deposit box at your local bank.

Don't forget to add photograph negatives – or archived copies of digital photograph files – to your original documents folder. Memories are valuable, too!

"Good filing systems are like snowflakes: each family's system is unique."

▶ **Flip and file.** "Vertical beats horizontal" is never more true than when handling paperwork. Hanging file folders allow you to locate paperwork with a quick peep.

Step 3 Create a retention schedule. Everyone has a friend or relative who will never part with paperwork – ever. Over the years, their household files become so bloated and cumbersome that it's impossible to find anything again.

Knowing what to keep and how long to keep it is the key to an efficient filing system. Professional records managers call this list a retention schedule. Develop one for your organized home; it will provide guidelines that will help you keep filing systems lean and mean. You'll need to check with legal and financial advisers for specific recommendations for your household, but use the list on page 236 as a general guide to how long to keep household files. A simple list – tax records (keep 7 years); credit card receipts (4 years); house documents (forever) – makes it easy to prune stale files.

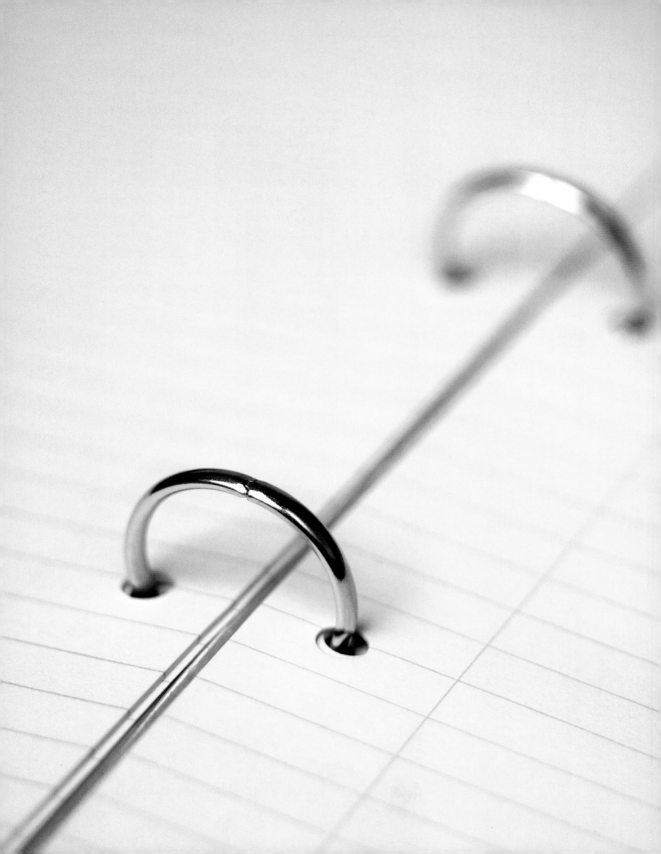

Start here for the basic planner pages for your Household Notebook. Forms cover daily, weekly, and master to-do lists; a shopping list; a freezer inventory; weekly and monthly menu planners, and emergency information.

Capture the flow of each day's chores with a simple daily planner. It includes "to go," "to do," "to call," and "what's for dinner?" Track each week with the Weekly To-do List, and round up nagging chores and niggling tasks on the Master To-Do List.

Posted on the refrigerator, the Shopping List holds a week's worth of to-buy notes; use the Freezer Inventory to keep track of freezer contents. Smart cooks know that menu planning saves time, money, and stress in the kitchen. Plan a week at a time with the Weekly Menu Planner. For organized menu planning, use the Monthly Menu Planner to decide on a month's worth of meals in a single planning session.

For more information on the subjects covered in this book, turn to Resources (*see pages 248–9*) for details of useful websites.

Emergency information

Emergency number:

1 Stay calm   **2** Describe the emergency   **3** Don't hang up the phone

Emergency medical

Police

Fire

Ambulance

This telephone number is

This address is

Directions to this address

Family doctor

Mum's work number

Mum's mobile phone/pager

Dad's work number

Dad's mobile phone/pager

Neighbour's name

Neighbour's phone

Friend/relative's name

Friend/relative's phone

Master to-do list

Date	To do	Category	Target date

■ List To-Do items and assign each to a Life Category (e.g. work, home, voluntary work, spouse, parent)

■ Each week, review the Master To-Do list and add a few To-Do items to each day's list. Use the Target Date and Category to help you choose.

Daily to-do list

Date

To do

To go

To buy

To call

What's for dinner?

Weekly to-do list

Week of:

Monday

Tuesday

Wednesday

Thursday

Friday

Saturday

Sunday

Shopping list

Item	✔	Item	✔	Item	✔
	☐		☐		☐
	☐		☐		☐
	☐		☐		☐
	☐		☐		☐
	☐		☐		☐
	☐		☐		☐
	☐		☐		☐
	☐		☐		☐
	☐		☐		☐
	☐		☐		☐
	☐		☐		☐
	☐		☐		☐
	☐		☐		☐
	☐		☐		☐
	☐		☐		☐
	☐		☐		☐
	☐		☐		☐
	☐		☐		☐
	☐		☐		☐
	☐		☐		☐
	☐		☐		☐
	☐		☐		☐
	☐		☐		☐
	☐		☐		☐

Freezer inventory

Item

Item

Use a slash mark to record each freezer meal or frozen item stored in the freezer. Cross out each item as it is used. You can also use this form for a pantry inventory.

 Item in   **Item out**

Weekly menu planner

Week of:	breakfast	lunch	dinner
Monday			
Tuesday			
Wednesday			
Thursday			
Friday			
Saturday			
Sunday			

Monthly menu planner

Month of:	Week 1	Week 2	Week 3	Week 4	Notes
Monday					
Tuesday					
Wednesday					
Thursday					
Friday					
Saturday					
Sunday					

Resources

Need more help to get organized at home? Try these online resources.

Declutter

Alt.Recovery.Clutter

http://groups-beta.google.com/group/alt.recovery.clutter/about
The granddaddy of online support groups for clutter sufferers began on Usenet in 1996. Now available on the Web, this mailing list provides information and support to hoarders and clutterers.

Planet Ark's "Recycling Near You"

http://www.recyclingnearyou.com.au
Find out what can be recycled in your area in Australia – from printer cartridges and mobile phones to garden organics and plastic bags. Hunt down your closest charity store where you can donate unwanted household goods and clothing.

Direct Marketing Association

http://www.dma.org.uk
To reduce junk mail, request that your name be removed from marketing mailing lists. Send a notice, including your name and address, to:
Mailing Preference Service (MPS)
DMA House
70 Margaret Street
London W1W 8SS
You can also register for this service online.

Australian Direct Marketing Association

http://www.adma.com.au
Use their online service to opt out of marketing mailing lists, or contact them at:
ADMA – Do Not Contact Service
Reply Paid 464
Kings Cross NSW 1340

Dress for Success

http://www.dressforsuccess.org
This nonprofit organization accepts donations of interview suits for low-income women entering or re-entering the workforce. Founded in New York in 1996, there are now affiliate locations in England, Wales, and New Zealand. Clean out your closet and give a sister a leg up!

Freecycle

http://freecycle.org/
An international grass-roots organization devoted to reducing the amount of waste in our landfills. Recycle unneeded items with others in your local area through the Freecycle network.

Organize

Home Made Simple: Organized Life

http://homemadesimple.com/organizedlife/
Articles, hints and tips for home organization.

The Holding Company

http://www.theholdingcompany.co.uk
Store solutions for every room in the house, including kitchens, bathrooms, bedrooms, children's rooms, and the home office.

MSN House and Home

http://houseandhome.msn.com
Check the "Decor and Home Living" area for storage and organization solutions for every room.

Howard's Storage World

http://www.howardsstorageworld.com.au
Franchise stores throughout Australia that offer simple storage solutions for your home. Their vast product range and customized service will solve your trickiest storage dilemmas.

Clean

Consumers Answer Line

http://www.extension.iastate.edu/answerline/

A service of the Iowa State University Cooperative Extension Agency, check this web resource for tips and articles on household cleaning, food safety, home management, and laundry.

National Soap and Detergent Association

http://cleaning101.com

This site from an association of cleaning product manufacturers offers guidance on laundry, household cleaning, washing up, and using cleaning products. Don't miss their annual survey of cleaning attitudes – it's always a good read!

The Clean Team

http://thecleanteam.com/

Jeff Campbell's professional cleaners can clean a two-bedroom apartment in 43 minutes. His books, products, articles, and advice will speed cleaning in any home. Be sure to check out the rules for speed cleaning and clutter control. Will ship worldwide.

Lakeland Limited

http://www.lakelandlimited.co.uk

A mail-order service covering kitchenware, cleaning tools and products, storage items, and much more.

Bald's Furniture Balm

http://www.baldsbalm.co.uk

Specialist product that restores woods and deals with scratches and scrapes. Will ship worldwide.

Plan

Getting Things Done by David Allen

http://davidco.com/

Productivity expert David Allen provides a road map through time chaos with principles for Getting Things Done. Discover the secret of 43 folders and clear the "stuff" from your life.

More good stuff

Consumers Union

http://consumersunion.org/

Publisher of Consumer Reports, this non-profit organization provides tips and advice on a range of topics

eHow: Homemaking

http://www.ehow.com/list_1096.html

Short and sweet, this homemaking resource offers how-to advice for myriad homemaking issues.

USDA Food Safety Information

http://www.foodsafety.gov/

From freezer cooking to pantry storage, get tips on safe cooking and food storage practices.

OrganizedChristmas.Com

http://organizedchristmas.com

Sister web site to OrganizedHome.Com, OrganizedChristmas.Com offers holiday organizing tips, free printable holiday planner forms, easy craft gifts, and recipes.

The Simple Living Network

http://www.simpleliving.net/

Robust resource site for simple living and financial freedom. Home of "Your Money or Your Life" and "Take Back Your Time" initiatives.

Index

Acknowledgments

Author's acknowledgments

Behind this book stands an entire community: the members who gather at OrganizedHome.Com to encourage one another to clean house and get organized at home. The heart and soul of the OH membership is a bright light in a world of chaos, and I am grateful for their friendship, inspiration, and example.

I send special thanks to members of the OH Mod Squad. These dedicated friends hold the unsung and uncompensated job of managing a large online community – and they were the sounding board and cheerleaders I relied upon throughout this project.

I offer honour and respect to my grandmother, Helen Betty Townley, for the homemaking heritage she embodies. She guided my first embroidery stitches, taught me to block a sweater, and has been a life-long role model on my journey to a clean and organized home.

I offer grateful kudos to super-cleaner Denise Davis, from Merry Maids. Always generous with her technical expertise and on-the-job know-how, she kept our home clean while I was too busy writing about cleaning to do any!

Last (first and always), I send love and acknowledgment to my husband, Dr. Steve Ewer. Without his unflagging encouragement and support, there would be no writer – and without his patient tolerance of my unending writerly megrims, there would have been no book. Every writer should be so blessed.

Publisher's acknowledgments

Dorling Kindersley would like to thank photographer Howard Shooter and his assistant, Michael Hart; models Alex Farrell, Jennifer Matter, Frances Wingate, Max Jones, and Luke Shooter; Karen Shooter, for her patience; stylist Bo Chapman; Shannon Beatty and Hilary Mandleberg for editorial assistance; Lynn Bresler for the index; Clara Latham for assisting on the photography shoot; Nick Lane for technical advice; and Sonia Charbonnier for all her DTP support.

All photographs by Howard Shooter except for the following: Andy Crawford and Steve Gorton: 128, 144r; Steve Gorton: 232l; Russell Sadur: 54, 96, 113, 116, 121, 150, 154, 169, 173, 175, 177; Pia Tryde 1, 200, 220, 232r, 233; Matthew Ward: 114. All images © DK Images. For further information see www.dk.images.com

About the author

Since 1990, Cynthia Townley Ewer has been writing online about home organization and management. As editor of OrganizedHome.com, Cynthia brings encouragement, information, and support to today's home managers. She has been widely quoted in print and in online media, including interviews on simplifying life at home in Modern Maturity magazine, Working Woman magazine, and the New York Times. She has appeared twice on the daytime TV show ABC's The View (awarded the Emmy for Outstanding Talk Show in 2003). OrganizedHome.com has received numerous web awards since its debut in 1998, including the coveted USA Today HotSite and USA Weekend "Best of the Web" awards.

Cynthia started her working life as a freelance legal writer while bringing up two children as a single mother, which required the highest level of home and personal organization. This provided an apprenticeship in the principles of home management that she teaches today. She now lives with her husband, cardiologist Dr. Stephen Ewer, in Richland, Washington, US.

Cynthia's juggling act of publishing web sites, writing projects, volunteer work, speaking engagements, and travel continues to require a high level of organization. "I'd still rather play than do laundry," she says.

Life, love, and cleaning the refrigerator. It's all in a day's work for Cynthia.